Java

A complete course

Also available from Continuum:

Java

A complete course

Stuart F. Lewis

CONTINUUM
London • New York

Continuum
The Tower Building
11 York Road
London SE1 7NX

370 Lexington Avenue
New York
NY 10017-6503

The author and publishers of this book have used their best efforts in preparing this book. These efforts include the development, research and testing of theories and programs to determine their effectiveness. The author and publishers make no warranty of any kind expressed or implicitly with regard to these programs or to the documentation contained in this book. The author and publishers should not be liable in any event for incidental or consequential damages in connection with or arising out of the final performance of use of these programs.

Sun, the Sun logo, Sun Microsystems, Solaris, HotJava, and Java are trademarks or registered trademarks of Sun Microsystems, Inc. in the US and certain other countries. All other product names mentioned herein are the trademarks of their respective owners.

First published 2002

British Library Cataloguing-in-Publication Data
A catalogue record for this book is available from the British Library.

ISBN: 0-8264-5927-7 (paperback)

Library of Congress Cataloging-in-Publication Data
A record of this book is available from the Library of Congress.

Typeset by Tech Set Limited, Gateshead
Printed and bound in Great Britain by Bookcraft, Midsomer Norton

Contents

Preface

This teaching text for software design and programming includes a comprehensive coverage of the Java language including plenty of fully designed and implemented examples. Designed for an advanced programming course delivered over 11 units, each chapter covers an aspect of object-oriented design and Java implementation in depth. This text is suitable for both undergraduate and postgraduate taught courses in universities and higher education colleges. Commercial programmers considering moving to the Java language will also find this text a useful resource.

The importance of separating the problem domain classes from the human computer interface classes is stressed in all examples. Each demonstrates six possible interfaces to every problem domain class.

1 Console output only

2 Command-line arguments passed to test classes

3 Console input and output

4 Graphical user interfaces using the Java 1.0 event model for applets running in almost any world wide web browser

5 Graphical user interfaces using the Java 1.1 event model for full stand-alone applications.

6 Graphical user interfaces featuring Swing platform-independent components from the Java Foundation Classes (JFC) included in the Java 2 platform. (Also known as 1.2.)

All example classes are fully javadoc commented, with the complete tested code for every class included.

Hypertext documentation generated directly from the text is available on the associated web site www.stuartflewis.co.uk. A consistent approach to designing and developing classes based on the Unified Modeling Language (UML) and well-proven structured techniques at the detailed method code level is used throughout. Several advanced features from Java 2 (version 1.2) are included in the later chapters.

Throughout the book there are in-text questions; review questions and exercises appear at the end of each chapter. The answers to the in-text questions are given at the end of the relevant chapter. The answers to the review questions are given in Appendix A and to selected exercises in Appendix B (these are flagged with an asterisk at the start of the question). The answers to the remaining exercises are given in the lecturer's supplement with other supporting material.

Dedication
To Tess, Nell, and Meg

1

Introduction

Overview

Computers are everywhere. With the rapid fall in hardware costs, the personal computer has become a standard part of the working and even home environment for many people. Computers are increasingly linked to company, national and international networks. Hence the saying 'the network is the computer'. To be able to solve problems using a computer some software is required. Many layers of software are needed to turn the computer into a useful machine. This software may be written in different languages. All languages share some common features. Problem solving is a skill independent of the language used and solutions can be expressed both in text and diagrams. Java and the Internet are closely related.

Using computers

If there is a problem which involves processing information it is likely that using a computer may help to solve the problem (Figure 1.1). However, the hardware alone will not provide any solutions. To be useful, computers need software. The software turns a computer from a collection of electrical and mechanical components into a useful tool for problem solving.

Many layers of software are needed and each provides more facilities than the layer below. An operating system is the basic layer that provides

- input using a keyboard and mouse
- processing of data using a central processing unit capable of simple instructions
- output on a screen or console
- storage of program instructions and data in memory and on one or more disks.

Many problems are solved using a variation on the sequence: input some data, process it, output some results and store both the raw data and results for later access. Some operating systems provide connections to other computers or printers on a network. Operating systems were originally closely linked to the hardware, with every different manufacturer providing their own operating system with names like VMS, MVS, BOSS, or TRSDOS. Early operating systems were written in a combination of machine code and assembly language.

When IBM agreed to license MSDOS from Microsoft for their personal computer, a *de facto* industry standard was set. Since then single-user personal computers have

1

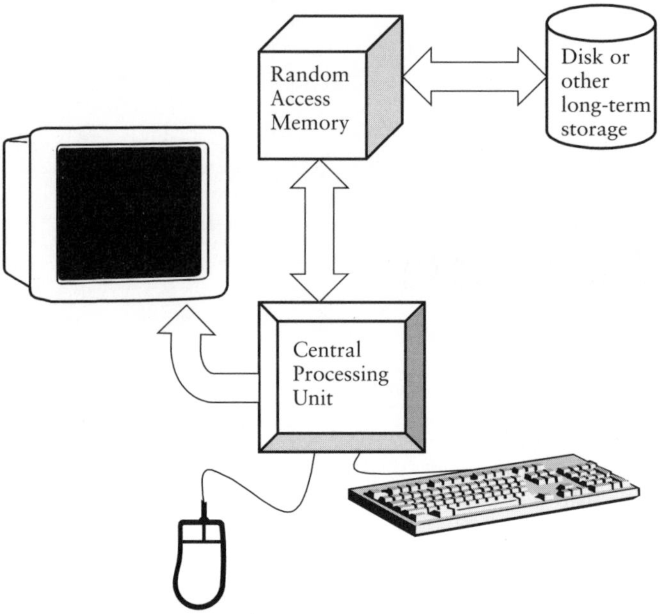

Figure 1.1   A simple computer system.

tended to run the same operating system regardless of who actually manufactures the hardware, although all are based on the same family of Intel central processing units or chips. The common operating system has led to various sophisticated application programs being developed that run on many personal computers.

?   **1.1**   Which operating systems have you used?

Input using a keyboard and mouse

The keyboard supplies alphanumeric characters that form the data to be processed by the computer. Certain special keys such as return, delete, alternate and control are used in different ways by different applications. When keys are pressed or released events are generated by the keyboard and processed by the operating system.

The graphical user interface (GUI) consists of pictures (or icons) representing the various programs and options. Using the mouse these icons can be selected by pointing the cursor (an arrow) at the icon and pressing (clicking) the mouse button. To start an application program (for example a word processor) a 'double-click' (pressing the mouse button twice in quick succession) is often used. To move items on the graphical user interface a technique called 'dragging' is used. First the item is selected by pressing the mouse button, then by keeping the button depressed the selected item will follow the cursor. These movements and pressing the mouse button generate events that are processed by the operating system. Some events are passed on to the application programs.

Processing of data

Using a central processing unit, the computer is capable of following simple instructions. All instructions are stored in memory in a machine code specific to the particular processor. Each instruction in a program is fetched from memory and loaded into the processor in turn. After an instruction has been executed, the next instruction is fetched. Many thousands of instructions are required to carry out even the simplest task. Some instructions request that data be moved around in memory, others carry out arithmetic or logic operations.

Output on a screen or console

Before graphical user interfaces were popular, most output from computer systems was to simple screen or console devices only capable of displaying alphanumeric text. Now the results of processing some input data can be displayed in many ways, as diagrams, pictures and charts as well as text.

Storage of program instructions and data

While a program is running the instructions are stored in memory. When a computer is turned on the first stage of 'booting-up' or starting the machine is to load the operating system from a long-term storage device such as a disk into memory. The operating system is the first program that is executed. The operating system will then load other programs when requested to by the user. While a computer is working the operating system is always running. Many computers have one or more disks and are connected to other storage devices using a network. Programs and data can be stored on any of these devices.

1.2 What other storage devices are used to store programs and data?

Networks

After the move from large central computer systems to small personal computers, the importance of networks to link these personal computers has increased dramatically. Within any one company, there may be many separate or connected internal networks known as intranets. Some networks require all the connected computers to run the same operating system but others will support many different operating systems.

1.3 What is the world-wide network of computers called?

Application programs

On top of the operating system various application programs may be run. These can be separated into two groups. Shrink-wrapped packages are generalized programs, which can be used for performing common tasks by many different users.

1.4 Which shrink-wrapped packages have you used?

If there is a particular problem that cannot be solved using a shrink-wrapped package then a bespoke solution can be developed. The process of building a bespoke system involves specification, design, implementation and testing. All are challenging tasks requiring analytical, logical, and organisational skills.

Central to this is a process of translation of the problem from the real world to the computer. The final aim is to provide instructions on how to solve the problem in a language the computer can use. The instructions are expressed in a special language known as a programming language using source code specific for that language.

The early stages of the process are the most difficult. Finding out what the users of a proposed system want and expressing that specification precisely is very difficult. Various methods have been proposed to help this process but the communication problem remains. Several different design paradigms with emphasis on different aspects of the problem solution have been developed. All aim to help reduce the complexity of systems by subdividing them into smaller parts. This may be on a functional basis as in functional decomposition or based on the structure of the underlying data as in structural or database oriented design methods. Different problems are more amenable to being solved by these different methods. Once a design for a system has been produced, the next stage is to implement that design on an actual computer system.

Programming languages

Implementation requires a programming language. There are many choices and, as with design methods, different languages suit different problems. Over time, there have been four generations of programming language.

The first was assembly language that was specific to the processor used by the computer system. Hence languages like Z80, 6502, 68000 assembler. The ratio between lines of source code and actual machine instructions is close to 1:1 with macros providing only simple subroutine facilities. Assembly language is symbolic machine code, in many cases oriented more towards the underlying machine code rather than the problem to be solved.

Second-generation languages such as COBOL and FORTRAN are independent of both the underlying processor and operating system. These languages were the first high-level languages. Some were designed by committee and standardised at an international level. Many legacy systems are still running that are written in these languages. One line of a high-level language is translated into many lines of machine code. The English-like nature of these languages allows the solution to a problem to be expressed in a problem-oriented way rather than in a machine-oriented way.

Third-generation languages introduced block structuring and limited the number of different constructs that could be used to build a program to three, sequence, selection, and iteration. Languages such as PASCAL, C, and MODULA-2 grew in popularity along with the personal computer. All languages in the first three generations require the program to express how to solve the problem in a detailed way.

Fourth-generation languages attempt to free the author from expressing the problem solution procedurally and move towards expressing what is required rather than how to achieve the solution.

All of the generations of languages along with the other specialized programming languages such as LISP and PROLOG share some common features. A source code file is prepared using an editor. The source code is a mixture of reserved words, user defined identifiers, comments and various other characters used as a form of punctuation. These are combined according to the syntax rules of the language.

Reserved words have a special meaning within that language such as PRINT, DISPLAY, WRITELN, if, for, printf. Reserved words must be used according to the syntax rules of the language. Reserved words are restricted and cannot be used as identifiers. Reserved words are also known as keywords in some languages. Some reserved words define the structure of the program; others represent instructions or commands in statements that manipulate data.

User-defined identifiers are names for variables, procedures and submodules such as VAT-RATE, $name, myPay. User-defined names must conform to rules for the language. If a programmer names their identifiers with meaningful and understandable names, the readability of the program can be enhanced.

In order to aid understanding of the program source code, comments or remarks that briefly outline the function of the code can be included. Comments are also used to identify the overall function of the program, version number and its author. Comments are written in natural language and do not have to conform to the syntax rules of the programming language.

Many symbols from mathematics are used in these different languages but often with different meanings. For processing numbers the standard +, -, *, and / characters are often used, but some languages provide ADD, SUBTRACT, MULTIPLY and DIVIDE as reserved words in an attempt to make the source code more readable. Various brackets are used to separate parts of the source code into blocks. Other combinations of characters such as (*, /**, or && have special meanings in some languages.

Some languages are closer to English than others. Many languages allow the source code to be stored in one or more files and often rely on supporting tools to manage and organise these files into projects or program libraries.

Before a computer can run or execute a program written in one of these languages, it must be translated into the machine code for that computer. Fortunately, there are many tools to help with this process. A compiler translates the whole program into an executable file. The executable file can then be run directly without the source code being present. An interpreter translates and then executes one line of the source code at a time. Both compilers and interpreters will inform the programmer if any of the syntax rules of the language have been broken.

The reasons why one language is chosen over another by a particular organisation to solve a particular problem are many and varied. But many companies use a pseudo code, structured English or program design language (PDL) to express the design in a form that, whilst not as precise as actual source code, can easily be translated into source code in most languages.

What computers can do

At the lowest level computers can do only three different things to help solve problems regardless of which operating system or programming language used.

Sequence

A computer can follow a sequence of instructions in order, performing each after the last is completed. A sequence will always be executed in the same order every time, with each instruction being performed once only. This can be expressed in pseudo code by a block of instructions such as

```
BEGIN
input data.
process data.
output results.
END
```

This pseudo code expresses the fact that the statements must be executed once each from the first to the last. This general sequence of input, process, output, occurs in many problems and can be expressed using a diagram based on Jackson Structured Programming or Structured Systems Analysis Design Method Entity Life History diagramming notation. Each box represents one or more lines of pseudo code that in turn is translated into one or more lines of source code depending on the language used (see Figure 1.2).

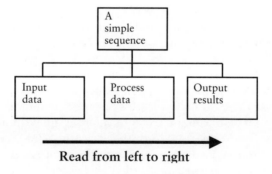

Read from left to right

Figure 1.2   A simple sequence.

Selection

A computer can make a simple choice or selection between two or more different tasks to perform. However, one and only one is chosen. The order in which the choices appear has no influence on which is chosen. Common pseudo code for expressing simple selection of doing a task or not is

```
IF (some condition is true) THEN do this task.
ENDIF
```

If the selection is between two alternatives then ELSE may be used:

```
IF (some condition is true)
    THEN do this task.
    ELSE do the alternative
ENDIF
```

Meaning that if the condition is true then do this task. If the condition is false then do the alternative. However, one and only one task is done. If there are a number of choices, a CASE statement is often used:

```
CASE (place in race)
1 : Award gold medal
2 : Award silver medal
3 : Award bronze medal
ENDCASE
```

Again only one selection is chosen from the alternatives. In this case, only one medal is awarded.

The simplest form of selection using the if statement can be expressed using a diagram based on Jackson Structured Programming and Structured Systems Analysis Design Method Entity Life History diagramming notation. Each box represents one or more lines of pseudo code that in turn is translated into one or more lines of source code. The small circle in the top right-hand side of the box indicates that this box is a selection of one and only one from the boxes on that branch. The order in which the boxes appear does not affect which is selected. The condition associated with each selection can be listed below the diagram (see Figures 1.3 and 1.4).

?   **1.5** Draw a structure diagram for the three-way case of awarding a medal.

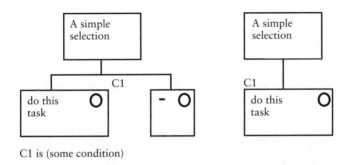

C1 is (some condition)

Figure 1.3   A selection with no alternative.

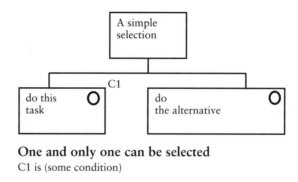

One and only one can be selected
C1 is (some condition)

Figure 1.4 A simple selection between two alternatives.

Iteration

Finally a computer can repeat or iterate over the same task or group of tasks zero or more times while some condition is true. The pseudo code for expressing iteration is

```
WHILE (more data) DO
     process data
     output results so far
     get more data
ENDWHILE
```

If there is no data to process at the start of the iteration the condition (more data) will be false and the body of the iteration will not be executed. This is the zero times situation which allows programs to deal gracefully with situations where no processing is required.

Iteration can also be expressed using a diagram based on Jackson Structured Programming and Structured Systems Analysis Design Method Entity Life History diagramming notation (Figure 1.5). The small asterisk in the top right-hand side of the box indicates that this box is an iterated component performed zero or more times.

Combining sequence, selection and iteration

These three structured design constructs can be combined to form a tree with each level being one of a sequence, selection or iteration. Each construct can be translated into almost any language. At the detailed low-level design stage, these diagrams can help ensure that the specification is accurately translated into source code. The combination of these three basic structures can be used to solve problems of increasing complexity.

A program is required for a bank to print a list of all account holders who are currently overdrawn. A possible solution to this problem as pseudo code may be:

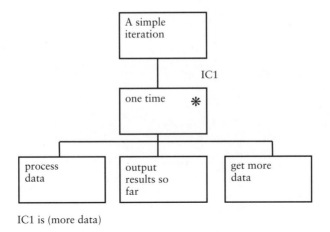

IC1 is (more data)

Figure 1.5   A simple iteration.

```
get first customer details
WHILE (more customers) DO
     IF (customer account overdrawn)
          THEN output customer name and balance
     ENDIF
     get next customer
ENDWHILE
```

The same solution expressed as a structure chart would be as shown in Figure 1.6.

To determine the type of each box look at two levels of the tree. The lower level determines the type of the box. The unlabelled boxes are the leaves of the tree and have no type. These leaves should contain operations that can easily be translated into pseudo code or source code.

1.6 A program is required by a sports team to print a list of the players who have not scored yet this season. Draw a structure chart to solve this problem and write the pseudo code.

To solve a complex problem using a computer there are two choices. Either break the large problem into smaller and smaller problems until each smaller problem can be solved separately using a computer, or provide more facilities for solving problems on the computer until they are sophisticated enough to solve the complex problem directly. These two approaches are known as top down or bottom up. In reality, a combination of both approaches is used.

Internet basics

Today there is an international computer network. It spans the globe and connects universities, researchers, computer workers and users around the world. The Internet represents a revolutionary medium for accessing and disseminating information. It

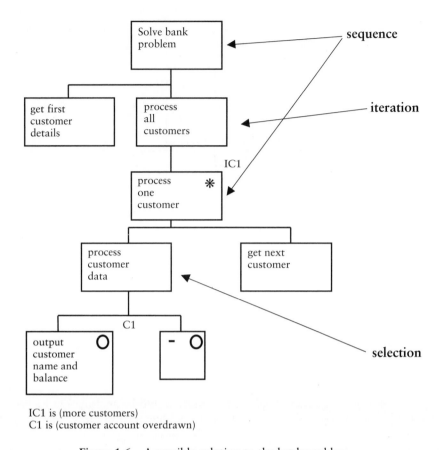

Figure 1.6   A possible solution to the bank problem.

consists of many computers running different operating systems and application programs. Most visible of these are those used to form the world-wide web. Web server software provides the service of making files on one computer available to other computers on the Internet. Client software such as Netscape and Internet Explorer is used to 'surf the Net' requesting files from the server computers.

1.7 What is the general name for software such as Netscape and Internet Explorer?

Initially the web servers gave only the service of providing static text and image files to be downloaded by clients. Every web resource has its own URL (Uniform Resource Locator) address, which consists of three parts. First, the type of server, either http (Hypertext transmission protocol), ftp (File transfer protocol), gopher (menu driven information seeker), telnet (remote login) or nttp or news (news site). Secondly, the server address (usually www..., which is now the most popular domain name in the world) similar to an Internet email address, e.g. www.glam.ac.uk. Finally, the actual resource name, usually an actual filename. The browser software interprets these files to allow them to be displayed on the local hardware (media independence). Many documents are hypertext documents with embedded links to other web documents. This makes 'surfing' the Net much easier for the first-time user who no longer needs to be concerned about the underlying software and network protocols.

Recently the number and range of interactive services provided via the web has increased dramatically. This requires application programs that can run on any client computer. By providing this functionality the Java language has grown in popularity along with the web itself. Java is designed for network programming and can easily work with common Internet protocols. Small Java programs known as Applets can be downloaded by any client with a Java virtual machine and run on the client machine.

Because Java and the Internet are so closely related, there is a vast amount of information about Java available on the Internet. The most common way of obtaining or updating the Java language itself is via the Internet from http://java.sun.com/.

An example Java Applet

Many web pages have small applets embedded in them (Figure 1.7). For example a minimum Applet could be:

```java
//: First.java
package chap01;

import java.applet.Applet;
import java.awt.TextField;

/** First implementation of a
* very simple class <code> First</code>
* @author Stuart F Lewis
* @version 1.00, 9/10/98
*/
public class First extends Applet {
/** A place to display a message
*/
TextField t = new TextField(20);
/**
* Initializes the applet. You never need to call this directly; it is
* called automatically by the system once the applet is created.
* Sets the text of the message and adds it to this Applet display area
*/
public void init() {
t.setText("Your message here");
this.add(t);
}
} ///:~
```

This would be loaded into a web page using a short piece of HTML similar to

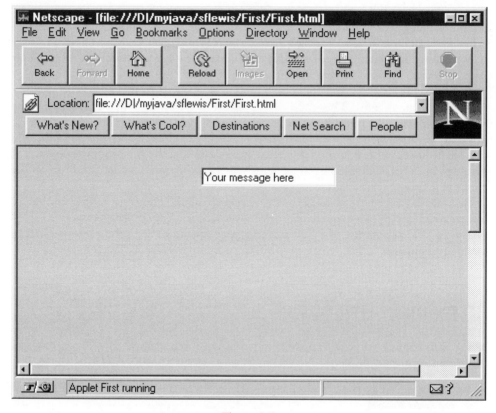

Figure 1.7

```
//: First.html
<applet
  name="First"
  code="First" codebase="file:/d:/myjava/sflewis/First"
  width="500"
  height="600"
  align="Top"
  alt="A java-enabled browser would show an applet here."
>   <hr>If your browser recognized the applet tag,
  you would see an applet here.<hr>
</applet>
} ///:~
```

Summary

Because of the rapid fall in hardware costs, the personal computer has become a standard part of the working and even home environment for many people. Computers are increasingly linked to company, national and international networks. To be able to solve problems using a computer some software is required. Many layers of software are needed to turn the computer into a useful machine. This software may be written in different languages. All languages share some common features. Problem solving is a skill independent of the language used and solutions can be expressed both in text and diagrams. Java and the Internet are closely related; as the popularity of the web has grown so has the Java language.

Answers to in-text questions

1 Many possible answers including MSDOS, UNIX, Windows 3.1, 95, 98, 2000, ME, MacOS, etc.

2 CD-ROM, magnetic tape, or optical disks.

3 Internet.

4 Many possible answers including Word, Office, Doom, Netscape, Excel, etc.

5 A structure diagram for the three-way case of awarding a medal is shown in Figure 1.8.

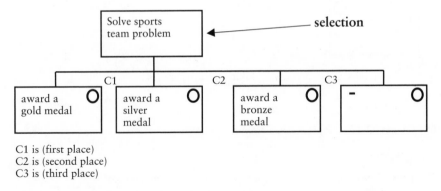

C1 is (first place)
C2 is (second place)
C3 is (third place)

Figure 1.8 A possible structure diagram for the three-way case of awarding a medal.

6 A possible solution to the sports team problem as a structure chart and pseudo code is shown in Figure 1.9.

```
get first player details
WHILE (more players) DO
      IF (player has not scored)
           THEN output player name
      ENDIF
      get next player
ENDWHILE
```

7 Browsers.

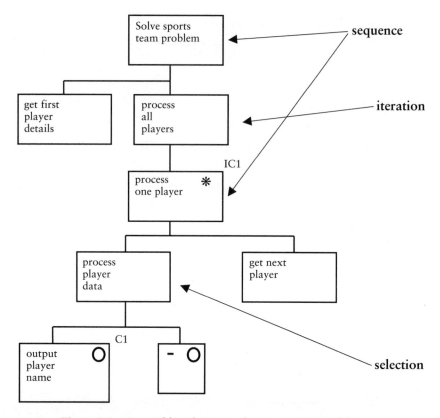

Figure 1.9   A possible solution to the sports team problem.

REVIEW QUESTIONS

Answers in Appendix A.

1 What physical devices are used to provide input to a computer system?

2 How does the operating system know that the user has pressed a key or mouse button?

3 What is the first program loaded when a computer is turned on?

4 Why are there so many different computer programming languages?

5 What kind of error will occur if a reserved word is spelt incorrectly?

6 Why are comments an important part of the program source code?

7 Explain the difference between an interpreter and a compiler.

8 What are the three logical structured constructs that can be used to write a program in any language?

9 Why has the growth of the Internet been so rapid?

10 Where on the Internet would you find information about Java?

EXERCISES

Answers to exercises flagged with an asterisk appear in Appendix B.

1* What is the difference between storing programs in memory or on disk?

2 Which computer programming languages are considered to belong to the fourth generation?

3 How many reserved words are there in a language you are familiar with?

4* What other diagrammatic notation can be used for expressing the low-level design constructs, sequence, selection and iteration?

2

Object-oriented basics

Overview

Before starting to design and write object-oriented programs, some basic under-standing of the terminology used is vital. Many of the words and ideas used in object-oriented systems are taken from everyday English but have a specialized meaning. After completing this chapter, you will have an insight into the words and concepts used in the object-oriented world and how some are achieved in Java.

What is an object?

Almost anything and everything can be an object. Every day we interact with objects around us. Some perform useful tasks for us. When we need to travel, we can choose between many objects that will transport us from one place to another. Cars, trains or buses are all useful travelling objects.

?   **2.1** What other travelling objects have you used?

The places we travel between are also objects. Some are places where we live. A house, flat, or bed-sit can all be a home. Others are places where we work. A factory, shop, warehouse, university, or garage can all be work places. Places are often classified by the facilities provided – restaurants to eat in, cinemas to watch films at, or sports complexes to play or watch many different activities.

Other objects provide us with information. Newspapers, radio or television offer different information in a variety of forms. Even people can be objects that provide a service for us – a doctor for diagnosing our illnesses, a teacher for help in learning, or a customer to buy something from us.

Some objects are complex. Some are simple. All computer-based systems consist of many objects that communicate with each other and with the users of the system. Any complete system can be considered as one very complex object made up of many simpler objects. By the process of abstraction we can ignore the non-essential details of a complex object and concentrate only on those that are relevant to the current problem. An architect requires a different plan of a house from an electrician or

16

plumber. Each ignores details that may be important to the others and concentrates only on the facts relevant to their particular interest.

2.2 What details about a house are important to an electrician?

This process of abstraction is further aided by the encapsulation of how an object achieves the services it provides. The object hides this information. We are only interested in what the object can do, not how it does it. By looking at the interface to an object we can see what services the object can provide. The objects in an object-oriented computer system are models or simulations of their real-world counterparts and the system itself is a dynamic model of the real world, that is a simulation.

2.3 Describe the interface presented to the occupiers of a house by the water supply system. What details about how the hot water is supplied are hidden?

To build a complex system we must start with simple component objects and assemble them into objects of increasing complexity. This composition can be performed with new or existing objects taken from a library, enabling considerable reuse of previously designed and developed components.

2.4 Which simple children's toy demonstrates the principle of building a complex system from very simple components?

An object is described by concentrating on what we can request the object to do and how those requests will change the object state. The behavior of an object is often described by listing the requests that an object can respond to or the methods that an object provides. We interact with everyday objects in many ways. This interaction can be considered as using the object's interface. By starting a car with a key, we change the car's engine state from stopped to running. When we tune a radio to a particular channel, we change the radio's state from untuned to tuned in. We can ascertain an object state by examining the attributes of the object. The values of these characteristics that describe the state of an object change as the state changes. In the car, we hear the engine running. On the radio, we can see the tuning display.

2.5 What possible states are there for a book in a library system? What attributes describe the state? How does the state change?

All cars have a common interface, state and behavior. The specific details of how any individual car interface is presented, and the behavior is implemented, differ from manufacturer to manufacturer. Even within cars made by the same company there are differences in the layout of the controls and the amount of information provided to the driver about the current state of the car. A typical interface used to control a car includes a steering wheel, accelerator, brake, clutch, and gear change. The dynamic state includes the current speed, gear selected, engine temperature, and fuel available. The current value of these attributes can sometimes be seen directly or may be communicated using a gauge. Once you understand how to use one particular car, the process of learning to use a different one is considerably eased by the common interface. Even if the car is a left-hand drive as opposed to right-hand, the interface is very similar and intuitive to use.

Objects adopt one of two roles within a system. Any object that uses the resources of another object is a 'client'. The object providing the resources is the 'server'. In different situations, one object can switch between these roles. The client sends a request to the server. The server responds by providing some sort of service.

? **2.6** In a restaurant, who are the clients and servers?

An object in an object-oriented system is more than just a model or simulation of the corresponding object in the real world system. Software objects do far more than their real counterparts. A software object represents what a system needs to know and do about the actual object. The functionality of the software objects within an object-oriented system achieves the goal of providing a working model of the real world.

Simple objects

The simplest objects have limited functionality and few states. A physical switch object can only be 'turned on' or 'turned off' and is normally used to control some other (usually physical) object. The operations or requests that the object can accept are known as the object methods. A software switch object can either be 'on' or 'off' and it knows its own state. A software switch object has only two states and only two methods that can change the state. The functionality of a simple switch may be further limited because if it is already 'on' it cannot be 'turned on'. Alternatively, if it can be 'turned on' when it is already 'on' then that operation does not affect the current state of the switch. By looking at the position of a physical switch, we can tell the state of the switch.

The switch described so far could be one of many possible types of switches or one particular switch of a particular type. This idea of an object belonging to a class of objects with similar attributes is explored later.

? **2.7** What other words are used for devices that carry out a similar function to a switch?

Each switch object is known as an 'instance' and given a name. Different instances are referred to by their names. The switch controlling the power to a particular physical device may be called powerSwitch. By convention in Java, object names start with a lower-case letter and use mixed case to separate the words in the name.

A software model of a switch would have to provide an additional method to inspect or return the current state of the switch. The simple switch has only two possible states and the general Java style for examining stateX is a method called isInStateX() using the Java data type boolean that can only have the values true or false. A boolean method such as isOn() would allow other objects to inspect the current state of a switch by saying if powerSwitch.isOn() then ask it to turn itself off by powerSwitch.off().

This Java syntax for using objects takes the general form objectname.method() where the objectname is the name of the object that provides the method. This is the server object that receives and responds to the request made by the client. The method is the name of the process that the client is requesting the server to perform.

2.8 Write the Java code to request the powerSwitch to turn itself on.

Enclosed in the round brackets () would be any arguments to the method. Arguments are information supplied by the client object to the server object to customize the way in which the server carries out some request. Arguments are also called parameters (Figure 2.1). A telephone directory object may provide a method to add a new name and number. The parameters would be the name and number inside the round brackets: myPhoneBook.add("Fred","123456") asks the myPhoneBook object to add Fred with the telephone number 123456.

2.9 How might you ask myPhoneBook to find John's number?

The switch object is a server to objects that send it requests, but is the client of the object that it controls. When the switch is turned on, it will then send a request to the object or device that it controls to perform some service.

A switch is such a simple object that it would probably be modelled as an attribute of another object with only two possible values in an object-oriented system.

2.10 List the possible attributes of a domestic television set. What other objects might make up a home entertainment system?

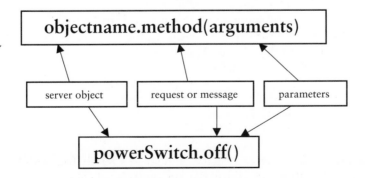

Figure 2.1   The general form of a request to an object.

Identifying objects

In a particular situation, often known as a problem domain, a common starting point for identifying objects is to start looking at the nouns. A noun is a word that names a person, thing, action, quality or state, which immediately implies that not all nouns are going to be objects. To decide which nouns are suitable for modelling as objects several criteria have been suggested.

- An object must have some attributes that together describe the object state and these need to be stored so the system model can function.
- An object must have a set of identifiable operations, methods or requests that can change these state attributes in some way.
- Most objects have more than one attribute. Objects with only one attribute are often so simple that they are best modelled as an attribute of another object.
- All of the attributes and operations for a particular object must apply to all occurrences of that object. This is captured in the definition of a class or template for defining new objects and is discussed below.

Identifying objects within a problem domain is relatively easy. Selecting the essential objects relevant to the system to be built is more problematic. Many texts on object-oriented analysis and design suggest criteria for identifying the essential objects. Java has only one type of object but during the identification stage it is worth classifying objects in different ways. Separating out the problem domain objects from the human interface objects, data management objects and system implementation objects at an early stage can pay dividends later.

What is a class?

From our earliest childhood, we start to group objects together in various ways. This process enables us to understand and use new objects more easily. Groups of objects that are similar make up a class in object-oriented systems. We have already met the classes of 'travelling objects', 'living spaces', 'workplaces', 'people' and 'information sources'. Within these large and complex classes, many possible subdivisions could be made to create a class hierarchy (see Figure 2.2).

It is by this process of subdividing that we seek to limit the complexity of the system. The process of abstraction allows us to focus on the essential characteristics of each class relative to the system. At each level of the hierarchy, the class may be used to create an object of that class.

? **2.11** Draw a class hierarchy diagram for 'information sources'.

The class hierarchy is a tree structure similar to a family tree with the root at the top known as the superclass. Each class below is a subclass of the superclass and inherits the attributes of its ancestors.

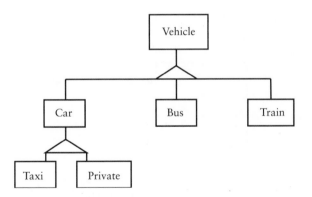

Figure 2.2 A possible hierarchy for 'travelling objects'.

The terms 'type' and 'class' are often used interchangeably. A class is more than a type because it defines the operations and the attributes of a type. A class can be considered as a specific implementation of a type. Many computer programming languages provide a number of simple basic types, including

- integers which are based on the whole numbers (0,1,2,3..)
- real or float values based on the numbers with decimal points (0.123, 1.967, 52321.4..)
- characters, including the alphabet and special symbols (A, b, c, ?, @..).

The language also defines the operations that are valid for each particular type. Basic arithmetic operations are provided for the number types. Ordering and comparison operations are available for the types with discrete values. Types that are more structured and complex are provided by some languages, including

- arrays for storing an indexed sequence of values of the same type
- records to hold groups of related values of different types
- lists and other abstract data types.

Again, the language defines the operations available to access and update these data structures. Java allows the class to define both the type or class for all attributes and the methods that can operate on members of the class. In this way the class is more than a type because the class defines the operations or methods available for all of its members.

?　**2.12** List the valid operations for whole numbers.

Later you will meet two Java classes, String and StringBuffer. Both implement different versions of the same generic computing type, a sequence of characters often known as a string. In many languages, the string type is implemented as an array of characters. Java uses an array of characters to actually store a string. However, all strings in Java are actually objects of the class String, StringBuffer, or one of their subclasses.

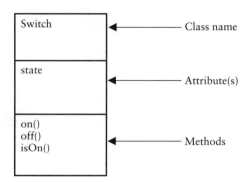

Figure 2.3   Diagram showing the basic Switch class.

The powerSwitch belongs to the class Switch. This class Switch describes the things that are common about all switches (Figure 2.3). All have a state but whilst you have to look at a physical switch to see its state, the software version knows its own state and can change it when asked to. How a switch reacts, if it is asked to change to a state it is already in, depends on the implementation.

The process of creating a new object from the class is called 'instantiation'. The new object is an 'instance' of that class. The class is a template which describes the attributes that make up the state of an instantiated object and the methods which that object performs. The class defines the things that each of its objects knows and does. Facts that an instantiated object knows are stored using 'instance variables'. Some of this definition can be hidden or encapsulated within the class. When defining the domestic water supply system in the earlier question the number and location of the hot and cold taps will be specified but the routes for pipes between them may be hidden.

2.13 What would a home owner need to define for the installation of a domestic lighting circuit?

The class interface defines what methods the object provides to any clients. The class implementation defines how the interface is achieved. A Java implementation of the simple switch can be programmed using a class.

Defining a simple class in Java

Returning to the Switch class let us consider the interface that is required.

2.14 What does a Switch need to know? What methods does a Switch need to provide?

To keep things simple let us assume that it is a valid operation to attempt to change a Switch to the state it is already in and that no error will result. When a new Switch is created, we will assume that it should be off.

Implementing a simple class in Java

Implementing a class in Java to model the switch object defined above takes only eleven lines of code. The numbered comments are added only to help you follow the explanation below and would not appear in an actual Java program. The special sequence of characters //: at the beginning of the program and ///:~ at the end are used to extract the source code from the original text for testing. The file name nocomnt.java and package statement are not required in this actual Java program. The name reflects the fact that all comments have been removed from this program leaving only the essential base code required by the compiler. The package statement is used to decide where the extracted source file is stored. The Java code, like many languages, is made up of reserved words that are actually part of the language, comments, and terms that we define to have a particular meaning.

```java
//: nocomnt.java
package chap02;                                     //Line number
class Switch {                                       //1

private static final int ON = 1;                     //2
private static final int OFF = 2;                    //3

private int state = OFF;                             //4

Switch() {state = OFF;}                              //5

void on() {state = ON;}                              //6

void off() {state = OFF;}                            //7

boolean isOn() {return (state == ON);}              //8

public String toString() {                           //9
if (this.isOn()) {return "This switch is ON";};     //10
return "This switch is OFF";}                        //11

public static void main(String args[]) {
Switch powerSwitch = new Switch();
System.out.println(powerSwitch);
System.out.println(powerSwitch.isOn());

System.out.println("Now turn the switch on");
powerSwitch.on();
System.out.println(powerSwitch);
System.out.println(powerSwitch.isOn());

System.out.println("Now turn the switch off again");
powerSwitch.off();
System.out.println(powerSwitch);
System.out.println(powerSwitch.isOn());
}//method main
} ///:~
```

Why are all of the rest of the lines needed? Simply to test the class and demonstrate how it might be used. Taking each line of the class definition in turn.

1. Reserved word 'class' indicates the start of a new class definition. The class is called Switch. Conventionally all class names begin with an upper-case letter. The opening { curly bracket marks the beginning of the class definition. Every

opening { curly bracket must have a matching closing } curly bracket. The closing } curly brackets are often commented using the // comment to the end of line to indicate which opening { curly bracket they match.

2. The sequence of reserved words 'private', 'static', 'final' defines a constant value that can not be changed or even accessed from outside the class. Conventionally all constants are named using all upper-case letters. The actual primitive type int and value 1 could be any primitive type and value because all other methods within the class refer to the name ON only. All static identifiers exist only once for a class. The semicolon ; is a statement terminator, not an end of line indicator. The simple assignment operator = is a binary operator and is read 'is assigned'. It assigns the variable on the left-hand side to store the value on the right-hand side. This would be read, the constant ON is assigned the value one.

3. Another constant, representing the state OFF.

4. The attributes of a class are stored in the instance variables. There is one set of instance variables for every object created from a class template. This state variable is private and cannot be accessed from outside the class. Here the declaration and initialization of the variable have been combined into a single definition statement.

5. Every class requires a constructor with the same name as the class to create new object instances. The empty round brackets () mean that this is a no-argument constructor. The opening { curly bracket marks the beginning of the constructor. This constructor sets the initial state of a switch to be OFF using the simple assignment operator =. This would be read, the instance variable state is assigned the value OFF. The closing } curly bracket marks the end of the constructor.

6. Return type 'void' means that this method does not return any information to the client that invoked it. Invoking one of the object methods may change the state of an object. When the method on() is invoked the switch state is assigned the value ON.

7. When the method off() is invoked the instance variable state is assigned the value OFF.

8. Return type boolean (true or false) means that this method does return information to the client that invoked it. A switch knows which state it is in, and can return that information as a boolean if requested to.

9. Reserved word 'public' means that this method can be called from outside the class. The return type 'String' means that this method returns information in the form of a character string. This is an example of overriding a method provided by the Object class.

10. Reserved word 'if' tests a boolean condition enclosed in round brackets. The expression (state == ON) uses the equivalence operator == to compare the instance variable state to the static class constant ON. If the result is true, the

next statement is executed. The reserved word 'this' refers to the switch itself. The early 'return' with the message 'This switch is ON' means that the next statement is executed only if the switch is off.

11. Return the message 'This switch is OFF'.

When the program is executed it will produce

```
This switch is OFF
false
Now turn the switch on
This switch is ON
true
Now turn the switch off again
This switch is OFF
false
```

This output is produced on the standard console output device, normally the screen, by the System.out.println() statements in the main() method of the class Switch. This code is used to test the Switch class and demonstrates how it can be used:

- a new switch is created
- the initial state is checked, it should be off
- the switch is turned on
- the state is checked again
- the switch is turned off
- finally, the state is checked again.

The System.out.println() statements are requests to a Java class System variable out, of class PrintStream. This server object accepts requests from any client object to display some text output on the standard console device. This class is provided primarily for use in debugging and provides a quick and easy way to display the output from our test program. Here you can see the importance of the toString() method that is used to convert the object powerSwitch to a meaningful string that 'textually represents' the current state of the switch.

Editing and compiling a simple class in Java

The details of editing and compiling a Java program depend on the software environment that you use. At a minimum a simple text editor to enter the code and the Java Development Kit (JDK) available from Sun will enable you to run any Java program. The cycle of edit, compile, run and test for Java is similar to all other programming languages (Figure 2.4).

The source code is entered into the editor and then saved to a file named Class.java (where Class is the name of any public class appearing in the file). Using the edit source file option of your Java development environment may well provide a template source file. If there are no public classes then any filename ending in .java may be used. Conventionally the source file is given the same name as the main class it contains.

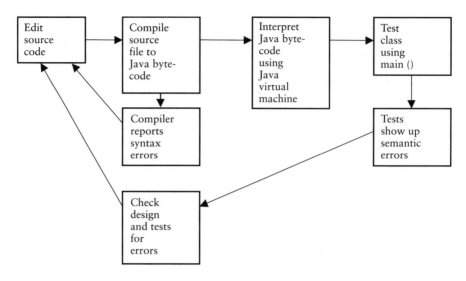

Figure 2.4   Edit, compile, run and test cycle.

This file is compiled to Java byte-code using a compiler command similar to javac filename.java.

2.15 What is the command to compile the Switch class defined above?

Either the compile or build option for your Java development environment will do this. A number of Java byte-code files will then be created, one for each class in the source file. These filenames will be Classname.class (where the Classname is taken from the source file contents). A Java byte-code file can be interpreted by a command similar to java Classname.

Either the run, interpret or execute option for your Java development environment will achieve the same result.

2.16 What is the command to run the Switch class defined above?

As there are many different environments on many different platforms for Java this book cannot explain how each one works. Most environments come with extensive on-line help facilities and tutorials that explain the above process for the particular environment. Once you have successfully completed the edit, compile, run cycle you will be able to enter and execute any Java program from this or any other text.

2.17 If you use an integrated Java development environment, what are the commands to perform the edit, compile, run cycle?

Documenting Java source code

Every Java program needs to contain much more than the bare bones above. Here is the same code with comments and documentation lines added.

```java
//: Switch.java
//package chap02

/** A very simple class <code>Switch</code>
* representing an on/off switch
* @author Stuart F Lewis
* @version 1.00, 19/02/98
*
*/
class Switch {

/**
* Constant to represent the switch state ON.
*/
private static final int ON = 1;
/**
* Constant to represent the switch state OFF.
*/
private static final int OFF = 2;

/**
* An instance variable to store the current state
* of this switch. Declared and initialized to OFF.
*/
private int state = OFF;

/**
* Constructs a new switch that is initially off.
*/
Switch() {
state = OFF;
}

/**
* Turn this switch on.
* Does not check that the switch is not already on.
* It is not an error to turn on a switch that is
* already on.
*/
void on() {
state = ON;
// Put hardware control code here to
// physically turn on the physical
// device that the switch controls
}
```

```
/**
 * Turn this switch off.
 * Does not check that the switch is not already off.
 * It is not an error to turn off a switch that is
 * already off.
 */
void off() {
state = OFF;
// Put hardware control code here to
// physically turn off the physical
// device that the switch controls
}

/**
 * Returns a boolean representation of the state
 * of this switch object.
 * @return boolean true if the switch is on
 */
boolean isOn() {
return (state == ON);
}

/**
 * Returns a string representation of the object.
 * In general, the
 * <code>toString</code> method returns a string that
 * "textually represents" this object. The result should
 * be a concise but informative representation that is
 * easy for a person to read.
 * It is recommended that all subclasses override
 * this method.
 * <p>
 * @return a string representation of the object.
 */
public String toString() {
if (this.isOn()) {return "This switch is ON";};
return "This switch is OFF";
}

/**
 * Test data for the Switch class.
 * Creates a new switch.
 * Check its initial state - should be off.
 * Turn the switch on.
 * Check the state again.
 * Turn off the switch.
 * Check the state again.
 */
public static void main(String args[]) {
Switch powerSwitch = new Switch();
System.out.println(powerSwitch);
System.out.println(powerSwitch.isOn());

System.out.println("Now turn the switch on");
powerSwitch.on();
System.out.println(powerSwitch);
System.out.println(powerSwitch.isOn());
```

```
System.out.println("Now turn the switch off again");
powerSwitch.off();
System.out.println(powerSwitch);
System.out.println(powerSwitch.isOn());
}//method main
} ///:~
```

This version is much longer than the one shown first. Because programs are read many more times than they are written you should aim to make your programs readable, understandable and maintainable.

2.18 Why are programs read many more times than they are written?

To achieve readable, understandable and maintainable source code

- select meaningful names for classes, methods, instances, and variables
- use comments to aid the understanding of the source code
- explain the purpose of methods
- lay code out in a consistent way following some coding standards.

The JDK utility program javadoc can help produce some basic documentation directly from the source code (Figure 2.5). When run with the command

javadoc -private -version -author Switch.java

the following output is produced and four files are created.

```
Constructing Javadoc information.
Generating tree.html
Generating index.html
Generating deprecatedlist.html
Generating Switch.html
```

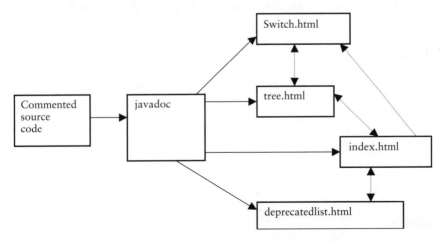

Figure 2.5   Generating documentation from source code.

Later versions of javadoc enable the generated documentation to be linked into the standard java application programming interface (API) documentation: javadoc -private -author -version -linkall Switch.java.
The following output is produced and several files are created.

```
Loading source file Switch.java...
Constructing Javadoc information...
Building tree for all the packages and classes...
Building index for all the packages and classes...
Generating tree.html...
Generating index-all.html...
Generating deprecatedlist.html...
Building index for all classes...
Generating allclasses-frame.html...
Generating index.html...
Generating Switch.html...
Generating serializedform.html...
Generating help.html...
Generating stylesheet.css...
```

tree.html

When viewed using any standard browser, such as Internet Explorer or Netscape, this file contains something similar to

```
All Packages  Index
```
_____

```
Class Hierarchy
•class java.lang.Object
     •class Switch
```

The three underlines are hyperlinks to the other three files. All Packages links to packages.html. Index links to Index.html. Switch links to Switch.html.

Switch.html

This, when viewed using a browser, contains something similar to

```
Class Switch
java.lang.Object
  |
  +——Switch
```
_____

```
class Switch
extends Object
A very simple class Switch representing an on/off switch
```

```
Author:
     Stuart F Lewis
```
_____

Variable Index

OFF
 Constant to represent the switch state OFF.
ON
 Constant to represent the switch state ON.
state
 An instance variable to store the current state of this switch.

Constructor Index

Switch()
 Constructs a new switch that is initially off.

Method Index

isOn()
 Returns a boolean representation of the state of this switch object.
main(String[])
 Test data for the Switch class.
off()
 Turn this switch off.
on()
 Turn this switch on.
toString()
 Returns a string representation of the object.

Variables

ON
 private static final int ON
     Constant to represent the switch state ON
OFF
 private static final int OFF
     Constant to represent the switch state OFF
state
 private int state

An instance variable to store the current state of this switch.
Declared and initialized to OFF.

Constructors

Switch
 Switch()
     Constructs a new switch that is initially off.

Methods

on
 void on()
     Turn this switch on. Does not check that the switch is not
     already on. It is not an error to turn on a switch that is
     already on.
off
 void off()
     Turn this switch off. Does not check that the switch is not
     already off. It is not an error to turn off a switch that is
     already off.
isOn
 boolean isOn()
     Returns a boolean representation of the state of this switch
     object.
 Returns:
 boolean true if the switch is on

toString
```
public String toString()
```
Returns a string representation of the object. In general, the
toString method returns a string that "textually represents" this
object. The result should be a concise but informative
representation that is easy for a person to read. It is
recommended that all subclasses override this method.
Returns:
a string representation of the object.
Overrides:
toString in class Object
main
```
public static void main(String args[])
```
Test data for the Switch class. Creates a new switch. Check its
initial state – should be off. Turn the switch on. Check the state
again. Turn off the switch. Check the state again.

The underlined words are hyperlinks within this file from the brief description in the
variable, constructor and method indexes to the longer descriptions later in the
document. The final hyperlink toString is a link to the Java documentation (all
produced with javadoc) at java.lang.Object.html#toString(). That is the method
overridden by this class.

Index.html

All packages   Class hierarchy

A B C D E F G H I J K L M N O P Q R S T U V W X Y Z

Index of all Fields and Methods
I
isOn(). Method in class Switch
Returns a boolean representation of the state of this switch object.
M

main(String[]). Static method in class Switch
Test data for the Switch class.

O
OFF. Static variable in class Switch
Constant to represent the switch state OFF
off(). Method in class Switch
Turn this switch off.
ON. Static variable in class Switch
Constant to represent the switch state ON
on(). Method in class Switch
Turn this switch on.

S
state. Variable in class Switch
An instance variable to store the current state of this switch.
Switch(). Constructor for class Switch
Constructs a new switch that is initially off.

T
toString(). Method in class Switch
Returns a string representation of the object.

The two underlines at the top are hyperlinks back to the other two files. <u>All packages</u> links to packages.html. <u>Class hierarchy</u> links to tree.html. The underlined letters are hyperlinks to the index letter. The underlined words are hyperlinks to the longer descriptions of the variables, constructors and methods in the class document, in this case Switch.html, but if there were more than one class then a Class.html file would be produced for each.

For the cost of adding some extra lines of comments to our program we can immediately reap the benefits of producing correct and up-to-date documentation. As the html format is very simple and highly portable this documentation can be viewed using any standard browser (Figures 2.6–7) either locally or over a network and quickly transferred to any other format.

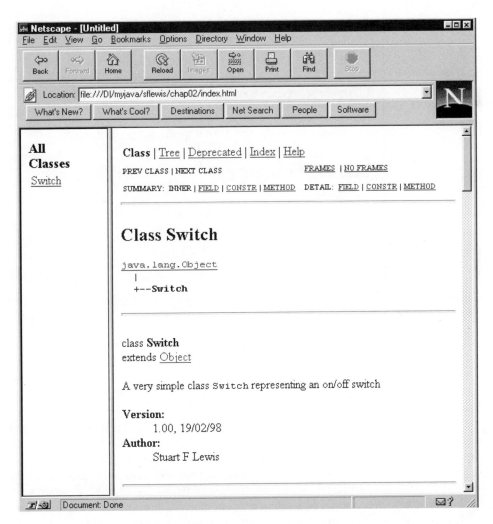

Figure 2.6   javadoc files viewed with a browser.

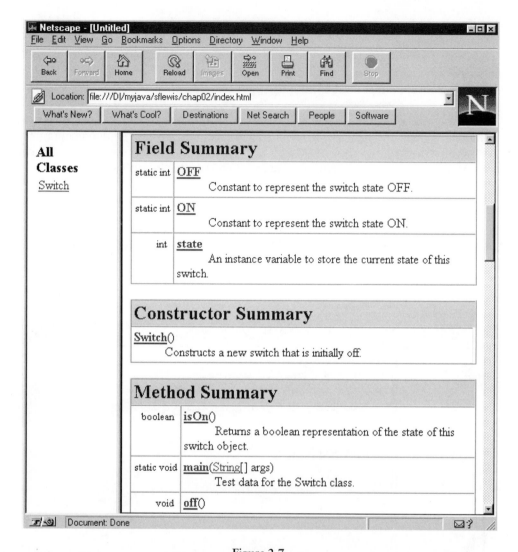

Figure 2.7

Having seen the output from javadoc for some Java source code this would be an ideal time to browse through the standard documentation for the Java Application Programming Interface (API). Start from the User's Guide provided by Sun as part of JDK. If you have not already downloaded or obtained a version of JDK then you will need to. It is available from http://java.sun.com/products/. Many Java texts repeat large sections of the on-line documentation from Sun. It is better to view this documentation using a browser. This ensures that the documentation for any particular class is correct for your installation of JDK. Every Java development environment has this or some equivalent documentation available to be viewed either using any browser or some built-in help system. As there are many different environments on many different platforms for Java this book cannot explain how each one works. To maximise your productivity in the Java language the ability to browse and find classes, interfaces, methods and other information quickly from the on-line documentation is vital.

2.19 By browsing the API documentation find the name of the method which inserts an integer into a StringBuffer.

Analysis and design

Before writing anything more than the simplest program, some analysis and design is vital. This is true for all software development methods. The process of building a software system is one of translation from the analysis through the design to the implementation. The object-oriented approach tries to minimise the amount of translation required by using the same notations and representations from the problem domain through to the implementation. The Unified Modeling Language (UML) typifies this single-model approach to analysis, design and programming. You can get the specification for UML from *www.rational.com*. Many of the reference sources for object-oriented analysis OOA, object-oriented design OOD and object-oriented programming OOP use notations based on or which have been incorporated into, UML. This book is no exception, although only a small subset is used. A class is drawn as a rectangle with three compartments separated by horizontal lines (Figure 2.8). The top name compartment holds the class name. The middle list compartment holds a list of attributes. The bottom list compartment holds a list of operations. Methods are implementations of operations in UML and are often called by the same name. These methods make up the object's interface.

A class diagram is a graphic view of the static model. Classes can be connected together to show the static relations between them that exist for a long time and are often fixed within the class hierarchy. Class hierarchies are built by using inheritance. This is one of the ways that OOP can deliver the potential of reusing large quantities of code and thus dramatically reduce development time. A class hierarchy is represented by an inverted tree diagram (Figure 2.9) with the root or simplest

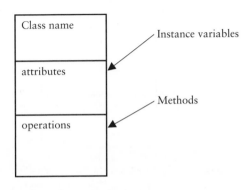

Figure 2.8   Diagram showing the basic UML class notation.

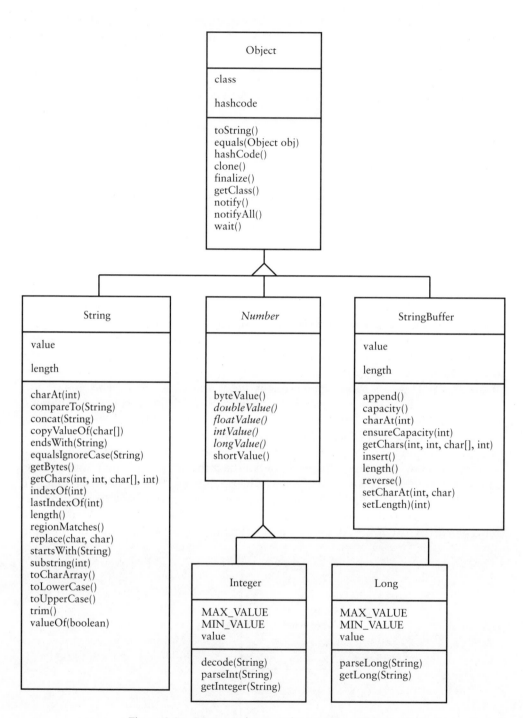

Figure 2.9   Diagram showing the Java class Object.

superclass at the top and increasingly specialized subclasses below it. The base or root class in all Java systems is the predefined class Object from which all classes inherit basic attributes and methods.

The object class hierarchy diagram shows only a tiny part of the Java hierarchy. A complete set can be found at *http://rendezvous.com/java/hierarchy*. The base class Object provides a set of nine methods that all objects in a Java program support either by overriding the original to provide their own version or inheriting the method provided by the Object class. This enables Java objects to have 'limited polymorphism' through the 'inheritance' hierarchy. This means that the client object requesting a service from another object does not need to know the server's class, only that it can provide the requested service.

The first three methods listed are public and may be called for any object of any class. The toString() method is particularly important in providing a standard way to 'see' any object. All subclasses should override the toString() method by providing their own version. toString() returns a string representation of the object. In general, the toString method returns a string that 'textually represents' this object. The result should be a concise but informative representation that is easy for a person to read.

The default implementation of equals() returns true only if the two objects are actually the same object. Again all subclasses should override equals() to compare the current values of each of the attributes of the two objects being compared.

Finally, hashCode() returns a single integer value that represents the entire value of an object. Hashcodes are used as key values when storing objects. The technique of hashing is widely discussed in many computer-programming texts. Essentially, hashing provides the fastest search and retrieval method from a data store.

The next two methods are protected. The default clone() method makes only a shallow copy of an object and should be overridden if a deep copy is required. The finalize() method is called automatically by the garbage collector when an object can be returned to the heap.

The getClass() method returns the runtime class of an object. The final three methods are all used in controlling access to synchronised resources.

The three classes shown inheriting attributes and methods from Object are String, Number, and StringBuffer. Every object is an instantiation of some class and every class inherits the attributes class and hashcode from the class Object. Every object in a Java system knows the class it belongs to and can produce a hashcode for itself.

The class *Number* is written in italics to show that it is an abstract class. Abstract classes cannot be used to create objects. There are no objects of class *Number* in a Java system nor can any be created. Abstract classes are used to capture what is the same about two or more subclasses. *Number* is a generalization describing the methods that all subclasses of *Number* must define.

Number actually has six subclasses in the java.lang package, although only two are shown. Both Integer and Long provide all of the methods defined by Object and Number plus some more specializations of their own. The generalization–specialization relationship between these classes in shown by the triangle pointing towards the generalization. The methods defined in the abstract class Number are all for different ways of presenting the same piece of data, a number. The attributes of the specialization classes Integer and Long are captured in the three variables MIN_VALUE, MAX_VALUE, and VALUE. Although these have the same names, they have very different values in each class. To describe the first two as variables is also a little misleading, as they are actually constants being defined as final. However, javadoc does not discriminate between variables and constants, listing both in the variable index or field summary.

The word static followed by the type is displayed before each static variable when the documentation is viewed using a browser. The variable value does not appear in the standard documentation because it is encapsulated by the Integer and Long class being defined as private. The methods provided by these subclasses apply only to objects of the subclass and would not be generally applicable to all members of the superclass.

There appears to be a slight anomaly in the naming of super- and subclasses in that the subclass knows and can do more than the superclass in most cases. In the Java documentation, the term 'direct superclass' refers to the immediate ancestor in the class hierarchy. The term 'superclass' can refer to any ancestors in the class hierarchy. A class is said to be a direct subclass of the class it extends. The term 'subclass' can refer to any descendants in the class hierarchy. If a class does not specify a direct superclass then the class Object is used by default.

The classes String and StringBuffer illustrate another way of achieving polymorphism. The methods charAt(int), getChars(int, int, char[ ], int), and length() are provided by both. This means that the client object requesting a service from another object does not need to know the server's class, only that it can provide the requested service. In this case, the server object may be an instance of the String or StringBuffer class. Both can provide the services charAt(int), getChars(int, int, char[ ], int), and length(). A client requesting any one of these services does not need to know whether it is sending the request to an object instance of class String or StringBuffer.

The method charAt(int) is an example of a method requiring an argument. The int value tells the server object which position in the character string the request applies to. The Java syntax for a client making this request to either a String or StringBuffer object could be someString.charAt(5), where someString is the name of the server object and the character the client is interested in is at position 5.

?

2.20 How could a client request that someString return the characters between positions 3 and 5 into a char array called midString? Hint: refer to the API documentation for getChars.

The System.out.println() statements in the main() method of the class Switch all used arguments. These arguments were different objects but each was converted to a meaningful string that 'textually represented' the object using the object's toString() method. Thus the System.out.println() statements could display some text output on the standard console device for the powerSwitch, a boolean and a literal string enclosed in double quotes. This class is provided primarily for use in debugging and provides a quick and easy way to display the output from our test program. Here you can see the importance of the toString() method that is used to convert any argument to a meaningful string that 'textually represents' the current state of the switch.

Summary

Almost anything and everything can be an object. Complex objects can be considered as consisting of many simpler objects. Every object has some functionality and state. We can ascertain an object state by examining the attributes of the object. During design concentrate on what the object can do not how it does it. Software objects do far more than their real counterparts. A software object represents what a system needs to know and do about the actual object. Separating out the problem domain objects from the human interface objects, data management objects and system implementation objects at an early stage can pay dividends later.

A class is a template that describes the attributes and methods of all objects of the class. A class hierarchy is used to subdivide and limit the complexity of the system The class Object is a superclass of all objects. A class is more than a type because it defines the operations and the attributes of a type. The class interface defines what methods the object provides to any clients. The class implementation defines how the interface is achieved. Adding some extra lines of comments to our program can immediately provide the benefits of producing correct and up-to-date documentation. The object-oriented approach tries to minimise the amount of translation required by using the same notations and representations from the problem domain through to the implementation. Abstract classes cannot be used to create objects.

Answers to in-text questions

1 Other travelling objects could include bicycle, motorcycle, ferry, ship, aeroplane etc.

2 The details about a house that are important to an electrician would include the fuse box, various lighting circuits, ring main and earth connections. The electrician's abstraction of a house is an electrical circuit.

3 The interface presented by a domestic water supply system is two taps, one hot, one cold, and possibly a mixer tap or shower that allows the hot and cold water to be mixed. The method of heating the water is hidden (encapsulated), you do not need to know whether the system uses gas, electricity, solar power or some other energy source. The timing of the water heating is also hidden, it may be on demand or may be stored in a tank.

4 Lego.

5 The possible states for a book in a library system are reserved, on loan or overdue. The attributes that describe the state are borrower, date due back, reservation date. The state can change when the book is borrowed, reserved, returned or when the date due back passes causing the book to become overdue. With each change of state one or more attributes may be changed.

6 In a restaurant, there are many clients and servers. The waiters serve the customers by taking their orders and bringing food and drinks to their table. The

chefs serve the waiters by responding to requests to prepare dishes. The bar staff prepare cocktails and drinks for the waiters to serve. The waiters are clients of the chefs and bar staff but servers to their clients, the customers.

7 Other names used for devices that carry out a similar function to a switch could include button, changer, remote control, selector, toggle, lever, etc.

8 powerSwitch.on().

9 myPhoneBook.find("John") assuming that a method find is provided by the myPhoneBook object where the parameter is the name of the person whose number we wish to find.

10 Possible attributes of a domestic television set could include current channel, volume, contrast, brightness, input source (aerial, satellite, video, laser disc), mode (teletext or picture), teletext page, etc. The other objects making up a home entertainment system could include video player, CD, satellite decoder, personal computer etc.

11 A possible class hierarchy for 'information sources' is shown in Figure 2.10.

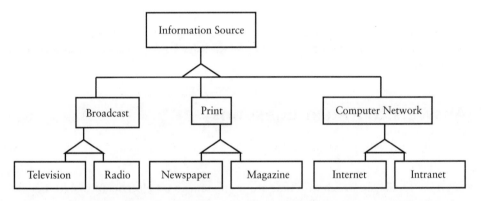

Figure 2.10   A possible class hierarchy for 'information sources'.

12 The valid operations for whole numbers are addition, subtraction, multiplication and modular division resulting in a whole number and remainder.

13 A home owner would need to define the location of all switches and lights for the installation of a domestic lighting circuit. An electrician would decide the routes for the cables and connections to the fuse box but these details may be hidden from the user.

14 A Switch needs to know if it is ON or OFF. A Switch needs to provide methods to turn it ON, turn it OFF, and tell a client whether it is ON or not.

15 javac Switch.java

16 java Switch

17 Depends on the Java development environment.

18 Programs are read many more times than they are written because they are rarely 'correct' the first time they are written.

19 The method is called insert. From the API documentation:

```
insert

public StringBuffer insert(int offset, int i)

    Inserts the string representation of the second int argument
into this string buffer.
```

20 A client would request that someString return the three characters between the third and fifth character into a char array called midString using the statement someString.getChars(2,5,midString,0); according to the API documentation:

```
public void getChars(int srcBegin,
                     int srcEnd,
                     char[] dst,
                     int dstBegin)

    Copies characters from this string into the destination
character array.

    The first character to be copied is at index srcBegin; the last
character to be copied is at index srcEnd-1 (thus the total number
of characters to be copied is srcEnd-srcBegin).

    The characters are copied into the subarray of dst starting at
index dstBegin and ending at index:

        dstbegin + (srcEnd-srcBegin) - 1
```

REVIEW QUESTIONS

Answers in Appendix A.

1 Which of the following could be considered as objects? CD player, Swimming, Bottle of wine, Weather, Big, One penny piece, Fly, Age, Window, Doctor.

2 What can we request the objects above to do?

3 How would those requests alter the object state?

4 What details about a house are important to a plumber?

5 Describe the interface presented to the occupiers of a house by the mains electrical system?

6 Which of the following could be considered as classes of objects? CD player, Homes, Swimming, Glass, Bottle of wine, Weather, Big, One penny piece, Money, Friends.

EXERCISES

Answers to exercises flagged with an asterisk appear in Appendix B.

1* List five everyday items that could be considered as simple objects.

2* What can we request the objects listed in 1 above to do?

3* How would those requests alter the object state?

4* How could the object state be stored?

5* Which are server objects?

6 Which are client objects?

7 What does the process of instantiation do?

8 Describe how the objects are related.

9 How could each object be seen as a text string?

3

Primitive data types and the String class

Overview

The Java language provides eight primitive data types that are not objects. These are vital in the construction of all programs. From variables of these data types all object attributes are constructed. By manipulating variables of these types object methods are developed. The primitive types are the boolean type, the four integer numeric types, the char type, and the two floating-point types. As Java is a strongly typed language every variable has a type. A variable of a primitive type always holds a value of that exact type. All other variables are reference types. The values of a reference type are references to objects. The Java class String is an interesting starting point for learning about the differences between Java primitive data types and Java objects. After completing this chapter, you will understand the range of primitive data types, their operations, and how they are used to build objects. Short test programs will be used to help explain operations using primitive data types. These are not object-oriented programs and contain no objects.

What is a variable?

A variable is the name of a location in the computer memory used to store a data value. A variable is one of many 'identifiers' used in Java to name classes, objects and methods. All Java identifiers are case sensitive. By convention variable names start with a lower-case letter and class names start with a capital letter. Rules and advice for naming variables apply to all Java identifiers. The rules are:

- The first character must be a Java letter.
- There is no limit on the length of an identifier.
- No spaces are allowed.
- All characters must be Java letters or Java digits.
- An identifier cannot have the same spelling as a keyword, boolean literal (true, false), or the null literal (null).

The advice is:

- All variables should be given short yet meaningful names.
- Meaningful mnemonic names that indicate the use or purpose of the variable are best.
- Conventionally, all variables start with a lower-case letter and use capital letters to break up words.
- The name of a variable will be read many times both in the code and generated documentation so it should be meaningful in both contexts.
- A little forethought in naming variables will pay tremendous dividends in the long term.
- Follow a standard naming convention.
- Single-character names should be avoided except for temporary 'throwaway' variables.

Common names for temporary variables are i, j, k, m, and n for integers or c, d, and e for characters. Other temporary variables seen in Java are b for a byte, c for a char, d for a double, e for an Exception or Event, f for a float, g for a graphics context, i, j, and k for integers, l for a long or listener, o for an Object, s for a String, and v for an arbitrary value of some type. Each will be discussed as they are used.

3.1 Comment on each of the following variable names: (a) 10percent; (b) My string; (c) aGoodName; (d) x; (e) true; (f) NotAClass.

Variables of the primitive data types always store the actual value at that named location. All other variables are reference types because they refer to other objects. The values of a reference type are references to objects. Reference types are sometimes referred to as 'pointers' or 'handles' in other texts. You cannot access the value of a reference variable directly. Reference variables are used only to access the object they refer to typically in the form objectname.method().

Boolean type

The boolean type has exactly two values, true and false. The most useful way to use the boolean type is as a return type of a method within a class to indicate that an object of that class is in or not in a particular state. All conditional statements and expressions in Java evaluate to a value of the boolean type.

3.2 Why does the statement return (someVariable == true); make little sense?

Four integer numeric types

Each of the four integer types byte, short, int, long, are integral types that can store a whole number in a given range. The range depends on the size of the storage location that is expressed in bits (binary digits) and is the same for all Java virtual machine implementations. The values are stored as signed two's-complement integers as shown in Table 3.1.

Table 3.1   The four integer numeric types.

Type	Range	Size
byte	−128 to 127	8-bit
short	−32768 to 32767	16-bit
int	−2147483648 to 2147483647	32-bit
long	−9223372036854775808 to 9223372036854775807	64-bit

char type

The char type is an integral type whose values are 16-bit unsigned integers (0 to 65535) representing Unicode characters. Information about this encoding may be found at: *http://www.unicode.org*. The first 128 characters of the Unicode character encoding are the ASCII characters. ASCII (ANSI X3.4) is the American Standard Code for Information Interchange.

The five integral primitive data types all share the common features that their values are stored exactly and are the same on every Java virtual machine implementation. The values of the integral ordinal types also follow the same sequence. For any value, you can always answer the questions: What is the next value in the sequence, known as the 'successor'? What was the previous value in the sequence, known as the 'predecessor'?

Java provides two special operators, increment ++ and decrement --, which change any variable of one of these five types to their next or previous value. For example, if a variable i of type int currently stores the value 5, the result of executing i++ will be to store the value 6 in i. These operators may be applied either before the variable (prefix) or after the variable (postfix). The difference is demonstrated by the following code segment.

```java
//: Test1.java
package chap03;

/** First of a series of examples
 * showing the difference in effect of prefix and postfix
 * operators used with the primitive data int.
 * Uses a class <code>Test1</code>
 * consisting only of a main method
 * @author Stuart F Lewis
 * @version 1.00, 21/02/98
 */
class Test1 {

/**
 * Test data for the file Test1.
 */
public static void main(String args[]) {
```

```
/**
 * Temporary variable
 */
  int i;
  i = 5;
  System.out.println(i);
  System.out.println(i++);
  System.out.println(i);
  i = 5;
  System.out.println(i);
  System.out.println(++i);
  System.out.println(i);
}//method main
} ///:~
```

An int variable is declared using the Java syntax primitiveType variableName. The initial value is assigned as 5 using the simple assignment operator = that assigns the value on the right-hand side to the variable on the left-hand side. This value is displayed. The postfix increment operator is used. The process is repeated using the prefix increment operator.

3.3 When the program is run what do you think it will display?

Using the postfix operator the increment operation is performed after the value is displayed. Using the prefix operator the increment operation is performed before the value is displayed.

Two floating-point types

The floating-point types are float and double, representing the single-precision 32-bit and double-precision 64-bit format IEEE 754 values and operations as specified in IEEE Standard for Binary Floating-Point Arithmetic, ANSI/IEEE Standard 754-1985 (IEEE, New York). This includes the special Not-a-Number value abbreviated to NaN, which is used to represent the result of operations whose result is not a number. NaN has no sign because it is not a number and therefore cannot be positive or negative.

The increment and decrement operators can also be applied to floating-point types. Because the value of a floating-point number cannot be stored exactly by the Java virtual machine, the result is not as precise as for integral types. The difference is demonstrated by the following code segment.

```
//: Test2.java
package chap03;
/** Second of a series of examples
 * showing how floating-point primitive values cannot
 * be stored with complete precision.
 * Uses a class <code>Test2</code>
 * consisting only of a main method.
 * @author Stuart F Lewis
 * @version 1.00, 19/02/98
 */
class Test2 {
```

```
/**
 * Test data for the file Test2.
 */
public static void main(String args[]) {
/**
 * Temporary variables d, f
 */
    double d = 5.123456789;
    float f = (float)d/10;
    d = d/10;
    System.out.println(f);
    System.out.println(d);

    System.out.println("increment");
    f++; d++;
    System.out.println(f);
    System.out.println(d);

    System.out.println("decrement");
    f--; d- -;
    System.out.println(f);
    System.out.println(d);
    System.out.println(d*10);
}//method main
} ///:~
```

A double variable d is defined using the Java syntax primitiveType variableName = value. The initial value is assigned as 5.123456789. A float variable f is defined using the Java syntax primitiveType variableName = (type to cast to)value. The initial value of f is the result of dividing d by 10. d is also divided by 10. These initial values are displayed. The postfix increment operator is used. The resulting values are displayed. The process is repeated using the postfix decrement operator. The program displays the float value f followed by the double value d before and after each operation. Finally, d is multiplied by 10:

```
0.5123457
0.5123456788999999
increment
1.5123457
1.5123456789
decrement
0.5123457
0.5123456789
5.1234567890000005
```

?

3.4 What is the problem with this output and what can you learn from it?

Numeric operators

A common set of operators can be used in expressions with all the numeric primitive types. These operators are sub-divided into groups.

Comparison operators

All comparison operators result in a value of type boolean that may be stored in a variable of type boolean, used in a conditional expression or returned as the result of a boolean method. The numerical comparison operators <, <=, >, and >= are spoken as less than, less than or equal to, greater than and greater than or equal to. The numerical equality operators == and != are spoken as equals or equal to and not equal to. These compare two numeric variables or values. The differences are demonstrated by the following code segment.

```
//: Test3.java
package chap03;

/** Third of a series of examples
 * showing the use of primitive data types
 * with the comparison operators.
 * Uses a class <code>Test3</code>
 * consisting only of a main method
 * @author Stuart F Lewis
 * @version 1.00, 19/02/98
 */
class Test3 {

/**
 * Test data for the file Test3.
 */
public static void main(String args[]) {

/**
 * Temporary variables d, f
 */
int i = 5;
double d = 5.123456789;
float f = (float)d/10;
d = d/10;
System.out.println(f + " is less than " + i + " is " + (f<i) );
System.out.println(d + " is less than or equal to "
+ f + " is " + (d<=f) );
System.out.println(f + " is greater than " + i + " is " + (f>i) );
System.out.println(d + " is greater than or equal to "
+ f + " is " + (d>=f) );
System.out.println(f + " is equal to " + d + " is " + (f==d) );
System.out.println(d + " is not equal to " + i + " is " + (d!=i) );
System.out.println(d + " is equal to " + f + " is " + (d==f) );
System.out.println(i + " is equal to " + 5 + " is " + (i==5) );
}//method main
} ///:~
```

3.5 When the program is run what do you think it will display?

The output again shows that neither float nor double values are stored exactly. Two floating-point variables should never be compared for equality. Only the integral data types will reliably return a result of true for the == operator. The test code in the main() method demonstrates the use of the System.out.println() method to display variables and values of the primitive data types to the standard console output device. The string concatenation operator + is used to concatenate the various strings.

Arithmetic operators

All arithmetic operators result in a value of a primitive numerical type, usually determined by the largest data type involved in the expression. If all of the operands are of type int then the result will be of type int. If you multiply a float and a double, the result will be double. If you add an int to a long, the result will be long.

The unary operators that require only one operand include plus (+), minus (-), increment (++), and decrement (--). From the earlier examples you know that increment and decrement can be applied either postfix or prefix. Plus (+) and minus (-) are always prefix operators used to indicate the sign of the operand. For integer values, negation (-) is the same as subtraction from zero. Unary minus (-) merely inverts the sign of a floating-point number. Special cases of interest:

- If the operand is a zero, the result is the zero of opposite sign.
- If the operand is infinity, the result is infinity of opposite sign.
- If the operand is NaN, the result is NaN (recall that NaN has no sign).

The binary operators that require two operands include the multiplicative operators multiplication (*), division (/), and remainder (%) and the additive operators addition (+) and subtraction (-). The differences are demonstrated by the following code segment.

```
//: Test4.java
package chap03;

/** Fourth of a series of examples
 * showing the use of primitive data types
 * with arithmetic operators.
 * Uses a class <code>Test4</code>
 * consisting only of a main method
 * @author Stuart F Lewis
 * @version 1.00, 19/02/98
 */
class Test4 {

/**
 * Test data for the file Test4.
 */
public static void main(String args[]) {

/**
 * Temporary variables izero, i, dzero, d, divideByZero, nan
 */
int izero = 0;
int i = 5;
```

```
double dzero = 0.0;
double d = 5.123456789;
double divideByZero = d/dzero;
double nan = divideByZero/divideByZero;

System.out.println(izero + " negated is " + (-izero) );
System.out.println(i + " negated is " + (-i) );
System.out.println();
System.out.println(d + " negated is " + (-d) );
System.out.println(dzero + " negated is " + (-dzero) );
System.out.println(divideByZero + " negated is " + (-divideByZero) );
System.out.println(nan + " negated is " + (-nan) );
System.out.println();

System.out.println(i + " squared is " + (i*i) );
System.out.println(d + " squared is " + (d*d) );
System.out.println();

System.out.println((i*i) + " divided by " + i + " is " + ((i*i)/i) );
System.out.println((d*d) + " divided by " + d + " is " + ((d*d)/d) );
System.out.println();

System.out.println((i*i) + " divided by " + i +
                " leaves remainder " + ((i*i)%i) );
System.out.println((d*d) + " divided by " + d +
                " leaves remainder " + ((d*d)%d) );
System.out.println(d + " divided by " + i +
                " leaves remainder " + (d%i) );

System.out.println(8 + " divided by " + i +
" leaves remainder " + (8%i) );
System.out.println(8 + " divided by " + d +
" leaves remainder " + (8%d) );
System.out.println();

System.out.println(i + " added to " + i + " is " + (i+i) );
System.out.println(d + " added to " + d + " is " + (d+d) );
System.out.println(d + " added to " + i + " is " + (d+i) );
System.out.println();

System.out.println(i + " subtracted from " + i + " is " + (i-i) );
System.out.println(d + " subtracted from " + d + " is " + (d-d) );
System.out.println(d + " subtracted from " + i + " is " + (i-d) );
System.out.println();

}//method main
} ///:~
```

The temporary variables divideByZero and NaN are assigned values of infinity and NaN by dividing by zero then dividing infinity by infinity. Long lines of code are written over two lines. The semicolon is a statement separator not an end-of-line indicator. Short lines could be written on the same line separated by a semicolon. Generous use of round brackets enhances the readability of code especially in the complex arithmetic expressions. The program displays the spoken version of each operation followed by the result:

```
0 negated is 0
5 negated is -5

5.123456789 negated is -5.123456789
0.0 negated is -0.0
Infinity negated is -Infinity
NaN negated is NaN

5 squared is 25
5.123456789 squared is 26.249809468750186

25 divided by 5 is 5
26.249809468750186 divided by 5.123456789 is 5.123456789

25 divided by 5 leaves remainder 0
26.249809468750186 divided by 5.123456789 leaves remainder
0.6325255237501883

5.123456789 divided by 5 leaves remainder 0.12345678899999957
8 divided by 5 leaves remainder 3
8 divided by 5.123456789 leaves remainder 2.8765432110000004

5 added to 5 is 10
5.123456789 added to 5.123456789 is 10.246913578
5.123456789 added to 5 is 10.123456788999999

5 subtracted from 5 is 0
5.123456789 subtracted from 5.123456789 is 0.0
5.123456789 subtracted from 5 is -0.12345678899999957
```

Zero of type int has no sign. Zero of a floating-point type can be either positive zero or negative zero. The special value Infinity can be negative or positive but NaN cannot. Although the remainder operator is available for floating-point values, the results suffer from an inevitable lack of precision. The result type of all expressions is dependent on the type of the operands.

3.6 Write a short piece of Java code to define and assign three values to three variables representing your score at darts then add these values together and display the total.

The solution to this problem is a simple sequence of statements that can be expressed as pseudo code.

```
Assign the values.
Calculate the total.
Display the total.
```

This pseudo code expresses the fact that the statements must be executed once each from the first to the last. This general sequence of input, process, output occurs in many methods and can be expressed using a diagram based on Jackson Structured Programming or Structured Systems Analysis Design Method Entity Life History diagramming notation. Each box represents one or more lines of pseudo code that in turn is translated into one or more lines of Java code (Figure 3.1).

3.7 Which line of Java code is the translation of the pseudo code 'Calculate the total'?

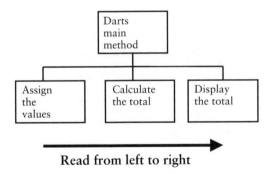

Read from left to right

Figure 3.1   A simple sequence.

Assignment operators

There are twelve assignment operators. The simple assignment operator = that assigns the value on the right-hand side to the variable on the left-hand side can be used with objects as well as primitive types. The two primitive variables are different variables assigned the same value. The two objects are the same object with two different names, any change in one results in the same change in the other. To copy two objects the clone() method must be used. The compound assignment operators require both operands to be a primitive type, except for +=, which allows the right-hand side to be of any type if the left-hand side is of type String. Each compound assignment operator consists of a binary operator (binaryOp) followed by the = symbol. Each is a shorthand way of writing

   variable = variable binaryOp right-hand side (aVar = aVar + 5)

as

   variable binaryOp= right-hand side (aVar += 5)

As with the simple assignment operator, the left-hand side must be a variable. It is this variable and the right-hand side that are used in the operation to produce the result that is stored in the variable. Each can be read as 'variable is assigned variable operation right-hand side'. In the example above, aVar is assigned aVar plus 5. The other eleven compound assignment operators are demonstrated by the code segment below.

?   **3.8** What is the compound assignment operator equivalent of a = a * b; ?

```
//: Test5.java
package chap03;

/** Fifth of a series of examples
 * showing the use of compound assignment operators.
 * Uses a class <code>Test5</code>
 * consisting only of a main method
 * @author Stuart F Lewis
 * @version 1.00, 19/02/98
 */
class Test5 {
```

```java
/**
 * Test data for the file Test5.
 */
public static void main(String args[]) {
/**
 * Temporary variables b,s,i,L,c,f,d, intResult and doubleResult
 */
byte b = 5;
short s = -195;
int i = 40000;
long L = 9876543210L;
char c = 'a';
float f = 200f;
double d = 5.123456789;

int intResult = 0;
double doubleResult = 0;

System.out.print("intResult of " + intResult );
intResult += b;
System.out.println(" plus " + b + " is " + intResult );

System.out.print("intResult of " + intResult );
intResult -= s;
System.out.println(" minus " + s + " is " + intResult );

System.out.print("intResult of " + intResult );
intResult *= i;
System.out.println(" multiplied by " + i + " is " + intResult );

System.out.print("intResult of " + intResult );
intResult /= i;
System.out.println(" divided " + i + " is " + intResult );

System.out.print("intResult of " + intResult );
intResult %= L;
System.out.println(" remainder when divided by " + L + " is " +
intResult );
intResult *= s;

System.out.print("intResult of " + intResult );
intResult <<= b;
System.out.print(" left shifted (<<) by " + b);
System.out.println(" is " + intResult );

System.out.print("intResult of " + intResult );
intResult >>= b;
System.out.print(" right shifted (>>) by () " + b);
System.out.println(" is " + intResult );
intResult <<= b;

System.out.print("intResult of " + intResult );
intResult >>>= b;
System.out.print(" unsigned right shifted (>>>) by " + b);
System.out.println(" is " + intResult );
intResult = b;

System.out.print("intResult of " + intResult );
intResult &= b;
System.out.println(" bitwise AND (&) of " + b + " is " +
intResult );
```

```
System.out.print("intResult of " + intResult );
intResult ^= b;
System.out.println(" bitwise exclusive OR (^) of " + b + " is " +
intResult );
System.out.print("intResult of " + intResult );
intResult |= b;
System.out.println(" bitwise inclusive OR (|) of " + b + " is " +
intResult );
System.out.print("doubleResult of " + doubleResult );
doubleResult += b;
System.out.println(" plus " + b + " is " + doubleResult );
System.out.print("doubleResult of " + doubleResult );
doubleResult -= s;
System.out.println(" minus " + s + " is " + doubleResult );
System.out.print("doubleResult of " + doubleResult );
doubleResult *= d;
System.out.println(" multiplied by " + d + " is " + doubleResult );
System.out.print("doubleResult of " + doubleResult );
doubleResult /= f;
System.out.println(" divided " + f + " is " + doubleResult );
doubleResult *= f;
System.out.print("doubleResult of " + doubleResult );
doubleResult %= f;
System.out.println(" remainder when divided by " + f + " is " +
doubleResult );
}//method main
} ///:~
```

Six temporary variables are defined and initialized, one for each of the numeric types. Note the alternative method of casting to float and long by adding a letter to the end of the numeric constant. Two variables are defined and initialized to store the results. Because of binary numeric promotion, the result of all the assignments not involving floating-point numbers will be of type int. The result of all the assignments involving floating-point numbers will be of type double. The program displays the spoken version of each operation followed by the result:

```
intResult of 0 plus 5 is 5
intResult of 5 minus -195 is 200
intResult of 200 multiplied by 40000 is 8000000
intResult of 8000000 divided 40000 is 200
intResult of 200 remainder when divided by 9876543210 is 200
intResult of -39000 left shifted (<<) by 5 is -1248000
intResult of -1248000 right shifted (>>) by 5 is -39000
intResult of -1248000 unsigned right shifted (>>>) by 5 is 134178728
intResult of 5 bitwise AND (&) of 5 is 5
intResult of 5 bitwise exclusive OR (^) of 5 is 0
intResult of 0 bitwise inclusive OR (|) of 5 is 5
doubleResult of 0.0 plus 5 is 5.0
doubleResult of 5.0 minus -195 is 200.0
doubleResult of 200.0 multiplied by 5.123456789 is 1024.6913577999999
doubleResult of 1024.6913577999999 divided 200.0 is 5.123456789
doubleResult of 1024.6913577999999 remainder when divided by 200.0 is
24.691357799999878
```

The bitwise operations shift, AND and OR are used only with the primitive integral types.

3.9 Rewrite the code to define and assign three values to three variables representing your score at darts then add these values together and display the total using the compound assignment operator +=.

String concatenation operator

The string concatenation operator (+) has been used in all of the examples to produce some output on the standard console device. If only one operand expression is of type String, then string conversion is performed on the other operand to produce a string at run time.

The character + is an overloaded operator in Java. It can be used as a unary or binary operator. It performs different operations according to the context in which it is used and the operands in that context.

3.10 What are the different operations that + performs?

3.11 What would you expect the statement

        System.out.println(5 + 7);

to display?

Wrapper classes

All the primitive data types have a related wrapper class to enable a primitive value to be stored as an object. A class is more than a type because it defines the operations and the attributes of a type, as can be seen from Figure 3.2.

String class

The Java String class is the template for all String objects. All strings in Java are objects of either the String or StringBuffer class. All objects in Java should be able to provide a String object to represent their class and state by overriding the toString() method provided by the Object class from which all Java classes are descended. To override an inherited method a class must provide a method with exactly the same signature as the inherited method. A method signature is made up of the visibility modifier, return type, method name, and parameter list. The signature for toString() is

        public String toString()

The toString() method from the class Object provides a default representation of all objects. If a class does not provide a version of toString() to produce a meaningful

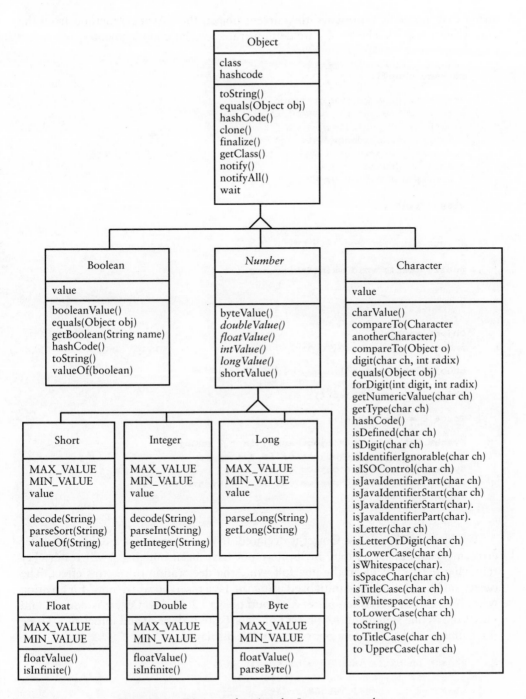

Figure 3.2 Diagram showing the Java wrapper classes.

string that 'textually represents' the current object, the toString() method from the class Object is used. The results are demonstrated by this code segment.

```
//: Test6.java
package chap03;

/** Sixth of a series of examples
* showing the use of System.out
* with simple objects.
* Uses a class <code>Test6</code>
* consisting only of a main method
* @author Stuart F Lewis
* @version 1.00, 19/02/98
*/
class Test6 {

/**
* Test data for the file Test6.
*/
public static void main(String args[]) {

/**
* Temporary variables o, o2, t
*/
Object anObj;
//System.out.println("object anObj is not yet initialized " + anObj);

anObj = new Object();

Object o2 = new Object();

Test6 t = new Test6();

System.out.println("object anObj is " + anObj );
System.out.println("object o2 is " + o2 );
System.out.println("object t is " + t);
System.out.println("System.out is " + System.out );
}//method main
} ///:~
```

An object anObj of class Object is declared. If you try to access anObj a compiler error message indicating that anObj may not have been initialized will result. Try removing the comment on the line following the declaration to see this effect. The object anObj is defined and initialized using the Java reserved word 'new' for creating new objects from a class template. A second object o2 of class Object is defined and initialized in one statement. An object t of class Test6 is defined and initialized. These three objects and the System.out object are all displayed.

```
object anObj is java.lang.Object@1cc767
object o2 is java.lang.Object@1cc768
object t is chap03.Test6@1cc769
System.out is java.io.PrintStream@1cc0fb
```

For each object the package and class followed by the @ symbol and the hashcode for that object are displayed.

Objects of class String can be created and displayed in this way and used to demonstrate the basic methods provided by the String class as seen in this code segment.

```java
//: Test7.java
package chap03;

/** Seventh of a series of examples
* showing the use of String class
* with simple objects.
* Uses a class <code>Test7</code>
* consisting only of a main method
* @author Stuart F Lewis
* @version 1.00, 29/02/98
*/
class Test7 {

/**
* Test data for the file Test7.
*/
public static void main(String args[]) {

/**
* Temporary variables s, s1, s2
*/
String s;
//System.out.println("string s is not yet initialized " + s );
s = new String();
String s1 = new String();
String s2 = new
String("one created with the one argument constructor");

System.out.println("string s is " +
s.getClass() + "@" + s.hashCode());
System.out.println("string s1 is " +
s1.getClass() + "@" + s1.hashCode());
System.out.println("string s2 is " +
s2.getClass() + "@" + s2.hashCode());

System.out.println("string s is " + s);
System.out.println("string s1 is " + s1 );
System.out.println("s is equal == to s1 is " + (s==s1) );
System.out.println("s equals s1 is " + (s.equals(s1)) );
System.out.println();

s = "a string";
s1 = "a string";
System.out.println("string s is " +
s.getClass() + "@" + s.hashCode());
System.out.println("string s1 is " +
s1.getClass() + "@" + s1.hashCode());
System.out.println(s + " s is equal == to " +
s1 + " s1 is " + (s==s1) );
System.out.println();

System.out.println("string s2 is " + s2);
s = s2;
System.out.println("string s is " + s );
```

```
System.out.println("s is equal == to s2 is " + (s==s2) );

System.out.println("string s2 is " + s2);
s = s2;
System.out.println("string s is " + s );
System.out.println("s is equal to s2 is " + (s==s2) );

System.out.println("string s is " +
s.getClass() + "@" + s.hashCode());
System.out.println("string s1 is " +
s1.getClass() + "@" + s1.hashCode());
System.out.println("string s2 is " +
s2.getClass() + "@" + s2.hashCode());
}//method main
} ///:~
```

Three string objects s, s1, and s2 are created based on the class String. The String class method toString() just returns the string. To see the class and hashcode of the string objects we can use the getClass() and hashCode() methods inherited from the Object class.

The string objects are compared using the equality operator ==. This will return true only if both objects are in fact the same object and the reference variable is a reference to the same object. Objects should always be compared using the equals() method normally overridden by all classes. For string objects the equals() method returns true if both are strings of the same length, containing the same characters.

The hashCode() for all three strings is displayed. The program displays the following:

```
string s is class java.lang.String@0
string s1 is class java.lang.String@0
string s2 is class java.lang.String@70749395
string s is
string s1 is
s is equal == to s1 is false
s equals s1 is true

string s is class java.lang.String@89011240
string s1 is class java.lang.String@89011240
a string s is equal == to a string s1 is true

string s2 is one created with the one argument constructor
string s is one created with the one argument constructor
s is equal == to s2 is true
string s is class java.lang.String@70749395
string s1 is class java.lang.String@89011240
string s2 is class java.lang.String@70749395
```

Although neither s nor s1 contains anything at first and have the same hashcode, they are not considered equal because they are different objects. The method astring.equals(anyObject) returns true because s and s1 are the same length and both contain no characters. Once they have been set to the same literal string they are now the same object and therefore equal. The first string s can be made equal to s2 using the assignment operator which assigns s to refer to the same string object as s2.

Again, this would be an ideal time to browse through the standard documentation for the Java Application Programming Interface for the class String.

3.13 How many constructors are there for the class String?

Comparing the documentation to the original source code for the class in the file jdk/src/java/lang/String.java gives an insight to the power of javadoc. This code also shows how a string object is stored using the private instance variables value[ ], offset, and count. The characters that make up the string are stored in an array of type char. The index of the first char is stored in the int variable offset. The number of characters in the string is stored in the int variable count.

The attributes of all objects must ultimately be stored using variables of primitive types. By encapsulating this storage within a class the attributes cannot be accessed directly.

Summary

Variables of primitive data types are not objects. The names of all identifiers will be read many times both in the code and generated documentation so they should be meaningful in both contexts. Variables of the primitive data types always store the actual value at that named location. All other variables are reference types because they refer to other objects. Neither float nor double values are stored exactly. The Java reserved word new is used for creating new objects, except for objects based on the String class that can be created using the assignment operator. Overloading occurs when the same operator or method performs a different operation depending on context and the operand(s). Overriding is when a method has exactly the same signature as an inherited method.

Answers to in-text questions

1 Each of the following variable names has a different problem:
   (a) 10percent is invalid because it starts with a digit.
   (b) My string is invalid because it has a space.
   (c) aGoodName is valid but not very meaningful.
   (d) x is also valid but not very meaningful, so it should be used only for a temporary variable.
   (e) true is invalid because it is a Java reserved word.
   (f) NotAClass is valid but does not follow the convention of starting a variable name with a lower-case letter.

2 Assuming someVariable is a boolean it can have only the values true or false so an equivalent statement would be return (someVariable); . It makes little sense to compare a boolean variable to either true or false.

3 The program displays:

```
5
5
6
5
6
6
```

4 The output shows that neither float nor double values are stored exactly. The result of an increment followed by a decrement and a division followed by a multiplication should be the original value.

5 The program displays the spoken version of each operation followed by either true or false:

```
0.5123457 is less than 5 is true
0.5123456788999999 is less than or equal to 0.5123457 is false
0.5123457 is greater than 5 is false
0.5123456788999999 is greater than or equal to 0.5123457 is true
0.5123457 is equal to 0.5123456788999999 is false
0.5123456788999999 is less than 5 is true
0.5123456788999999 is equal to 0.5123457 is false
5 is equal to 5 is true
```

6 A possible solution is:

```
//:Darts.java

package chap03;

/** Defines and assigns three values to three variables
* representing a score at darts.
* Adds these values together and displays the total
* Uses a class <code>Test1</code>
* consisting only of a main method
* @author Stuart F Lewis
* @version 1.00, 21/08/98
*/

class Darts {
/** Test data for the file Darts.
*/

public static void main(String args[]) {
/**
* Temporary variables
*/

    int dartOne = 20;
    int dartTwo = 10;
    int dartThree = 12;

    int totalScore = dartOne + dartTwo + dartThree;

    System.out.println("The total is " + totalScore);

}//method main
} ///:~
```

7 This line is the translation of the pseudo code "Calculate the total".

```
int totalScore = dartOne + dartTwo + dartThree;
```

8 The compound assignment operator equivalent of a = a * b; is a *= b;

9 As above except change the line

```
int totalScore = dartOne + dartTwo + dartThree;
```

to separate the declaration of totalScore from the calculation over four lines.

```
int totalScore = 0;
totalScore += dartOne;
totalScore += dartTwo;
totalScore += dartThree;
```

10 The + character is either used as an operator to concatenate String objects and perform addition of numeric values, or as part of the increment operator ++ and the compound assignment operator +=. The + character may also be used as a prefix operator used to indicate a positive sign for an operand, but as positive is the default, it is rarely used.

11 The statement System.out.println(5 + 7); will display 12. To achieve a display of 5 7 use System.out.println(5 + " " + 7);

12 The output may be different for other versions of the Java virtual machine.

13 There are 11 constructors for the class String in Java 1.2 (There may be more or less in different versions of the API.)

REVIEW QUESTIONS

Answers in Appendix A.

1 Why are the ranges of primitive data types the same for all Java platforms?

2 What is the difference between byte and Byte?

3 Which are the primitive integral data types?

4 Which are the primitive floating-point data types?

5 What is the difference between the primitive integral data types and primitive floating-point data types?

EXERCISES

Answers to exercises flagged with an asterisk appear in Appendix B.

1* In which package can you find the class StringBuffer?

2* What is the name of the method that finds a character within a String?

3* What does the method trim() do?

4 How many constructors does the StringBuffer class have?

5 What is MAX_VALUE?

6* Which class does Integer inherit from?

7 Can you create objects described by the OutputStream class?

8* Does the class Integer have a constructor which has a String argument?

9 What is a PrintStream?

4

Basic control structures

Overview

The basic control structures (Table 4.1) for primitive types used by objects to construct, accept data, set attributes, provide data, and the client server roles of different objects are introduced as are methods used by objects to select between one of several alternatives, including boolean expressions, relational operators, precedence, and multi-way selection. Initializing and continuing iterative constructs using various methods are considered.

Summary of basic control structures

Table 4.1   Summary of basic control structures.

Statement	Keyword
decision making or selection	if-else, switch-case
loop or iteration	while, for, do-while
exception	try-catch-finally, throw
miscellaneous	break, continue, return

Selecting one of several alternatives

The if-else statement

The if-else statement provides programs with the ability to selectively execute other statements based on some criteria. For example, suppose that a program printed debugging information based on the value of some boolean variable named DEBUG. If DEBUG were set to true, then the program would print debugging information.

```
if (DEBUG) {
System.out.println("DEBUG statement ");
}
```

This is the simplest version of the if statement. The statement governed by the if is executed if some boolean expression evaluates to true. An else can be added as part of the if statement. The statement governed by the else is executed if the boolean expression evaluates to false.

```
//: Test41.java
package chap04;

/** First of a series of examples
 * showing the use of the primitive data type boolean
 * with the if statement.
 * Uses a class <code>Test4</code>
 * consisting only of a main method
 * @author Stuart F Lewis
 * @version 1.00,
 */
class Test41 {
/**
 * Test data for the file Test41.
 */
public static void main(String args[]) {
/**
 * Constant DEBUG
 */
boolean DEBUG = true;

if (DEBUG) {
   System.out.println("DEBUG statement ");
}
else {
   System.out.println("Debugging is not enabled ");
}
}//method main
} ///:~
```

4.1 What will the program display when it is run?

4.2 How would you change the program to display the other message?

The simplest form of selection using the if statement can be expressed using a diagram based on Jackson Structured Programming and Structured Systems Analysis Design Method Entity Life History diagramming notation. Each box represents one or more lines of pseudo code that in turn is translated into one or more lines of Java code (Figure 4.1). The small circle in the top right-hand side of the box indicates that this box is a selection of one and only one from the boxes on that branch. The order in which the boxes appear does not affect which is selected. The condition associated with each selection can be listed below the diagram.

Another form of the else statement, else if, executes a statement based on another boolean expression. To write a program that assigns grades based on the value of a percentage score, an A1 for 90% or above, an A2 for 80% or above and so on, use an if statement with a series of companion else if statements, and an else.

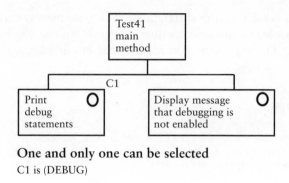

One and only one can be selected
C1 is (DEBUG)

Figure 4.1   A simple selection.

So far, all of the examples have produced only output. To be useful all programs carry out a variation on the input, process, output cycle. The first method of providing input to a Java program is via a command-line argument. To enable this program to be tested with several different values read the percentage value from the command line. This is the simplest form of input. Java byte-code files are interpreted by a command similar to

> java Classname

To add one or more command-line arguments to the program use a command like

> java Classname argumentZero argumentOne argumentTwo argumentThree

where argumentZero, argumentOne, argumentTwo, and argumentThree are String values to be passed to the program. These can be changed each time the program is run to produce different results.

This program demonstrates both the if-else statement and reading a single command-line argument representing the percentage score.

```
//: Test42.java
package chap04;

/** Second of a series of examples
* showing the use of primitive data types
* with the if-else statement and
* a numerical comparison operator.
* Uses a class <code>Test42</code>
* consisting only of a main method
* @author Stuart F Lewis
* @version 1.00,
*/
class Test42 {
/**
* Test data for the file Test42.
*/
public static void main(String args[]) {
/**
* Temporary variable percentage
*/
int percentage;
```

```
/**
 * Temporary variable grade
 */
String grade = "Unknown";
percentage = Integer.parseInt(args[0]);
if (percentage >= 90) {
  grade = "A1";
} else if (percentage >= 80) {
  grade = "A2";
} else if (percentage >= 70) {
  grade = "A3";
} else if (percentage >= 67) {
  grade = "B1";
} else if (percentage >= 64) {
  grade = "B2";
} else if (percentage >= 60) {
  grade = "B3";
} else if (percentage >= 57) {
  grade = "C1";
} else if (percentage >= 54) {
  grade = "C2";
} else if (percentage >= 50) {
  grade = "C3";
} else if (percentage >= 47) {
  grade = "D1";
} else if (percentage >= 44) {
  grade = "D2";
} else if (percentage >= 40) {
  grade = "D3";
} else if (percentage >= 35) {
  grade = "F1";
} else {
  grade = "F2";
}
System.out.println(grade);
}//method main
} ///:~
```

An if statement can have any number of companion else if statements, but only one else. The statement

```
percentage = Integer.parseInt(args[0]);
```

shows how a String command-line argument can be converted to an int in a program. The standard documentation for the Java Application Programming Interface (API) describes the method parseInt(String) in detail in the class Integer.

4.3 What will the program display when run with the command

java Test42 64

This multi-way selection (Figure 4.2) using the if statement can also be expressed using a diagram based on Jackson Structured Programming and Structured Systems

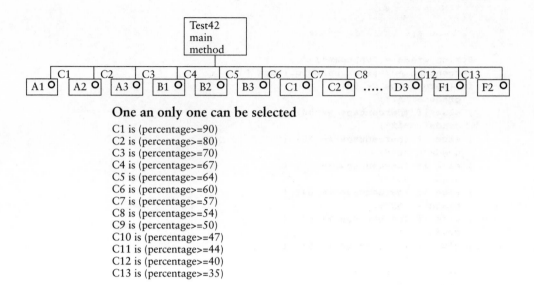

One an only one can be selected

C1 is (percentage>=90)
C2 is (percentage>=80)
C3 is (percentage>=70)
C4 is (percentage>=67)
C5 is (percentage>=64)
C6 is (percentage>=60)
C7 is (percentage>=57)
C8 is (percentage>=54)
C9 is (percentage>=50)
C10 is (percentage>=47)
C11 is (percentage>=44)
C12 is (percentage>=40)
C13 is (percentage>=35)

Figure 4.2   A multi-way selection.

Analysis Design Method Entity Life History diagramming notation. The small circle in the top right-hand side of the box again indicates that this box is a selection of one and only one from the boxes on that branch. The order in which the boxes appear does not affect which is selected. The condition associated with each selection can be listed below the diagram.

4.4 Write a program to assign grades based on a simpler system where the value of the percentage score is converted as a D for 70% or above, an M for 60% or above, a P for 40% or above and an F for less than 40%.

All of the different conditional operators from the previous chapter can be used with the if statement.

```
//: Test43.java
package chap04;

/** Third of a series of examples
 * showing the use of primitive data types
 * with the comparison operators in
 * several if statements.
 * Uses a class <code>Test43</code>
 * consisting only of a main method
 * @author Stuart F Lewis
 * @version 1.00, 19/02/98
 */
class Test43 {
```

```
/**
 * Test data for the file Test43.
 */
public static void main(String args[]) {
/**
 * Temporary variables d, f
 */
int i = 5;
double d = 5.123456789;
float f = (float)d/10;
d = d/10;

if (f<i) {
System.out.println(f + " is less than " + i );
}

if (d<=f) {
System.out.println(d + " is less than or equal to " + f );
}

if (f>i) {
System.out.println(f + " is greater than " + i );
}

if (d>=f) {
System.out.println(d + " is greater than or equal to " + f );
}

if (f==d) {
System.out.println(f + " is equal to " + d );
}

if (d!=i) {
System.out.println(d + " is not equal to " + i );
}

if (d==f) {
System.out.println(d + " is equal to " + f );
}

if (i==5) {
System.out.println(i + " is equal to " + 5 );
}

}//method main
} ///:~
```

?   **4.5** When the program is run what do you think it will display?

Several if statements can be nested inside one another.

```
//: Test44.java
package chap04;

/** Fourth of a series of examples
* showing the use of primitive data types
* with a nested if and comparison operator.
* Uses a class <code>Test4</code>
* consisting only of a main method
* @author Stuart F Lewis
* @version 1.00,
*/
class Test44 {
/**
* Test data for the file Test44.
*/
public static void main(String args[]) {
/**
* Temporary variables DEBUG and i
*/
boolean DEBUG = true;
int i = 5;

if (i==5) {
System.out.println("i is five so check DEBUG ");
if (DEBUG) {
        System.out.println("DEBUG statement ");
   }//if
}//if
}//method main
} ///:~
```

4.6 When the program is run what do you think it will display?

The switch statement

Use the switch statement to conditionally perform statements based on some constant expression of one of the integral types char, byte, short, or int. To display the long description of each of the grades from the question above based on its coded equivalent use the switch statement

```
//: Test45.java
package chap04;

/** Fifth of a series of examples
* showing the use of primitive data types
* with the case statement.
* Uses a class <code>Test45</code>
* consisting only of a main method
* @author Stuart F Lewis
* @version 1.00,
*/
class Test45 {
/** Test data for the file Test45.
*/
```

```
public static void main(String args[]) {

/** Temporary variable grade
*/
char grade;

grade = args[0].charAt(0);
switch (grade) {
case 'D': System.out.println("Distinction"); break;
case 'M': System.out.println("Merit"); break;
case 'P': System.out.println("Pass"); break;
case 'F': System.out.println("Fail"); break;
default: System.out.println("not a valid grade");
}
}//method main

} ///:~
```

The switch statement evaluates its expression, the value of grade, and executes the appropriate case statement. The break statements are necessary because case statements fall through. Finally, the default statement at the end of the switch handles all values that are not explicitly handled by one of the case statements.

4.7 Why could the switch statement not be used to display the long description of each of the grades in the example above (A1, A2 etc.)?

4.8 How could such a display be achieved?

The break statements cause control to break out of the switch and continue with the first statement following the switch. Sometimes you do want control to proceed sequentially through case statements as in the following code that calculates the number of days in a month according to the old rhyme that starts 'Thirty days hath September...'.

```
//: Test46.java
package chap04;

/** Sixth of a series of examples
* showing the use of primitive data types
* with the case statement.
* Uses a class <code>Test46</code>
* consisting only of a main method
* @author Stuart F Lewis
* @version 1.00,
*/
class Test46 {
/**
* Test data for the file Test46.
*/
```

```java
public static void main(String args[]) {
/**
* Temporary variable month
*/
int month = 0;
month = Integer.parseInt(args[0]);
int year = 1998;
year = Integer.parseInt(args[1]);
switch (month) {
case 1: System.out.print("January"); break;
case 2: System.out.print("February"); break;
case 3: System.out.print("March"); break;
case 4: System.out.print("April"); break;
case 5: System.out.print("May"); break;
case 6: System.out.print("June"); break;
case 7: System.out.print("July"); break;
case 8: System.out.print("August"); break;
case 9: System.out.print("September"); break;
case 10: System.out.print("October"); break;
case 11: System.out.print("November"); break;
case 12: System.out.print("December"); break;
default: System.out.print("not a valid month");
}
int numDays = 0;

switch (month) {
case 1:
case 3:
case 5:
case 7:
case 8:
case 10:
case 12: numDays = 31; break;
case 4:
case 6:
case 9:
case 11: numDays = 30; break;
case 2:
 if (((year % 4 == 0) && !(year % 100 == 0)) || (year % 400 == 0)) {
    numDays = 29;
 } else {
    numDays = 28;
 }
 break;
}//switch
System.out.println(" has " + numDays + " days in " + year);
}//method main
} ///:~
```

4.9 What does the expression

((((year % 4 == 0) && !(year % 100 == 0)) || (year % 400 == 0))

mean in English?

4.10 What will the program display when run with the commands

java Test46 2 1994

java Test46 2 2000

Combining the sequence and selection diagrams already introduced in a tree diagram (Figure 4.3) or using pseudo code can represent the design of this method.

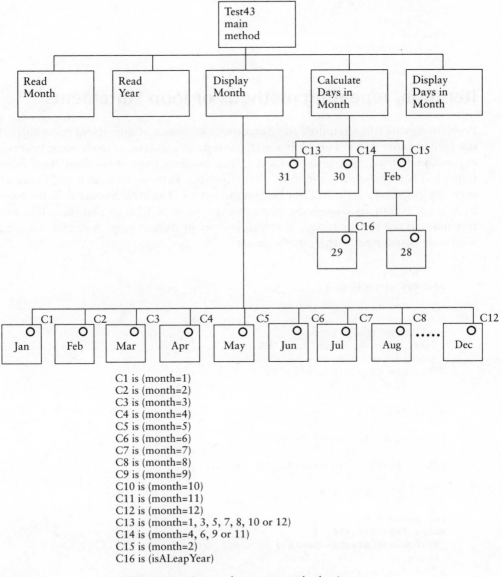

C1 is (month=1)
C2 is (month=2)
C3 is (month=3)
C4 is (month=4)
C5 is (month=5)
C6 is (month=6)
C7 is (month=7)
C8 is (month=8)
C9 is (month=9)
C10 is (month=10)
C11 is (month=11)
C12 is (month=12)
C13 is (month=1, 3, 5, 7, 8, 10 or 12)
C14 is (month=4, 6, 9 or 11)
C15 is (month=2)
C16 is (isALeapYear)

Figure 4.3 A nested sequence and selection.

```
Read month number from the command line.
Read year from the command line.
CASE month OF
1 : Print January.
..etc.
12 : Print December.
ENDCASE
CASE month OF
1,3,5,7,8,10,12 : NumberOfDays = 31;
4,6,9,11 : NumberOfDays = 30;
2: IF itsALeapYear
   NumberOfDays = 29;
   ELSE
   NumberOfDays = 28;
ENDCASE
Print NumberOfDays.
```

Iteration, repeating methods or loop statements

Problem solving often requires an operation or sequence of operations to be carried out zero or more times. The while statement repeats a statement while some boolean expression is true. The variable used in the boolean expression must have been initialized before entering the loop. If the boolean expression is false at the outset then the loop body code will not be executed at all. The code executed in the loop body must eventually change the boolean expression to false so that the while will terminate. If not the iteration will run forever in an endless loop. A simple counting loop is demonstrated by this code segment:

```
//: Test47.java
package chap04;

/** Seventh of a series of examples
* showing the use of primitive data types
* with the while loop.
* Uses a class <code>Test47</code>
* consisting only of a main method
* @author Stuart F Lewis
* @version 1.00,
*/
class Test47 {
/**
* Test data for the file Test47.
*/
public static void main(String args[]) {
/**
* Temporary variable month
*/
int month = 0;
while (month++ <10) {
 System.out.println(month);
 }//while
}//method main
} ///:~
```

4.11 What will the program display?

When the condition becomes false the looping terminates and the statement following the closing brace } of the while statement is executed next.

```
//: Test48.java
package chap04;

/** Eighth of a series of examples
 * showing the use of primitive data types
 * with the while loop
 * Uses a class <code>Test48</code>
 * consisting only of a main method
 * @author Stuart F Lewis
 * @version 1.00,
 */
class Test48 {

/** Test data for the file Test48.
 */
public static void main(String args[]) {

/**Temporary variables miles and kms
 */
int miles = 0;
double kms = 0.0;

System.out.println("Miles  Kms");

while (miles <60) {
 miles += 10;
 kms = miles * 1.609 ;
 System.out.println(miles + "   : " + kms);
}//while
}//method main

} ///:~
```

4.12 What will the program display?

This iteration can also be expressed using a diagram based on Jackson Structured Programming and Structured Systems Analysis Design Method Entity Life History diagramming notation. The small asterisk in the top right-hand side of the box (Figure 4.4) indicates that this box is an iterated component performed zero or more times.

There are two other iterative constructs, the for loop and the do-while loop. Both can be implemented using the while loop. Use the for loop when you know the constraints of the iteration (its initialization instruction, termination criteria, and increment instruction). A for loop can be used to iterate over the characters in a string.

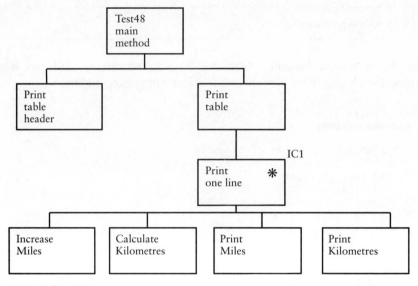

IC1 is (miles <60)

Figure 4.4 A simple iteration.

```
//: Test49.java
package chap04;

/** Ninth of a series of examples
* showing the use of primitive data types
* with the while loop.
* Uses a class <code>Test49</code>
* consisting only of a main method
* @author Stuart F Lewis
* @version 1.00,
*/
class Test49 {
/**
* Test data for the file Test49.
*/
public static void main(String args[]) {
/**
* Temporary variable aString
*/
String aString = args[0];
for (int i = 0; i < aString.length(); i++) {
  System.out.println(aString.charAt(i));
}
System.out.println();
}//method main
} ///:~
```

4.13 What will the program display when run with the command
java Test49 Hello

The initialization statement is executed once at the beginning of the loop to declare a variable i with a value of zero. The termination statement is a boolean expression that terminates the loop when it becomes false. This boolean expression is evaluated at the top of each iteration of the loop. When the expression evaluates to false, the for loop terminates. The increment statement is an expression that is invoked for each iteration through the loop. Any (or all) of these components can be empty statements (a single semicolon by itself).

The do-while loop is similar to the while loop except that the expression is evaluated at the bottom of the loop:

```
do {
    statements
} while (booleanExpression);
```

The do-while is convenient to use when the statements within the loop must be executed at least once.

Exception-handling statements

When an error occurs a method can throw an exception to indicate to its caller that an error occurred and the type of error that occurred. The calling method can use the try, catch, and finally statements to catch and handle the exception.

Errors of two types occur in software programs. Some are due to mistakes made by the designer or programmer; these logical errors must be corrected by maintaining the program. Others may be exceptional circumstances, some of which can be anticipated by the programmer. It is for these extraordinary, exceptional situations that exception handling is intended. After the error occurs the exception is either handled or passed up to the calling method to be handled.

Exceptions provide a means to separate all the details handling an error from the main logic of the program. Exceptions are instances of the class Throwable or any Throwable descendant. Check the API documentation for the full description of these classes.

4.14 How many constructors are there for the class Throwable?

The second way of providing input data to a program is by entering the input using the keyboard. If the program expects a number and the user enters a sequence of letters what should the program do? Some programming languages let the program crash or terminate abnormally in this situation, others ignore the letters and wait for a number to be entered, and others assume a default value, often zero. All of these effects are possible using exception handling. This example demonstrates one approach.

```
//: Test4A.java
package chap04;
import java.io.*;

/** Tenth of a series of examples
 * showing the use of primitive data types
 * with the while loop.
 * Uses a class <code>Test4A</code>
 * consisting only of a main method
 * @author Stuart F Lewis
 * @version 1.00,
 */
class Test4A {

/** Example of exception handling in input
 * Tries to read an integer from the console input.
 * If anything other than a number in the valid
 * range is entered a helpful message is
 * displayed and the chance is offered again.
 * @exception NumberFormatException ;
 * If the value entered is not an integer.
 * @exception IOException If an I/O error occurs.
 * @see java.io.BufferedReader
 * @see java.io.InputStreamReader
 */
public int getInt() throws IOException {
BufferedReader stdin = new BufferedReader
    (new InputStreamReader(System.in));
int anInt = 0;
while (!validPositiveWholeNumber(anInt)) {
  System.out.print("Enter a positive whole number ");
  try {
   anInt = Integer.parseInt(stdin.readLine());
  }
  catch (NumberFormatException e) {
   anInt = 0;
   System.out.println("Not a number. ");
  }
  if (!validPositiveWholeNumber(anInt)) {
   System.out.println("Not a valid positive whole number. Please" +
     " enter a number between 1 and " + Integer.MAX_VALUE);
  }//if
}//while
return anInt;
}//method getInt

boolean validPositiveWholeNumber(int i) {
return (i > 0 && i < Integer.MAX_VALUE);
}

/**
* Test data for the file Test4A.
*/
public static void main(String args[]) throws IOException {
Test4A testObj = new Test4A();
System.out.println(testObj.getInt());
}//method main
} ///:~
```

?

4.15 When is the message "Not a number." displayed?

?

4.16 How does the program recover from this exceptional situation?

System.in, a static field of class java.io.InputStream in the System class, provides keyboard input. This is the standard input stream. This stream is already open and ready to supply input data. It is the partner of System.out, a static field of class java.io.PrintStream which we have used to output all data so far. This is also known as the standard output stream.

Using System.in is slightly more involved than using System.out because an InputStream works in raw bytes. By wrapping the InputStream in an InputStreamReader bytes are read and translated into characters according to the default character encoding for the system. Finally, wrapping the InputStreamReader in a BufferedReader means that text from the character-input stream will be buffered so as to provide efficient reading of characters and lines. Check the API documentation for full details of these classes for your current version of Java.

Array data type

An array is a data structure for holding a related group of data items of the same data type or class. Each individual element of the array is like a simple data item of a primitive data type. The scores of the 11 batsmen in an innings of a cricket match will require a group of 11 int values. Accessing the individual elements can process these scores.

```java
//: Test4B.java
package chap04;
import java.io.*;

/** Eleventh of a series of examples
* showing the use of an array
* Uses a class <code>Test4B</code>
* consisting only of a main method
* @author Stuart F Lewis
* @version 1.00,
*/

class Test4B {
/** Test data for the file Test4B.
*/

public static void main(String args[]) throws IOException {

  BufferedReader stdin = new BufferedReader
    (new InputStreamReader(System.in));

  int NUMBER_OF_VALUES = 11;
  int[] allScores = new int[NUMBER_OF_VALUES];
```

```
int sum = 0 ;
for (int i = 1; (i <= NUMBER_OF_VALUES); i++) {
 System.out.print("Enter score for batsman " + i + "> ");
 int score;
 try {
  score = Integer.parseInt(stdin.readLine());
  sum += score;
  allScores[i-1] = score;
 }
 catch (NumberFormatException e) {
  score = 0;
 }
 System.out.println();
}//for
System.out.print("The sum of the " + NUMBER_OF_VALUES);
System.out.println(" scores is " + sum);
System.out.println("Their average is " + sum / NUMBER_OF_VALUES );
System.out.println("Score by Batsman");
for (int i = 1; (i <= NUMBER_OF_VALUES); i++) {
 System.out.println(allScores[i-1] + " by " + i);
}
}//method main
} ///:~
```

4.17 What will the program display?

4.18 Change this code to report the highest-scoring batsman.

Vector class and Enumeration

The class Vector provides a way of storing objects. Like an array, it contains components that can be accessed using an integer index. However, the size of a Vector can grow or shrink as needed to accommodate adding and removing items after the Vector has been created. An Enumeration is an interface that generates a series of elements, one at a time.

Successive calls to the nextElement method return successive elements of the series. To print all elements of a vector v:

```
for (Enumeration e = v.elements(); e.hasMoreElements();) {
    System.out.println(e.nextElement());
}
```

These classes will be discussed in more depth later.

4.19 How does a Vector differ from an array?

Summary

A number of different code constructs are used by objects to select between one of several alternatives. These include boolean expressions, relational operators, precedence, and multi-way selection. Initializing and continuing iterative constructs using various methods were considered. Exception handling is an important aspect of developing robust programs.

Answers to in-text questions

1 The program will display

```
DEBUG statement
```

2 To display the other message change the definition of DEBUG to be:

```
boolean DEBUG = false;
```

3 The program will display B2 when run with the command java Test42 64.

4 A possible solution is

```
//: Question4.java
package chap04;
/** One possible solution
* showing the use of primitive data types
* with the if-else statement and
* a numerical comparison operator.
* Uses a class <code> Question4</code>
* consisting only of a main method
* @author Stuart F Lewis
* @version 1.00,
*/
class Question4 {
/** Test data for the file Question4.
*/
public static void main(String args[]) {
/** Temporary variable percentage
*/
int percentage;
/** Temporary variable grade
*/
char grade = '?';
percentage = Integer.parseInt(args[0]);
if (percentage >= 70) {
  grade = 'D';
} else if (percentage >= 60) {
  grade = 'M';
} else if (percentage >= 40) {
  grade = 'P';
} else {
  grade = 'F';
}
System.out.println(grade);
}//method main
} ///:~
```

5 The program displays

```
0.5123457 is less than 5
0.5123456788999999 is greater than or equal to 0.5123457
0.5123456788999999 is less than 5
5 is equal to 5
```

6 The program displays:

```
i is five so check DEBUG
DEBUG statement
```

7 The switch statement could not be used to display the long description of each of the grades (A1, A2 etc.) because "A1" is a String but switch only works with constant expressions of one of the integral types char, byte, short, or int.

8 Such a display could be achieved using if, else-if and else statements.

9 If year is a leap year this expression will evaluate to true.

10 The program displays

```
February has 28 days in 1994
February has 29 days in 2000
```

11 The program displays

```
1
2
3
4
5
6
7
8
9
10
```

12 The program displays

```
Miles     Kms
10    :   16.09
20    :   32.18
30    :   48.269999999999996
40    :   64.36
50    :   80.45
60    :   96.53999999999999
```

13 The program displays

```
H
e
l
l
o
```

14 There are two constructors for the class Throwable, one with a String argument.

15 When a NumberFormatException occurs.

16 By setting the value entered to zero and requesting the input again.

17 The program will repeat the prompt 11 times asking for a score. Then a summary will be printed with the question marks replaced by actual values from the input.

```
The sum of the 11 scores is ???
and their average is ??
Score by Batsman
?? by 1.
etc..to
?? by 11.
```

18 Add lines similar to

```
//declare extra variables
int sum = 0, highest = 0, highScorer = 0;
//in the body of the loop
if (allScores[i-1] > highest) {
   highest = allScores[i-1];
   highScorer = i;
 }
//at the end
System.out.println("Highest Score by Batsman " + highScorer +
                   " with " + allScores[highScorer-1]);
```

19 A Vector can increase in size, an array is declared with a fixed size. A Vector can be iterated over using an Enumeration.

REVIEW QUESTIONS

Answers in Appendix A.

1 What must always appear around a boolean expression?

2 How can a multi-way selection be coded?

3 Command-line arguments are stored in what type of object?

4 Which is the easiest multi-way selection to read?

EXERCISES

Answers to exercises flagged with an asterisk appear in Appendix B.

1* What possible values do boolean expressions evaluate to?

2 What is the difference between a switch statement with and without break statements?

3 How many boolean expressions are used to form an if statement?

4* What is the scope of i when declared in for (int i = 0; ?

5* What is the difference between Switch and switch?

5

Implementation of one object

Overview

A simple Count class is used to relate the OO design concepts of state, attributes and methods to concrete implementation in Java. The importance of commenting code for readability, understandability, maintainability and to produce documentation is reinforced. The basic methods used by objects to construct, accept data, set attributes, provide data, and the client/server roles of different objects are introduced. The first of three human interaction classes is implemented to show how the same object can be viewed in different ways. The three choices are the standard console interface and graphical user interfaces (GUI) for both applets and applications.

Analysis and design for the Count class

The class Count is a software model of a simple real-world object often attached to turnstiles, car park entrances, or even held by club bouncers. It is used to provide the service of counting the number of people or cars entering and leaving a particular location.

5.1 What other counting objects have you seen in the real world or in a software system?

For a simple object, the amount of analysis and design is minimal but a careful approach will pay dividends in the future when trying to reuse classes. Consider what a Count knows and what services it can provide to potential clients. Essentially a Count object knows the current value of its own count and can increment, decrement, or reset that value when asked to by a client. To enable the count to be reset to a particular value each Count object will know its own reset value. Every Count object will be able to tell any client its current count value. Expressing this Count class using a UML class diagram (Figure 5.1) shows the class name, a list of attributes, and list of methods.

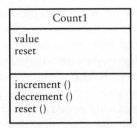

Figure 5.1   Diagram showing the Count1 class.

Three additional methods will be implemented by the class: setResetValue(int), setValue(int), and getValue(). These set or get methods are not normally shown on a class diagram because every class with attribute values needs these basic access methods. The informal standard for naming these accessor methods is 'get' or 'set' followed by the attribute name. This is vital for developing reusable Java software components known as Java Beans. Adhering to this naming standard enables component editors to access, change and save the attributes, allowing Java Beans to be customized without having the source code available.

5.2 What additional accessor method may be required for the Count class?

Implementation for the Count class

When moving from design to code retain the vocabulary of the problem domain. The selection of identifier names can have a huge impact on the readability, understandability, and maintainability of code. Add comments to code as it is written for two distinct purposes. Firstly to enhance the readability of the code itself. Secondly to gain the benefit of automatically producing documentation with the javadoc utility. All Java library code is documented using this utility.

Three ways of including comments are available in Java and are used for different purposes. The simple double forward slash // marks everything to the end of the current line as a comment. This is useful for commenting out sections of code. This is used in this text for examples that include code lines that do not compile. Other uses are for adding short comments to help the reader understand the code and for marking the closing curly brackets } of longer methods and classes.

The single forward slash followed by an asterisk /* marks the beginning of a multiline comment which ends with an asterisk followed by a forward slash /. Often every line between the /* and */ are started with an asterisk * to show that all these lines are comments too. Many modern language-sensitive editors display comments in a different colour or text style but this is not so often true for program listings or textbooks. This style of commenting is often used for including copyright notices and other information in the source code. Both of these commenting styles were inherited from C++.

Finally, javadoc comments start with a single forward slash followed by two asterisks /** and end with an asterisk followed by a forward slash */. Again, every line between the /** and */ is started with an asterisk * to show that all these lines are comments (these asterisks are ignored by javadoc). The documentation produced by javadoc links each comment with the class, variable, constructor or method immediately following it in the source code. Within a javadoc comment, there are two ways of enhancing the output. Embedded Hypertext Markup Language (HTML) markers can be used for formatting. Any line that begins with the character @ followed by one of a few special keywords starts a tagged paragraph. These tagged paragraphs identify specific information related to the class, variable, constructor or method.

? **5.3** Where is HTML most widely used?

The state of a Count object is stored using two primitive variables of type int. Java allows the provision of more than one constructor for creating new objects based on a class template. The Count class provides three constructors, a default no-argument constructor Count(), a constructor that provides an initial value Count(int) and finally a constructor that provides an initial value and a reset value Count(int, int). Here is the fully commented code for the Count class. It is called Count1 to indicate that it is a first attempt.

```
//: Count1.java
package chap05;

/** First implementation of a
* very simple class <code>Count1</code>
* representing a Counting object.
* @author Stuart F Lewis
* @version 1.00, 9/03/98
*/
public class Count1 {

/**
* Current <code>value</code> of this Count1.
*/
private int value;

/**
* Current <code>reset</code> value for this Count1.
*/
private int reset;

/**
* Constructs a new Count1 with initial value zero.
* Reset value is also zero.
*/
public Count1() {
this(0);
}
```

```java
/**
 * Constructs a new Count1 with initial value provided.
 * Reset value is also the initial value provided.
 * @param val the initial value for this <code>Count</code>
 */
public Count1(int val) {
this(val,val);
}


/**
 * Constructs a new Count1 with initial value and
 * a reset value provided.
 * Reset value is also the initial value provided.
 * @param val the initial value for this <code>Count</code>
 * @param reset the reset value for this <code>Count</code>
 */
public Count1(int val, int reset) {
this.value = val;
this.reset = reset;
}

/**
 * Increases the value of this Count1.
 */
public void increment() {
value++;
}

/**
 * Decreases the value of this Count1.
 */
public void decrement() {
value--;
}

/**
 * Resets the value of this Count1.
 */
public void reset() {
setValue(reset);
}

/**
 * Sets the reset value of this Count1.
 * @param val the reset value for this <code>Count</code>
 */
public void setResetValue(int val) {
reset = val;
}

/**
 * Sets the current value of this Count1.
 * @param val the current value for this <code>Count</code>
 */
public void setValue(int val) {
value = val;
}
```

```
/**
 * Gets the current value of this Count1.
 * @return the current value of this Count1.
 */
public int getValue() {
return value;
}

/**
 * Test data and code for Count1.
 * Creates a new Count1 a and displays Count1 a.
 * Sets the Count1 a to 10.
 * Displays Count1 a.
 * Increases Count1 a twice and displays Count1 a.
 * Decreases Count1 a and displays Count1 a.
 * Changes the reset value of Count1 a.
 * Resets Count1 a and displays Count1 a.
 * Sets the Count1 a to the maximum integer available.
 * Displays Count1 a, increases Count1 a, displays Count1 a.
 * Creates a new Count1 b initially set to 24 and displays it.
 * Creates a new Count1 c initially set to 4 and resets it to 10.
 */
public static void main(String args[]) {

Count1 a = new Count1();
 System.out.println(a.getValue());
 a.setValue(10);
 System.out.println(a.getValue());
 a.increment();
 a.increment();
 System.out.println(a.getValue());
 a.decrement();
 System.out.println(a.getValue());
 a.setResetValue(23);
 a.reset();
 System.out.println(a.getValue());
 a.setValue(Integer.MAX_VALUE);
 System.out.println(a.getValue());
 a.increment();
 System.out.println(a.getValue());
Count1 b = new Count1(24);
 System.out.println(b.getValue());
 System.out.println(b);
Count1 c = new Count1(4,10);
 System.out.println(c.getValue());
 c.reset();
 System.out.println(c.getValue());
}//method main
} ///:~
```

The first constructor Count1() uses the Java reserved word 'this' to refer to this Count object itself and call the second constructor with an initial value of zero. The second constructor Count1(int) calls the third constructor. The third constructor Count1(int,int) is thus called to create every object of class Count1. The two instance variables used to store the state of 'this' Count are initialized. The reserved word this is used in the constructors to refer to the object being created and call the other constructors to actually create the new Count1.

? **5.4** What reset value will a Count1 constructed with the second constructor Count1(int) have?

All of the methods are declared as public and are available to any client object of this class. All of the methods except getValue() have a return type of void because they do not return any information to the client. The service is achieved in each case by changing the current state of the Count object. The only method that does not change the state of the Count object is getValue() which simply returns the current count to the client that requested it. The test code provided in the static class method main() is described in the comment immediately before the method.

? **5.5** When the program is executed what it will produce?

The output demonstrates that the class works as designed and illustrates the wrap-round nature of the increment (++) and decrement (--) operators when used with the primitive type int. The final line shows that Count1 has inherited a toString() method (and hashCode()) from the superclass Object. The inherited method however is not displaying a meaningful string that 'textually represents' the current state of the count. To improve the class Count1 the methods inherited from Object should be overridden to provide appropriate functionality for a Count object. The first three methods to consider overriding from Object are toString(), equals() and hashCode(). Usually only the first two methods are actually overridden as the inherited hashCode() is satisfactory in most cases.

To override an inherited method the method signature must be identical to the inherited method signature. A method signature consists of the visibility modifier, return type, name and argument list or parameters. If any part of the signature differs from the inherited method then the method will be considered a new method.

Here the overloaded operator + is used to convert the value returned from getValue() to a String by concatenating it to an empty string constant " ":

```
/**
 * Returns the current value of this Count as a String.
 * @return a string representing the current value of this Count
 */
public String toString() {
return getValue()+"";
}
```

To override the equals() method you must first decide what makes two Count objects equal.

? **5.6** What conditions need to be true for two Count objects to be equal?

The simple equality == operator will only return true if the two objects are indeed the same object. If two objects are equal according to == then any change in the state of one will also be the same change in the state of the other because they are just different references or variable names for the same object. The equals() method could be called by any object with any other object as an argument. Using a general form for an equals() method ensures that the simple cases are taken care of first. Using an if conditional statement and comparison operators check that the other object is not the null object and is actually an instance of the same class. The Java reserved word 'null' refers to an object that has not been initialized or defined as referring to any particular instance of a class. The Java reserved word 'instanceof' is a binary comparison operator that returns a boolean true if the object is an instance of the class. Having ensured that the other object is a Count, cast it to a temporary Count object and compare the instance variables representing the state to each other. If all the instance variables have the same values in both objects, then these two Count objects can be considered equal.

```
/**
 * Compares this Count to the specified object.
 * The result is <code>true</code> if and only if the argument is not
 * <code>null</code> and is a <code>Count</code> object that has
 * the same current value and reset value as this <code>Count</code>.
 *
 * @param  anObject  the object to compare this <code>Count</code> to.
 * @return <code>true</code> if the <code>Counts </code>are equal;
 *      <code>false</code> otherwise.
 */
public boolean equals(Object anObject) {
if ((anObject != null) && (anObject instanceof Count)) {
  Count anotherCount = (Count)anObject;
  if ((value == anotherCount.value) &&
      (reset == anotherCount.reset)) {
    return true;
  }//if
}//if
return false;
}//method equals
```

With these two overridden methods added the test method main() can be altered and extended to test the equals() method. All of the calls to the getValue() method can be removed and replaced in System.out.println() statements by just the Count object reference. The Count toString() method will be called to convert the Count object to a string when required. The following code is added to the test method main():

```
a.setResetValue(24);
a.reset();
System.out.println("Count a is " + a);
a.increment();
System.out.println("Count a is " + a);
b = new Count(24);
System.out.println(b);
System.out.println("Count a.equals(b) is " + a.equals(b));
System.out.println("Count b is " + b);
b.increment();
```

```
System.out.println("Count b is " + b);
System.out.println("Count a.equals(b) is " + a.equals(b));
System.out.println("Count a==b is " + (a==b));
b=a;
System.out.println("Count a==b is " + (a==b));
System.out.println("Only increment b");
b.increment();
System.out.println("Count a is " + a);
```

5.7 What will the program will display?

The output shows that two instances of the Count class are only equal if they are in the same state. Until a is actually assigned to b using the assignment operator = the equality operator == always considers a and b to be different objects because they are. After the assignment a and b are now references to the same object. When the object referred by b changes state so does the object referred to by a. The reference variables refer to the same object and therefore have the same value.

5.8 Combine the first attempt Count1 with the overriding methods toString() and equals() to provide a complete class Count as per the UML diagram of the Count class (Figure 5.2).

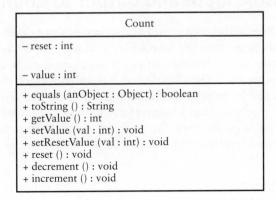

Figure 5.2 Count class with full UML operation signatures.

Adding an interface to Count

The Switch and Count classes have been tested using the main() method to create objects, call methods and display the state using the System.out object. This has allowed us to see that our problem domain classes can be used to create objects that have the required functionality. For a software system to be useful, it must have an interface to the real world. The interface is provided by human interaction components. In OOA, OOD and OOP we strive to keep the human interaction components separated from the problem domain components. Separation of these concerns will facilitate change and reuse.

Java has several options for providing an interface to objects. Standard console input is provided to enhance the output-only and command-line versions used so far. Graphical user interfaces (GUIs) can be built for both stand-alone applications and applets viewed using standard web browsers. A GUI builder tool could be used to develop the interface by direct manipulation of AWT components or JavaBeans on a design view surface followed by automatic code generation. This process is outside the scope of this text but is often clearly explained by the help system of many GUI builders. All four interface choices have different purposes.

Standard console output only

A Java source file can contain far more than just the executable lines of code that are converted by the compiler into Java byte code. The comments to be processed by javadoc provide basic, standard, portable documentation. The test code in the main() class can both reassure the designer that objects of the class do indeed perform correctly and provide valuable examples of how those objects might be used. When a class is modified it can be immediately tested simply by running the class itself. As the class static method main() is part of the class itself, access to private helper methods and even private variables is possible for testing purposes.

Adding console input and output to Count

Before the graphic capabilities of personal computers were developed, most human interaction with software systems was achieved using simple console input/output systems. As a quicker and easier alternative for developing a human interaction class for a problem domain class the console still has an important role. Prototypes can demonstrate early results using a simple interface that can be replaced with a more sophisticated GUI interface later. As interface design has become a discipline in its own right, the clear separation of the problem from the interface can pay many dividends. Automated testing using this type of interface is also considerably easier than when using GUIs.

5.9 Why is it easier to automatically test classes using the console interface?

It is always important to retain the separation between the problem domain classes and the human interaction classes. In a program that uses standard console input and output, the program typically prompts the user for input and then executes a statement that reads some input from the console. When the input is read and validated as being acceptable it is then processed. In an OO system, processing usually involves requesting a problem domain object to perform some service. The flow of control in this situation is easy to follow.

Rather than develop a console interface directly for the Count class, start with a generalized interface class that can be specialized for the Count class. One of the most common tasks a human interface must support is selecting or choosing between a number of alternatives. To make a choice of one from several alternatives requires the choices to be presented and the choice can be made. A selection often involves one or more choices from between a number of alternatives.

5.10 How are selection choices often presented on GUI interfaces?

5.11 What must a generalized choice class know?

It must store a number of choices, a prompt requesting the user to make a choice and the currently chosen item. To keep the input simple let us assume the choice will be made using a primitive of type int. The choices themselves and prompt can all be stored using the String type.

5.12 What must a generalized choice class do?

It must provide services to allow a client to add the choices and the prompt. Clients will also need to be able to request choice objects to get a new choice from the user. To ensure that only valid choices are made the class must be able to validate any choice made. As the current choice is part of the state of every choice object, clients may need to get it at any time. Expressing this ConsoleChoice class using a UML class diagram (Figure 5.3) shows the class name, a list of attributes, and list of methods.

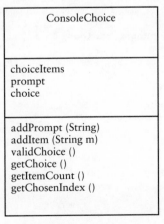

Figure 5.3 Diagram showing the ConsoleChoice class.

Implementation for the ConsoleChoice class

The state of a ConsoleChoice object is stored using a number of items and a prompt all of class String plus one primitive variable of type int. Java allows the provision of more than one constructor for creating new objects based on a class template. The ConsoleChoice class provides two constructors, a default no-argument constructor ConsoleChoice() and a constructor that provides an initial value for the number of items ConsoleChoice(int). Here is the fully commented code for the ConsoleChoice class.

```
//: ConsoleChoice.java
package chap05;
//uses Vector and Enumeration from java.util
import java.util.*;
//uses BufferedReader and InputStreamReader from java.io
import java.io.*;
/** A simple console Choice menu class.
 * The Choice menu initially has no items in it.
 * Some items and a prompt should be added before
 * a choice is made.
 * By default, the first item added to the choice menu
 * becomes the chosen item,
 * until a different choice is made by the user by
 * calling the getChoice() method.
 * @see java.util.Vector
 * @see java.util.Enumeration
 * @see java.io.BufferedReader
 * @see java.io.InputStreamReader
 * @author Stuart F Lewis
 * @version 1.00, 12/03/98
 */

public class ConsoleChoice {

/** Storage for the choiceItems.
 * @see java.util.Vector
 */
private Vector choiceItems;
/** Prompt to ask the user to enter a number.
 * Represents their choice from the choiceItems.
 * Initialized to a default used if none is supplied.
 */
private String prompt = "Enter choice";
/** Currently chosen item.
 * Used by subclasses to actually execute methods.
 */
protected int choice = 0;

/** Current standard input.
 * Used by getChoice() to actually select choice.
 */
BufferedReader stdin;
/**
 * Constructs a new <code>ConsoleChoice</code>
 * with initial space for four items.
 */
public ConsoleChoice() {
this(4);
}
```

```
/**
 * Constructs a new <code>ConsoleChoice</code>
 * with initial space for the given number of items.
 * @param    size    the initial number of items.
 */
public ConsoleChoice(int size) {
choiceItems = new Vector(size);
stdin = new BufferedReader
    (new InputStreamReader(System.in));
}


/**
 * Adds the prompt string to the <code>ConsoleChoice</code>.
 * @param    p    the specified string
 */
public void addPrompt(String p) {
prompt = p;
}


/**
 * Adds a Choice item to the <code>ConsoleChoice</code>.
 * if this is the first item added to
 * the <code>ConsoleChoice</code> menu
 * it becomes the chosen item.
 * @param    m    the Choice menu item string
 */
public void addItem(String m) {
choiceItems.addElement(m);
if (choiceItems.size() == 1) {
  choice = 1;
}//if
}


/**
 * Display all the Choice items and prompt.
 * @see java.util.Enumeration
 */
void displayChoice() {
Enumeration e = choiceItems.elements();
int i = 1;
while(e.hasMoreElements()) {
  System.out.println(i++ + " " + e.nextElement());
}//while
System.out.println();
System.out.print(prompt + " ");
}//method displayChoice


/**
 * Validates a choice.
 * @return true if the current choice is a valid choice ;
 *         from this <code>ConsoleChoice</code> menu
 */
boolean validChoice() {
return ((choice <= choiceItems.size()) && (choice > 0));
}
```

```java
/**
 * Displays all the Choice items and prompt.
 * Tries to read an integer from the console input.
 * If anything other than a number in the valid
 * choice range is entered a helpful message is
 * displayed and the <code>ConsoleChoice</code> is offered again.
 * @return a valid choice from this <code>ConsoleChoice</code> menu.
 * @exception NumberFormatException ;
 * If the value entered is not an integer.
 * @exception IOException If an I/O error occurs.
 * @see java.io.BufferedReader
 * @see java.io.InputStreamReader
 */
public int getChoice() throws IOException {
BufferedReader stdin = new BufferedReader
    (new InputStreamReader(System.in));
choice = 0;
while (!validChoice()) {
  displayChoice();
  try {
      String response = stdin.readLine();
      choice = Integer.parseInt(response);   }
  catch (NumberFormatException e) {
      choice = 0;
  }
  if (!validChoice()) {
      System.out.println("Not a valid choice. Please" +
          " enter a number between 1 and " + choiceItems.size());
  }//if
}//while
return choice;
}//method getChoice

/**
 * Returns the number of items in this <code>ConsoleChoice</code> menu.
 * @return the number of items in this <code>ConsoleChoice</code> menu.
 */
public int getItemCount() {
return choiceItems.size();
}

/**
 * Returns the index of the currently chosen item.
 * @return the index of the currently chosen item.
 */
public int getChosenIndex() {
return choice;
}

/**
 * Test data for <code>ConsoleChoice</code> menu.
 * Creates a new <code>ConsoleChoice</code> menu.
 * Adds three items and a prompt.
 * While the currently chosen item is less than the number of
 * items in the <code>ConsoleChoice</code>.
 * Display the index of the currently chosen item.
 * Exit when the last item is chosen because the
 * last item is the exit choice.
 */
```

```
public static void main(String args[])throws IOException {

ConsoleChoice c = new ConsoleChoice();
c.addItem("First Choice item");
c.addItem("Second Choice item");
c.addItem("Exit");
c.addPrompt("Enter choice");
 while (c.getChoice() < c.getItemCount()){
  System.out.println("The currently chosen item is " +
                     c.getChosenIndex());
 }//while
}//method main
} ///:~
```

The various constructs in this code were covered using primitive types in the previous chapters. Their use with objects is discussed more deeply in later chapters. The import statements make classes available from the standard Java libraries. The util library contains various utilities. The io library contains additional input and output classes. All are fully documented using HTML generated by javadoc in the standard documentation for the Java Application Programming Interface. This would be an ideal time to browse through this documentation for the classes Vector, Enumeration, BufferedReader, and InputStreamReader. The keyword @see starts a tagged paragraph to indicate a cross-reference to a class, interface, method, constructor, field, or URL.

The references to the String items that present the choice menu are all stored in a private instance variable of class Vector. The prompt is defined to have an initial value and is stored as a reference to a String. The currently selected choice is stored in a primitive int. The reason for choice being protected rather than private will be investigated when the specialization of ConsoleChoice for the class Count is implemented.

The two constructors show how the reserved word 'this' is used to refer to the instance of the class itself. The keyword @param starts a tagged paragraph describing the parameters passed to the method. The usual convention is that there should be one @param paragraph for each parameter of the method or constructor. These normally appear in the order in which the parameters are declared. Each consists of the name of the parameter followed by a short description.

The method addItem(String) shows how an item is added to a Vector and uses a simple if statement to set the currently chosen item to the first item added. The method displayChoice() uses an Enumeration to return successive items from the Vector storing the menu items. Each is displayed along with a number indicating the value that should be entered to make that choice. Finally the prompt is displayed. The method validChoice() returns the boolean result of comparing the choice to the number of available choices and zero. If the choice is within the valid range validChoice() returns true.

The keyword @exception starts a tagged paragraph describing the exception that may be thrown by the method getChoice(). This consists of the name of an exception class followed by a short description of the circumstances that cause the exception to be thrown. The reasonably complex code of getChoice() ensures that only a valid choice is stored in the instance variable choice. The topics of input and exception handling for objects are covered in depth in later chapters.

The last two methods getItemCount() and getChosenIndex() are used to return parts of the current state of a Choice object. The first is very useful assuming that the last item in the Choice menu is the exit option. The second allows any client to access the current choice without having to ask the user for a new choice.

The main() method demonstrates the class in action. Using a while construct the user is asked for a choice. While that choice is not the exit choice, the choice made is displayed and the user is asked again. When the program is executed, it will produce:

```
1 First Choice item
2 Second Choice item
3 Exit

Enter choice 1
The currently chosen item is 1
1 First Choice item
2 Second Choice item
3 Exit

Enter choice 2
The currently chosen item is 2
1 First Choice item
2 Second Choice item
3 Exit

Enter choice 3
```

The values 1, 2 and 3 are all entered using the keyboard followed by the enter or carriage return key. The resulting String is parsed for an int value and stored in the choice variable. Following the 3 being entered the program exits. This test method assures us that objects of the ConsoleChoice class deliver the required functionality for a basic console choice component.

Specialization of the ConsoleChoice class

The ConsoleChoice class can be specialized to provide a human interaction component for the Count class.

5.13 How much more than a ConsoleChoice object does a CountConsoleChoice object need to know?

5.14 How much more than a ConsoleChoice object does a CountConsoleChoice object need to do?

There is also a need to feed back to the user the current state of the count. This task should be carried out by the Count informing some object responsible for the user's view of the Count that the state of the Count has changed. The view object would then update the user view. Because the program is managing the flow of control, this task has been incorporated into the main() method. In the GUI interface in later chapters, the task will be performed by a view object.

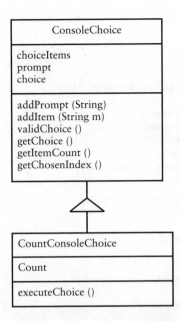

Figure 5.4   Diagram showing the CountConsoleChoice class.

The only additional attribute a CountConsoleChoice needs is the Count. The only additional method needed is to executeChoice(). Expressing this CountConsoleChoice class using a UML class diagram (Figure 5.4) shows the class name, the extra attribute, and the extra method.

Implementation for the CountConsoleChoice class

One of the strengths of OOP is the ability to inherit from generalized classes to provide more specialized classes. In Java this is achieved using the 'extends' reserved word as can be seen in the fully commented code for the CountConsoleChoice class.

```
//: CountConsoleChoice.java
package chap05;
//only needs IOException from java.io
import java.io.IOException;

/** A CountConsoleChoice menu class.
 * showing the use of extends to inherit
 * from the ConsoleChoice superclass
 * @see java.io.IOException
 * @author Stuart F Lewis
 * @version 1.00, 12/03/98
 */
public class CountConsoleChoice extends ConsoleChoice {
/** Count for which this is the Console Choice interface.
 * @see chap05.Count
 */
private Count c;
```

```
/** Constructs a new <code>CountConsoleChoice</code>
 * as interface to Count c
 * with initial menu of four items and prompt.
 * @param c Count for which this is the Console Choice interface.
 */
public CountConsoleChoice(Count c) {
this.c = c;
this.addItem("Increment");
this.addItem("Decrement");
this.addItem("Reset");
this.addItem("Exit");
this.addPrompt("Enter choice");
}

/** Executes the currently chosen Choice item.
 * Requests the Count c to perform appropriate method.
 */
void executeChoice() {
switch (choice)
{
 case 1 : c.increment();
     break;
 case 2 : c.decrement();
     break;
 case 3 : c.reset();
     break;
}//switch
}//executeChoice

/** Test data for the file CountConsoleChoice.
 * Creates a new Count and CountConsoleChoice.
 * While not exit option, executes choice.
 * Display a view of the Count.
 */
public static void main(String args[]) throws IOException {
Count ic = new Count();
CountConsoleChoice ccm = new CountConsoleChoice(ic);
 while (ccm.getChoice() < ccm.getItemCount()) {
   ccm.executeChoice();
   System.out.println("Current count is " + ic);
 }//while
}//method main
} ///:~
```

The import statement is used in a slightly different form as only the single exception IOException is required rather than the wildcard * used when several items are required from a library package. The private instance variable c couples this CountConsoleChoice class to the corresponding Count class.

The constructor shows how much more a CountConsoleChoice knows about its own appearance than a ConsoleChoice menu did. A CountConsoleChoice adds the required menu items and prompt to itself. This is important because the order in which the items are added determines which int value will be associated with each choice. In the executeChoice() method CountConsoleChoice requests the Count c to perform the required methods using a switch statement. Here access is made to the variable choice, inherited from the super class ConsoleChoice, which is the reason choice was declared as protected rather than private. The static method main() provides some testing for the class and an example of how a CountConsoleChoice object maybe used.

When the program is run it will display

```
1 Increment
2 Decrement
3 Reset
4 Exit

Enter choice 1
Current count is 1
1 Increment
2 Decrement
3 Reset
4 Exit

Enter choice 1
Current count is 2
1 Increment
2 Decrement
3 Reset
4 Exit

Enter choice 2
Current count is 1
1 Increment
2 Decrement
3 Reset
4 Exit

Enter choice 3
Current count is 0
1 Increment
2 Decrement
3 Reset
4 Exit

Enter choice 4
```

This demonstrates that all of the requests to the Count object are being correctly handled and that the inherited interface works.

5.15 How could the ConsoleChoice class be used as an interface to a Switch?

Summary

When designing a class, consider what an object of that class knows and what services it could provide to potential clients. A class is a template that describes the attributes and methods of all objects of the class. The class Object is a superclass of all objects. The set or get methods are not normally shown on a class diagram because every class with attribute values needs these basic access methods. When moving from design to code retain the vocabulary of the problem domain. It is useful to have more than one constructor for creating new objects based on a class template. The Java reserved word this refers to the object itself. All methods declared as public are available to any client of this class. Include test code in the static class method main() and describe it in the comment immediately before. The simple equality == operator will only return true if the two objects are indeed the same object. The Java reserved word 'instanceof' is a binary comparison operator that returns a boolean true if the object is an instance of the class. In a program that uses standard console input and output, the program typically prompts the user for input and then executes a statement that reads some input from the console. The flow of control in this situation is easy to follow.

Answers to in-text questions

1 Real-world counting objects could include traffic-flow detectors, access-control systems, and vote calculators. In software systems there are printed page counters, document analysis statistics, website access logs.

2 getResetValue().

3 To prepare World Wide Web documents read with the Hyper Text Transmission Protocol (http:).

4 The reset value will be the same as the initial value.

5 When the program is executed it will produce:

```
0
10
12
11
23
2147483647
-2147483648
24
chap05.Count1@1cc792
4
10
```

6 Both Count objects must have the same current value and the same reset value to be considered equal.

7 When the program is executed it will display

```
Count a is 24
Count a is 25
24
Count a.equals(b) is false
Count b is 24
Count b is 25
Count a.equals(b) is true
Count a==b is false
Count a==b is true
Only increment b
Count a is 26
```

8 The full Count class source code is

```
//: Count.java
package chap05;

/** First implementation of a
 * very simple class <code>Count</code>
 * representing a Counting object.
 * @author Stuart F Lewis
 * @version 1.00, 9/03/98
 */
public class Count {

/**
 * Current <code>value</code> of this Count.
 */
private int value;

/**
 * Current <code>reset</code> value for this Count.
 */
private int reset;

/**
 * Constructs a new Count with initial value zero.
 * Reset value is also zero.
 */
public Count() {
this(0);
}

/**
 * Constructs a new Count with initial value provided.
 * Reset value is also the initial value provided.
 * @param val the initial value for this <code>Count</code>
 */
public Count(int val) {
this(val,val);
}

/**
 * Constructs a new Count with initial value and
 * a reset value provided.
 * Reset value is also the initial value provided.
 * @param val the initial value for this <code>Count</code>
 * @param reset the reset value for this <code>Count</code>
 */
public Count(int val, int reset) {
this.value = val;
this.reset = reset;
}

/**
 * Increases the value of this Count.
 */
public void increment() {
value++;
}
```

```java
/**
 * Decreases the value of this Count.
 */
public void decrement() {
value--;
}

/**
 * Resets the value of this Count.
 */
public void reset() {
setValue(reset);
}

/**
 * Sets the reset value of this Count.
 * @param val the reset value for this <code>Count</code>
 */
public void setResetValue(int val) {
reset = val;
}

/**
 * Sets the current value of this Count.
 * @param val the current value for this <code>Count</code>
 */
public void setValue(int val) {
value = val;
}

/**
 * Gets the current value of this Count.
 * @return the current value of this Count.
 */
public int getValue() {
return value;
}

/**
 * Returns the current value of this Count as a String.
 * @return a string representing the current value of this Count
 */
public String toString() {
return getValue()+"";
}

/**
 * Compares this Count to the specified object.
 * The result is <code>true</code> if and only if the argument is not
 * <code>null</code> and is a <code>Count</code> object that has
 * the same current value and reset value as this <code>Count</code>.
 *
 * @param  anObject  the object to compare this <code>Count</code> to.
 * @return <code>true</code> if the <code>Counts </code>are equal;
 *       <code>false</code> otherwise.
 */
public boolean equals(Object anObject) {
if ((anObject != null) && (anObject instanceof Count)) {
```

```
      Count anotherCount = (Count)anObject;
      if ((value == anotherCount.value) &&
    (reset == anotherCount.reset)) {
    return true;
      }//if
}//if
return false;
}//method equals

/**
* Test data and code for Count.
* Creates a new Count a and displays Count a.
* Sets the Count a to 10 and displays Count a.
* Displays Count a.
* Increases Count a twice and displays Count a.
* Decreases Count a and displays Count a.
* Changes the reset value of Count a.
* Resets Count a and displays Count a.
* Sets the Count a to the maximum integer available.
* Displays Count a, increases Count a, displays Count a.
* Creates a new Count b initially set to 24 and displays it.
* Compares Count a to b using equals and ==
public static void main(String args[]) {

Count a = new Count();
 System.out.println(a.getValue());
 a.setValue(10);
 System.out.println(a.getValue());
 a.increment();
 a.increment();
 System.out.println(a.getValue());
 a.decrement();
 System.out.println(a.getValue());
 a.setResetValue(23);
 a.reset();
 System.out.println(a.getValue());
 a.setValue(Integer.MAX_VALUE);
 System.out.println(a.getValue());
 a.increment();
 System.out.println(a.getValue());
Count b = new Count(24);
 System.out.println(b.getValue());
 System.out.println(b);
Count c = new Count(4,10);
 System.out.println(c.getValue());
 c.reset();
 System.out.println(c.getValue());
 a.setResetValue(24);
 a.reset();
 System.out.println("Count a is " + a);
 a.increment();
 System.out.println("Count a is " + a);
 b = new Count(24);
 System.out.println(b);
 System.out.println("Count a.equals(b) is " + a.equals(b));
 System.out.println("Count b is " + b);
 b.increment();
```

```
        System.out.println("Count b is " + b);
        System.out.println("Count a.equals(b) is " + a.equals(b));
        System.out.println("Count a==b is " + (a==b));
        b=a;
        System.out.println("Count a==b is " + (a==b));
        System.out.println("Only increment b");
        b.increment();
        System.out.println("Count a is " + a);
    }//method main
    } ///:~.
```

9 Input data can be re-directed to the interpreted Java program using simple operating system facilities. Results can also be captured in this way and compared to expected or previous output using file comparison utilities.

10 GUIs present selection choices using pull-down or pop-up menus.

11 The number of and text of each choice plus which is currently chosen.

12 Enable the user to make a choice.

13 It needs to know the Count it is an interface for and the choice items it provides.

14 It needs to request the Count to update its state in response to user choices.

15 By extending the ConsoleChoice class to implement a SwitchConsoleChoice class offering options to turn the switch on or off and inspect its current state. The constructor for a SwitchConsoleChoice would accept a Switch as a parameter.

REVIEW QUESTIONS

Answers in Appendix A.

1 What does an object of the following classes need to know?
   (a) From the Java API – Object, String, StringBuffer, System.out.
   (b) General generic computing classes – stack, list, queue, array.
   (c) Real-world classes – invoice, bank account, address book.

2 What services could the objects above provide?

3 How would those requests alter the object state?

EXERCISES

Answers to exercises flagged with an asterisk appear in Appendix B.

1* What are the four choices for providing an interface to Java objects?

2* Which three methods are usually overridden by classes extending Object?

3* Explain the differences between the three styles of commenting available in Java?

4 When are two objects equal?

5 What is the difference between a Vector and an array?

6* When is the tagged paragraph @see used?

7* Which two questions can help in designing or extending classes?

6

Adding graphical user input and output

Overview

Graphical user interfaces are the preferred option for many systems. The simple Count class is reused to demonstrate separation of the problem domain from human interaction. The other two human interaction classes are implemented to show how the same object can be viewed in different ways. These are the graphical user interfaces (GUI) for both applications and applets. Both the Java version 1.0 and 1.1 event-handling models are introduced.

Graphical user interface (GUI)

Ever since SketchPad was developed, the graphical interface has been considered more intuitive to use than text-based interfaces. The rapid fall in the cost of hardware and move away from vector graphics devices to the ubiquitous high-resolution raster display of the modern personal computer has made the GUI the *de facto* standard interface (Figure 6.1). The success of the Macintosh computers and then Microsoft is often attributed to the usability of the GUI. The arrival of the World Wide Web (www or just Web) has further enhanced the role of GUI interfaces of increasing sophistication.

6.1 Why are GUIs so popular?

The various standards from the Graphical Kernel System (GKS), Programmer's Hierarchical Interactive Graphics System (PHIGS), Windows, Motif, X, etc., to the Java Abstract Windowing Toolkit (AWT) have all provided similar human interaction components classified in various ways. Logical generic input devices to enter text, numeric values, make choices, pick objects, and provide sequences of co-ordinates are specified. The physical input devices used by the user (keyboard, mouse, or joystick) can generate events from these different logical classes. All GUIs are 'event driven'. This means that the flow of control is more unpredictable than in

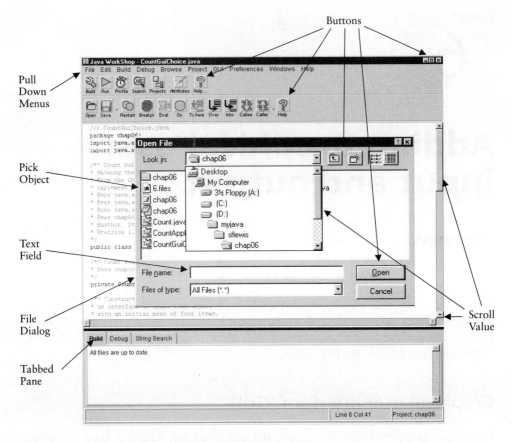

Figure 6.1   A typical graphical user interface.

a console-driven system where the program rather than the user dictates the sequence of events. A successful GUI can give a system a modern look and feel but at the cost of being more difficult to build, maintain and test.

The three basic elements of implementing a GUI are: define the components; add them to a container; handle the events generated by the components. Whether the GUI is developed by writing code or using a GUI builder tool to directly manipulate the components the stages are the same.

Stand-alone applications with a graphical user interface

To add console input and output a generalized choice class was developed first. A similar approach will be taken to add graphical user input and output. Instead of developing a generalized choice class use the one provided by the Java GUI library. This library is called the Abstract Windowing Toolkit (AWT) and is fully documented using javadoc in the packages java.awt, java.awt.datatransfer, java.awt.event, and java.awt.image. The class to specialize is java.awt.Choice that presents a pop-up menu of choices. This is an ideal time to browse through the documentation for the class java.awt.Choice. The Choice class is a direct subclass of java.awt.Component. All java.awt building blocks are descended from java.awt.Component, which is why they are known as components.

Unfortunately, the UML uses the term 'component' to refer to a representation of a source file, a library, or an executable. Java source code components are .java files. Java executable components are applications and applets. The UML component view maps elements from the logical view using component diagrams.

A component in java.awt terms is an object having a graphical representation that can be displayed on the screen and that can interact with the user. Examples of java.awt components are the buttons, checkboxes, and scrollbars of a typical graphical user interface.

The three basic elements of implementing a GUI are: define the components; add them to a container; handle the events generated by the components.

Specialization of the java.awt.Choice class to the CountGuiChoice class

6.2 How much more than a Choice object does a CountGuiChoice object need to know?

6.3 How much more than a Choice object does a CountGuiChoice object need to do?

The only additional attribute a CountGuiChoice needs is the Count. The only additional method needed is one to ask the count object to execute the user's requests. This is provided by itemStateChanged(ItemEvent e) which is invoked every time the Choice object changes state.

Expressing this CountGuiChoice class using a UML class diagram (Figure 6.2) shows the class name, the extra attribute, and the extra method. This also shows the hierarchical relationships between the other java.awt classes used to implement CountGuiChoice.

Implementation for the CountGuiChoice class

The combination of the java.awt classes and the previously developed Count class involves considerable reuse as can be seen in the fully commented code for the CountGuiChoice.

```
//: CountGuiChoice.java
package chap06;
import java.awt.*;
import java.awt.event.*;
```

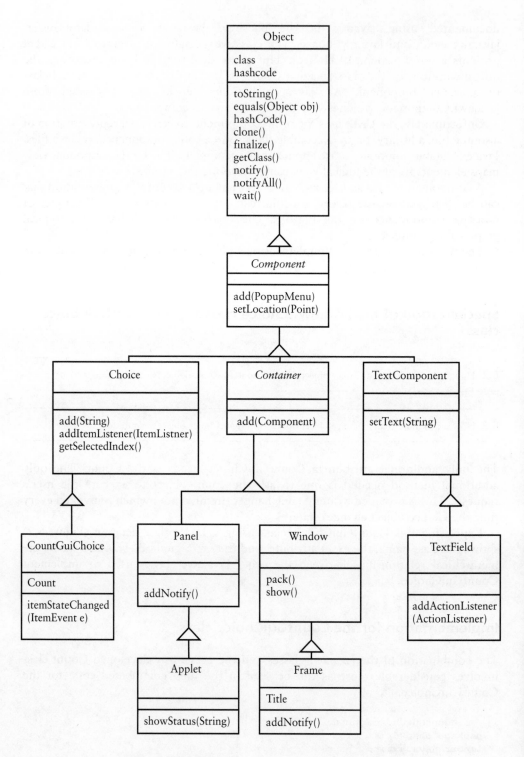

Figure 6.2   Diagram showing the CountGuiChoice class.

```java
/** CountGuiChoice menu implementation
* showing the use of extends to inherit
* from the Choice superclass and implements to
* implement the ItemListener interface.
* @see java.awt.Panel
* @see java.awt.Choice
* @see java.awt.event.ItemListener
* @see chap06.Count
* @author Stuart F Lewis
* @version 1.00, 29/02/98
*/
public class CountGuiChoice extends Choice implements ItemListener {

/** Count for which this is the Gui Choice interface.
* @see chap06.Count
*/
private Count c;

/** Constructs a new <code>CountGuiChoice</code>
* as interface to Count countObject
* with an initial menu of four items.
* Registers this <code>CountGuiChoice</code> as
* a listener for any events generated by the user on this Choice
* @param countObject Count for which this is the Gui Choice interface.
*/
public CountGuiChoice(Count countObject) {
c = countObject;
this.add("Increment");
this.add("Decrement");
this.add("Reset");
this.add("Exit");
this.addItemListener(this);
}//constructor

/** Executes the newly selected Choice item.
* Requests the Count c to perform appropriate method.
* Called when user generates an ItemEvent by selecting from this Choice
* @param e ItemEvent generated by CountGuiChoice.
*/
public void itemStateChanged(ItemEvent e) {
switch (getSelectedIndex())
{
  case 0 :  c.increment();
       break;
  case 1 :  c.decrement();
       break;
  case 2 :  c.reset();
       break;
  case 3 :  System.exit(0);
}//switch
}//itemStateChanged

/** Test data for the file CountGuiChoice.
* Creates a new Count and an interface to it using CountGuiChoice.
* Adds the CountGuiChoice to a frame and shows it
* make a choice, the only one working should be exit.
*/
public static void main(String args[]) {
Count ic = new Count();
```

```
Frame f = new Frame("Count Gui Choice test");
Panel p = new Panel();
Choice countActionChooser = new CountGuiChoice(ic);
p.add(countActionChooser);
f.add(p);
f.setLocation(100,100);
f.pack();
f.show();
}//method main
} ///:~
```

The import statement is used to access the java.awt in two library packages. The private instance variable c couples this CountGuiChoice class to the corresponding Count class.

The constructor shows how much more a CountGuiChoice knows about its own appearance than a Choice component does. A CountGuiChoice adds the required menu items itself. This is important because the order in which the items are added determines which int value will be associated with each choice. In the itemStateChanged(ItemEvent e) method CountGuiChoice requests the Count c to perform the required methods using a switch statement. Here access is made to this.getSelectedIndex(), inherited from the superclass Choice. The static method main() provides some testing for the class and an example of how a CountGuiChoice object may be used (Figure 6.3).

When the program is run it will display just a pulldown or popup menu. Although selecting the choices does change the state of the dependent Count, the only option that appears to work is the exit.

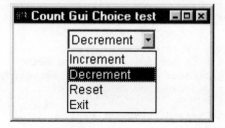

Figure 6.3   CountGuiChoice test.

6.4 How could you see the changing state of the Count?

Specialization of the java.awt.TextField class to the CountGuiDisplay class

There is a need to feed back to the user the current state of the Count. The Count is a model object in the problem domain and to maximise reusability it has no way of displaying itself other than the basic toString() method. This follows the division of responsibilities in the Model-View-Controller (MVC) design pattern often used for developing GUI OO interfaces. The task of displaying a view of the Count will be performed by an object of the CountGuiDisplay class. The Count class needs to notify the CountGuiDisplay class responsible for the user's view of the Count that the state of the model Count has changed. The view object updates the user view of the model.

Enhancing the Count class for use with a GUI

This is achieved by making a very slight modification to the original Count class so that it inherits from the class java.util.Observable (Figure 6.4). This class represents an observable object, or model in the model-view paradigm. See the API documentation for a full specification of java.util.Observable.

java.util.Observable can be subclassed to represent an object that the application wants to have observed, in this case, objects of the Count class. The modified and

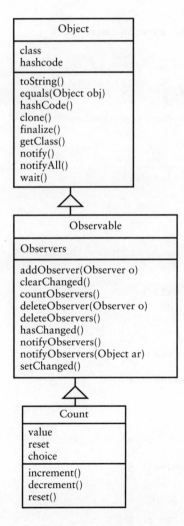

Figure 6.4   Count inheriting from java.util.Observable.

fully commented code shows that Count objects now notify any observers if their state has changed by calling the setChanged() and notifyObservers() methods inherited from java.util.Observable.

```java
//: Count.java
package chap06;
import java.util.Observable;

/** Second implementation of a
 * simple class <code>Count</code>.
 * representing a Counting object now extending
 * Observable to inform any interested observers of
 * any change of state.
 * @see java.util.Observable
 * @author Stuart F Lewis
 * @version 2.00, 9/04/98
 */

public class Count extends Observable {

/**
 * Current <code>value</code> of this Count.
 */
private int value;
/**
 * Current <code>reset</code> value for this Count.
 */
private int reset;

/** Constructs a new Count with initial value zero.
 * Reset value is also zero.
 */
public Count() {
this(0);
}

/** Constructs a new Count with initial value provided.
 * Reset value is also the initial value provided.
 */
public Count(int val) {
value = val;
reset = value;
}

/** Increases the value of this Count.
 */
public void increment() {
value++;
changed();
}

/** Decreases the value of this Count.
 */
public void decrement() {
value--;
changed();
}
/** Resets the value of this Count.
 */
```

```java
public void reset() {
setValue(reset);
changed();
}


/** Sets the reset value of this Count.
*/
public void setResetValue(int val) {
reset = val;
changed();
}


/** Sets the current value of this Count.
*/
public void setValue(int val) {
value = val;
changed();
}


/** Gets the current value of this Count.
* @return the current value of this Count.
*/
public int getValue() {
return value;
}


/** Returns the current value of this Count as a String.
* @return a string representing the current value of this Count
*/
public String toString() {
return getValue()+"";
}


/** Compares this Count to the specified object.
* The result is <code>true</code> if and only if the argument is not
* <code>null</code> and is a <code>Count</code> object that has
* the current value and reset value as this <code>Count</code>.
*
* @param  anObject  the object to compare this <code>Count</code> to.
* @return <code>true</code> if the <code>Counts </code>are equal;
*       <code>false</code> otherwise.
*/
public boolean equals(Object anObject) {
if ((anObject != null) && (anObject instanceof Count)) {
  Count anotherCount = (Count)anObject;
  if ((value == anotherCount.value) &&
   (reset == anotherCount.reset)) {
   return true;
   }//if
}//if
return false;
}//method equals
/** Called whenever any instance variables are changed.
* Notifies all Observers of the change of state.
* @see java.util.Observable
*/
```

```
private void changed() {
setChanged();
notifyObservers();
}

/**Test data and code for Count.
* Creates a new Count a and displays Count a.
* Sets the Count a to 10.
* Displays Count a.
* Increases Count a twice and displays Count a.
* Decreases Count a and displays Count a.
* Changes the reset value of Count a.
* Resets Count a and displays Count a.
* Sets the Count a to the maximum integer available.
* Displays Count a, increases Count a, displays Count a.
* Creates a new Count b initially set to 24 and displays Count b.
*/

public static void main(String args[]) {

Count a = new Count();
 System.out.println(a);
 a.setValue(10);
 System.out.println(a);
 a.increment();
 a.increment();
 System.out.println(a);
 a.decrement();
 System.out.println(a);
 a.setResetValue(24);
 a.reset();
 System.out.println("Count a is " + a);
 a.increment();
 System.out.println("Count a is " + a);
Count b = new Count(24);
 System.out.println(b);
 System.out.println("Count a.equals(b) is " + a.equals(b));
 System.out.println("Count b is " + b);
 b.increment();
 System.out.println("Count b is " + b);
 System.out.println("Count a.equals(b) is " + a.equals(b));
 System.out.println("Count a==b is " + (a==b));
 b=a;
 System.out.println("Count a==b is " + (a==b));
 System.out.println("Only increment b");
 b.increment();
 System.out.println("Count a is " + a);
}//method main
} ///:~
```

The change has been localised into a private helper method only available to the class
Count named changed(). This method is called by any other method that changes any
instance variables and hence the state of the Count. The two methods called by
changed(), setChanged() and notifyObservers(), are inherited from the superclass
Observable.

Now Count is observable, the view class will be able to observe and be notified of
any changes in the model. As Count objects can be displayed using a String returned
from the toString() method the most appropriate GUI component would be one that

can display a String object. For this purpose, java.awt.TextField is ideal. The view class also needs to be able to observe the model. For this, the java.util.Observer interface is required.

6.5 How much more than a TextField object does a CountGuiDisplay object need to know?

6.6 How much more than a TextField object does a CountGuiDisplay object need to do?

The only additional attribute a CountGuiDisplay needs is the Count (Figure 6.5). The only additional method needed is one to display the count every time that the state of the Count changes. This is provided by update(Observable o, Object arg) which is invoked every time the Count object changes state and notifies observers of the change.

The composition of Count with CountGuiDisplay is shown on the UML diagram as a simple association by a single line linking the classes. CountGuiDisplay is shown to implement the Observer interface by the <<conforms>> arrow from the interface to the class.

Implementation for the CountGuiDisplay class

CountGuiDisplay is required to implement update(Observable o,Object arg) as part of the Observer interface. The combination of the java.awt classes and the previously enhanced Count class involves considerable reuse as can be seen in the fully commented code for the CountGuiDisplay.

```
//: CountGuiDisplay.java
package chap06;
import java.util.*;
import java.awt.*;

/** CountGuiDisplay implementation
 * showing the use of extends to inherit
 * from the TextField superclass and implements to
 * implement the Observer interface allowing this
 * TextField to watch for and be notified of any change
 * in the state of the related Count.
 * @see java.util.Observer
 * @see java.awt.TextField
 * @see chap06.Count
 * @author Stuart F Lewis
 * @version 1.00, 02/04/98
 */
public class CountGuiDisplay extends TextField implements Observer {

/** Count for which this is the Gui Display interface.
 * @see chap06.Count
 */
private Count c;
```

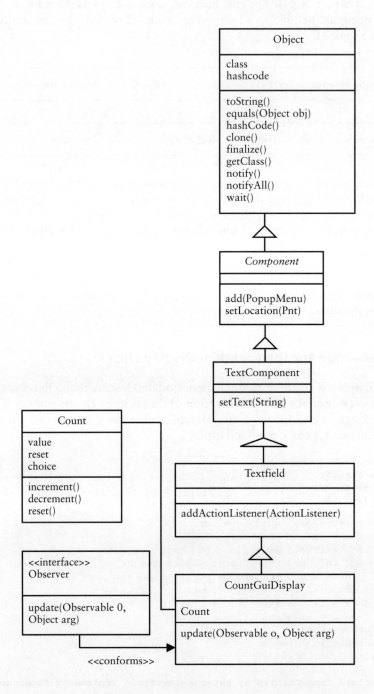

Figure 6.5   Diagram showing the CountGuiDisplay class.

```
/** Constructs a new <code>CountGuiDisplay</code>
* as interface to Count countObject.
* Blanks the display field.
* Registers this <code>CountGuiDisplay</code> as
* an Observer for any changes generated by countObject.
* Gets and displays the initial value of countObject.
* Sets this <code>CountGuiDisplay</code> as not editable.
* @param countObject Count for which this is the Gui Display interface.
* @see java.util.Observer
* @see java.awt.TextField
*/
public CountGuiDisplay(Count countObject) {
c = countObject;
c.addObserver(this);
setText(c+"");
setEditable(false);
}//constructor

/** Displays the new Count state.
* Called when the Count c being observed notifies
* observers of a state change.
* @param Observable o the observable object ie. the Count.
* @param Object arg an optional argument passed to the ;
*     notifyObservers method, always null in this case.
*/
public void update(Observable o,Object arg) {
//get the value and display it. Not necessary as toString() works.
//setText(c.getValue()+"");
setText(o+"");
}

/** Test data for the file CountGuiDisplay.
* Creates a new Count ic and a view tv on to it using CountGuiDisplay.
* Creates another new Count ic2 with a value 12345
* and a view tv2 on to it using CountGuiDisplay.
* Adds tv and tv2 to a Panel p.
* Adds the panel p to a frame and shows it.
* @see java.awt.Panel
* @see java.awt.Frame
* @see java.awt.TextField
*/
public static void main(String args[]) {
Count ic = new Count();
TextField tv = new CountGuiDisplay(ic);
Count ic2 = new Count(12345);
TextField tv2 = new CountGuiDisplay(ic2);
Frame f = new Frame("Count Gui Display test");
Panel p = new Panel();
p.add(tv);
p.add(tv2);
f.add(p);
f.setLocation(100,100);
f.pack();
f.show();
}//method main
} ///:~
```

For CountGuiDisplay to inherit methods from two superclasses is not possible in Java. CountGuiDisplay is a specialization of java.awt.TextField and inherits methods from this superclass only. The interface java.util.Observer is an example of how an object by implementing an interface can appear to 'belong' to two superclasses.

The java.util.Observer interface is the other side of the java.util.Observable class that Count extends. The CountGuiDisplay is a view of the Count model that is referenced by private instance variable c. This dependency is set up by the only constructor for new CountGuiDisplay objects. A reference to the countObject argument is assigned to the instance variable c. The count object is asked to add this CountGuiDisplay as an observer. The text of this CountGuiDisplay is initialized as the current toString() representation of the count. The +"" concatenates the String returned by c.toString() to the empty String "". It is a shorter alternative to setText(c.toString()); with the added advantage that it works for variables of primitive types too as was seen in the Count method toString(). This CountGuiDisplay is set not to be editable because the only way that this view should change is to reflect changes in the model count. Both setText(String t) and setEditable(boolean b) are actually inherited from java.awt.TextComponent the superclass of java.awt.TextField. This is an example where the superclass TextField actually provides more functionality than is required by the subclass CountGuiDisplay. Setting CountGuiDisplay to prevent editing reduces the number of unused methods available from the superclass.

?   **6.7** What functionality could be added if the user was allowed to edit the CountGuiDisplay?

The only method required to implement the interface java.util.Observer is update(Observable o, Object arg). The first parameter is the observed object, in this case always the count c. The second parameter is an optional parameter that the observed object can pass when calling the notifyObservers() method, in this case always null. The Observer CountGuiDisplay could request the model to supply information about the new state before updating the user view. Here CountGuiDisplay just displays the count as passed to the update() method.

The static method main() provides some testing for the class and an example of how a CountGuiDisplay object may be used. Two different counts are created each with a view. These views are added to a Panel that is added to a Frame and displayed. When the program is run it will display the two views with the initial values of their dependent counts (Figure 6.6).

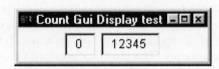

Figure 6.6   CountGuiDisplay test.

Specialization of the java.awt.Panel class to the CountViewContainer class

To bring together the components CountGuiChoice and CountGuiDisplay in the 'add them to a container element' of implementing the GUI a container is required. The abstract class java.awt.Container is the superclass of several AWT components that can contain other AWT components. Panel is the simplest container class. A panel provides space in which an application can attach any other component. Panels have already been used to test the components in their main() methods.

6.8 How much more than a java.awt.Panel object does a CountViewContainer object need to know?

6.9 How much more than a java.awt.Panel object does a CountViewContainer object need to do?

The only additional attribute a CountViewContainer (Figure 6.7) might need is the Count, but as the components themselves both know the Count it is not required. No additional methods are needed.

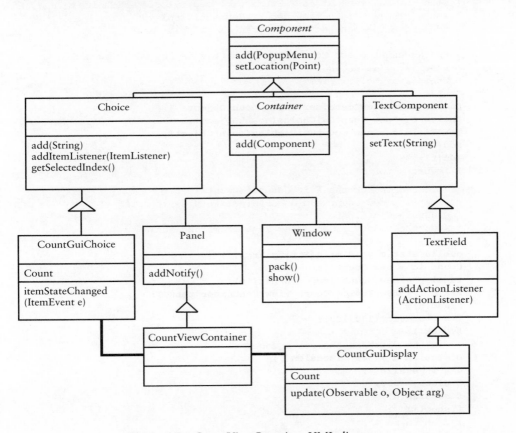

Figure 6.7   CountViewContainer UML diagram.

Implementation for the CountViewContainer class

The combination of the java.awt classes and the previously developed Count, CountGuiChoice, and CountGuiDisplay classes involves considerable reuse as can be seen in the fully commented code for the CountViewContainer.

```java
//: CountViewContainer.java
package chap06;
import java.awt.*;

/** CountViewContainer implementation
* showing the use of extends to inherit
* from the Panel superclass.
* Knows nothing about the state, methods, or interface
* of a Count apart from the existence of the CountGui
* Choice and Display classes.
* @see java.awt.Panel
* @author Stuart F Lewis
* @version 1.00, 29/04/98
*/
public class CountViewContainer extends Panel {

/** Constructs a new <code>CountViewContainer</code>
* as interface to Count countObject.
* with initial menu of four items provided by CountGuiChoice
* and a display field provided by CountGuiDisplay.
* Adds both the menu and display field to this Panel.
*
* @param countObject Count for which this is the Gui ViewContainer.
* @see java.awt.Choice
* @see java.awt.TextField
*/
public CountViewContainer(Count countObject) {
Choice c = new CountGuiChoice(countObject);
TextField t = new CountGuiDisplay(countObject);
add(c);
add(t);
}//constructor

/** Test data for the file CountViewContainer.
* Creates a new Count and a container to view it using
* CountViewContainer.
* Adds the CountViewContainer to a frame and shows it
*/
public static void main(String args[]) {
Count ic = new Count();
Panel p = new CountViewContainer(ic);
Frame f = new Frame("Count View Container test");
f.add(p);
f.setLocation(100,100);
f.pack();
//fix the width so the title shows
Dimension d = new Dimension();
d = f.getSize();
d.width = 250;
f.setSize(d);
f.show();
}//method main
} ///:~
```

This class consists of only a constructor that accepts a Count object as an argument and creates a Choice object and view object for the Count. These are both added to this CountViewContainer. The add(Component) method is inherited from java.awt.Container the superclass of java.awt.Panel.

The test method main() creates a new Count and a CountViewContainer for it. This CountViewContainer is then added to a Frame that is displayed after adjusting the width so the title shows correctly. When the program is run the GUI is displayed and all of the options can be tested to ensure they work correctly (Figure 6.8).

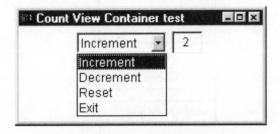

Figure 6.8   CountViewContainer test.

Applets

All applets have a graphical user interface.

6.10 How did applets contribute to the rapid rise in the popularity of the Java language?

Although the class Applet (Figure 6.9) is imported from the library java.applet it does in fact extend java.awt.Panel and inherits all the methods from Panel and the awt superclasses Container and Component.

An applet is a small program that is intended not to be run on its own, but rather to be embedded inside another application. The Applet class must be the superclass of any applet that is to be embedded in a Web page or viewed by a Java Applet Viewer.

Many Java development environments will provide a skeleton class structure for applet code. This consists of importing the class java.applet.Applet; a public class that extends Applet, and up to six public methods init(), start(), stop(), destroy(), getAppletInfo(), and getParameterInfo() which an applet may wish to override.

Applets are run inside another application that controls any access to resources on the host machine. To do this every applet relies on the Java virtual machine implementation of the host application. Unfortunately, many browsers still only support the Java version 1.0 event-handling model. This means that the java.awt.ItemListener interface is not available. Of the three classes involved in CountViewContainer only CountGuiChoice uses the Java version 1.1 event-handling model. The other two classes CountGuiDisplay and Count can be reused directly.

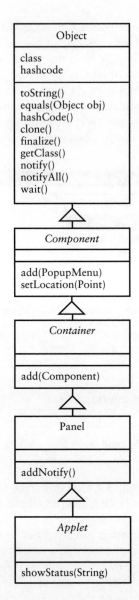

Figure 6.9   Diagram showing the Applet class.

Specialization of the java.awt.Choice class to the V10Choice class

6.11 How much more than a Choice object does a V10Choice object need to know?

6.12 How much more than a Choice object does a V10Choice object need to do?

The only additional attribute a V10Choice needs is the Count. The only additional method needed is one to ask the Count object to execute the user's requests. This is provided by action(Event e, Object o) which is invoked every time the Choice object changes state.

The same Choice class (Figure 6.10) is being specialized as was used to provide the class CountGuiChoice but using different event handling. The Java version 1.0 event-handling model works with applications too but was changed in version 1.1 to support more complex interfaces. The Java version 1.0 event model is simpler than 1.1. All events are handled by a single method.

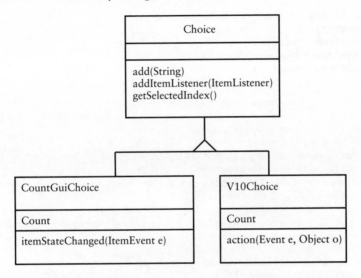

Figure 6.10   Diagram showing the V10Choice class.

Implementation of the V10Choice class

The combination of the java.awt classes and the previously developed Count class involves considerable reuse as can be seen in the fully commented code for the V10Choice.

```java
//: V10Choice.java
package chap06;
import java.awt.*;

/** Count Choice using Version 1.0 event handling model
* menu implementation
* showing the use of extends to inherit
* from the Choice superclass and uses the 1.0 event model.
* @see java.awt.Panel
* @see java.awt.Choice
* @see chap06.Count
* @author Stuart F Lewis
* @version 1.00, 02/05/98
*/
public class V10Choice extends Choice {
```

```
/** Count for which this is the Gui Choice interface.
 * @see chap06.Count
 */
private Count c;

/** Constructs a new <code>V10Choice</code>
 * as interface to Count countObject
 * with initial menu of three items.
 * An applet does not need an exit option.
 * @param countObject Count for which this is the Gui Choice
 * interface.
 */
public V10Choice(Count countObject) {
c = countObject;
this.addItem("Increment");
this.addItem("Decrement");
this.addItem("Reset");
}//constructor

/** Executes the newly selected Choice item.
 * Requests the Count c to perform appropriate method.
 * Called when user generates an ActionEvent
 * by selecting from this Choice
 * @param e ActionEvent generated by V10Choice.
 * @param o Object generated by V10Choice.
 * @return a boolean indicating that the event has been handled
 * @deprecated As of JDK version 1.1,
 *   should register this component as ItemListener
 *   on the Choice component which fires Item events.
 * @see chap06.CountGuiChoice
 */
public boolean action(Event e, Object o) {
if (o.equals("Increment")) {
c.increment();
}
if (o.equals("Decrement")) {
c.decrement();
}
if (o.equals("Reset")) {
c.reset();
}
return true;
}//action

/**Test data for the file V10Choice.
 * Creates a new Count and an interface to it using V10Choice.
 * Adds the V10Choice to a panel
 * Adds a view onto the Count using CountGuiDisplay to the panel
 * adds the panel to a frame and shows it
 * make a choice, see the view change
 * the only problem is that the exit choice
 * has been removed because an applet does not need it so
 * this test cannot be exited from.
 */
public static void main(String args[]) {
Count ic = new Count();
Frame f = new Frame("Count version 1.0 Choice test");
Panel p = new Panel();
```

```
Choice countActionChooser = new V10Choice(ic);
p.add(countActionChooser);
TextField t = new CountGuiDisplay(ic);
p.add(t);
f.add(p);
f.setLocation(100,100);
f.pack();
f.show();
}//method main
} ///:~
```

The import statement is used to access the java.awt from the library package. The private instance variable c couples this V10Choice class to the corresponding Count class. The constructor shows how much more a V10Choice knows about its own appearance than a Choice component does. A V10Choice adds the required menu items itself using addItem(String) which has been supplemented by add(String) in Java version 1.1. Only three menu items are required because an applet does not need or normally have an exit option.

6.13 Why does an applet not require an exit option?

The Java version 1.0 event model is simpler than 1.1. All events are represented by the java.awt.Event class. Events are first dispatched to the handleEvent() method of the component or a superclass of the component on which they occurred. An event contains an id field that indicates what type of event it is and which other Event variables are relevant for the event. The default implementation of the handleEvent() method checks the id field of the Event object and dispatches the most commonly used types of events to various type-specific methods. A Choice object generates an event with id ACTION_EVENT when the user selects an item. An ACTION_EVENT indicates that the user wants some action to occur. ACTION_EVENT is a constant in the class java.awt.Event. In this case the superclass java.awt.Component implements both the handleEvent(Event evt) method and the action(Event evt, Object what). Both are deprecated having been replaced in the Java version 1.1 event-handling model.

V10Choice overrides action() to handle events generated by itself. The arguments e and o can be displayed to the standard console using System.out.println() during the debugging stage of implementation. This is possible if the applet constructing V10Choice is running under an applet viewer or if V10Choice is constructed using an application. Either, o a String object containing the text of the menu item or e.arg containing the same String can be used to act on the user's choice. V10Choice requests the dependent Count to perform the required methods using a series of exclusive if statements. Finally action() returns true to indicate that it has handled the event.

The static method main() provides some testing for the class and an example of how a V10Choice object may be used by an application (Figure 6.11). When the program is run it will display a pulldown or popup menu and a CountGuiDisplay. Selecting the choices changes the state of the dependent Count, the change can be seen because a view onto the Count has been added. This test is thus a Count View Container itself.

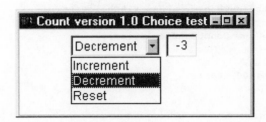

Figure 6.11   Diagram showing V10Choice test.

Specialization of the java.applet.Applet class to provide a Count View Container class

Now all of the components have been implemented to provide a Count View Container class. A container is required to bring together the components V10Choice and CountGuiDisplay in the 'add them to a container element' of implementing the GUI. Another class could be implemented, but an Applet is a direct subclass of the java.awt.Panel container. Remove one level from the hierarchy by specializing directly from an Applet to Count Applet View.

Panel is the simplest container class. A panel provides space in which an application can attach any other component. Panels have already been used to test the components in their main() methods.

?   **6.14** How much more than a java.awt.Applet object does a CountAppletView object need to know?

?   **6.15** How much more than a java.awt.Applet object does a CountAppletView object need to do?

The only additional attribute a CountAppletView might need is the Count, but as the components themselves both know the Count it is not required (Figure 6.12).

Implementation of the CountAppletView class using the V10Choice and CountGuiDisplay classes

Implementing an applet involves overriding the six public methods init(), start(), stop(), destroy(), getAppletInfo(), and getParameterInfo(). The first four are called automatically by the system that is hosting the applet. The last two may be called by the user of an applet viewer or more sophisticated browser to provide textual information about the applet. Further details of applets are discussed in later chapters.

The init() method is typically used in place of a constructor to set up the applet when it is first created. Applets can accept parameters from the environment hosting them. For a Web browser this is achieved using some HTML like this:

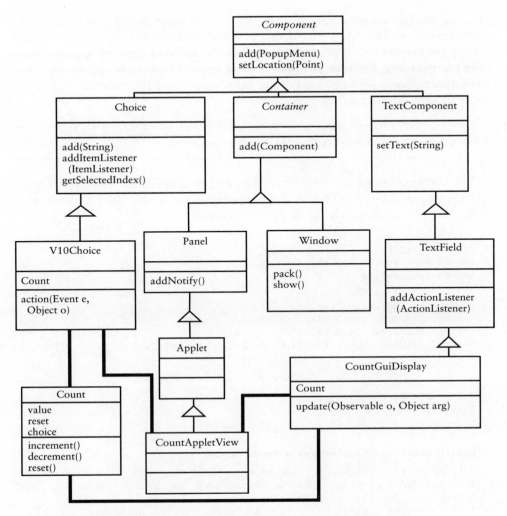

Figure 6.12   Diagram showing the CountAppletView class.

```
//: CountAppletView.html
<! CountAppletView.html >
<html>
<applet
  name="chap06"
  code="chap06.CountAppletView"
  codebase="file:/d:/myjava/sflewis/chap06"
  width="500"
  height="600"
  align="Top"
>
<param name="countStart" value="234">
</applet>
</html>
```

Here countStart is a parameter with the value 234. Some applet viewers and Java development environments have facilities for generating HTML for setting and passing parameters to applets. As there are many different environments on many different platforms for Java this book cannot explain how each one works. Most environments come with extensive online help facilities and tutorials that explain the above process for the particular environment.

6.16 How does the environment you use pass parameters to applets?

The combination of the java.awt classes and the previously developed Count, V10Choice, and CountGuiDisplay classes involves considerable reuse as can be seen in the fully commented code for the CountAppletView.

```java
//: CountAppletView.java
package chap06;
import java.applet.Applet;
import java.awt.*;

/** A test class for
 * the CountAppletView implementation.
 * showing how a CountAppletView extends Applet
 * Uses V10Choice class using version 1.0 events and CountGuiDisplay.
 * Knows nothing about the state, methods, or interface
 * of a Count apart from the existence of the V10Choice and
 * the CountGuiDisplay classes
 * @see chap06.CountGuiDisplay
 * @see chap06.V10Choice
 * @author Stuart F Lewis
 * @version 1.00, 02/05/98
 */

public class CountAppletView extends Applet {

/** Initializes the applet. You never need to call this directly; it
 * is called automatically by the system once the applet is created.
 * Test data for the CountAppletView class.
 * Tries to get a start value for the count from the parameter,
 * if that is not possible, defaults to zero.
 * Creates a new Count and a CountGuiDisplay to view it.
 * Uses V10Choice to make the Choice with version 1.0 events.
 * Adds these Count Views to a frame and shows it
 */
public void init() {
int start = 0;
try {
  start =Integer.parseInt(getParameter("countStart"));
  }
  catch (NumberFormatException e) {
     start = 0;
  }
Count ic = new Count(start);
Choice c = new V10Choice(ic);
TextField t = new CountGuiDisplay(ic);
add(c);
add(t);
}
```

```
/** Called to start the applet. You never need to call this directly;
 * it is called when the applet's document is visited.
 */
public void start() {
}
/** Called to stop the applet. This is called when the applet's
 * document is no longer on the screen. It is guaranteed to be
 * called before destroy() is called. You never need to call
 * this method directly
 */
public void stop() {
}
/** Cleans up whatever resources are being held.
 * If the applet is active, it is stopped.
 */
public void destroy() {
}
/**
 * Returns information about this applet. This applet overrides
 * this method to return a <code>String</code> containing information
 * about the author, version, and copyright of the applet.
 * <p>
 * The implementation of this method provided by the
 * <code>Applet</code> class returns <code>null</code>.
 *
 * @return a string containing information about ;
 *        the author, version, and copyright of the applet.
 */
public String getAppletInfo() {
return "Written by Stuart F Lewis. Version 1.00, 02/05/98\n" +
    " (c) 1998 Stuart F Lewis All Rights Reserved.";
}
/**
 * Returns information about the parameters than are understood by
 * this applet. This applet overrides this method to return an
 * array of <code>Strings</code> describing these parameters.
 * <p>
 * Each element of the array is a set of three
 * <code>Strings</code> containing the name, the type, and a
 * description. For example:
 * <p><blockquote><pre>
 * String pinfo[][] = {
 *     {"name", "range and type", "description"},
 *     {"countStart", "any integer",  "start value for this count"}
 * };
 * </pre></blockquote>
 * <p>
 * The implementation of this method provided by the
 * <code>Applet</code> class returns <code>null</code>.
 *
 * @return an array describing the parameters this applet looks for.
 */
public String[][] getParameterInfo() {
String pinfo[][] = {
  {"name", "range and type", "description"},
  {"countStart", "any integer",  "start value for this count"}
};
return pinfo;
}
} ///:~
```

All applets must import java.applet.Applet. Applet is the superclass of all applets.

The init() method has a similar role to the constructor for CountViewContainer. It creates a new Count object using the parameter supplied if it is a number and creates a V10Choice object and view object for the Count. These are both added to this applet. The add(Component) method is inherited from java.awt.Container, the superclass of java.awt.Panel. When the program is run under either a browser or applet viewer the GUI (Figure 6.13) is displayed and all of the options can be tested to ensure they work correctly.

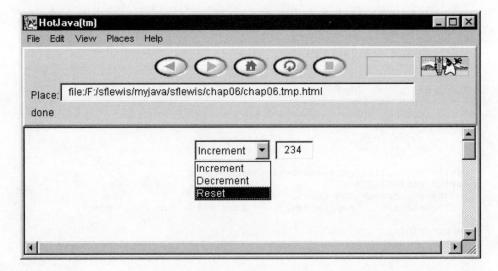

Figure 6.13   Count AppletView test.

Summary

A successful GUI can give a system a modern look and feel but at the cost of being more difficult to build, maintain and test. There are two ways of providing graphical user interfaces (GUI) to Java classes: stand-alone applications or applets embedded within either an applet viewer or Web browser. The three basic elements of implementing a GUI are: define the components; add them to a container; handle the events generated by the components. A component in java.awt terms is an object having a graphical representation that can be displayed on the screen and that can interact with the user. When specializing a class, consider what is the same and what is different about the two classes. Always ask two questions about these differences. How much more does a subclass know than the superclass? What additional services could the subclass provide to potential clients? An object implementing a Java interface can appear to 'belong' to two superclasses. Sometimes a superclass actually provides more functionality than is required by the subclass. The abstract class java.awt.Container is the superclass of several AWT components that can contain other AWT components. All applets must import java.applet.Applet. Applet is the superclass of all applets. The applet init() method has a similar role to the constructor for other objects.

Answers to in-text questions

1 The success of Windows and the Web has made the GUI the most popular interface.

2 CountGuiChoice needs to know the Count it is a choice object for and the choice items it provides.

3 CountGuiChoice needs to request the Count to update its state in response to user choices.

4 By adding a debug statement such as

```
System.out.println(c);
```

to the itemStateChanged method.

5 CountGuiDisplay needs to know the Count it is a view of.

6 CountGuiDisplay needs to display the Count every time that the state of the Count changes. That is every time that it is notified of a change.

7 The user could change the value of the Count directly.

8 A CountViewContainer only needs to know enough to add the choice and view objects to itself. As both of these need to know the Count they are dependent on, so does a CountViewContainer object.

9 A CountViewContainer only needs add the choice and view objects to itself.

10 The ability to write applets that can be embedded in Web pages was one of the reasons for the rapid rise in the popularity of the Java language.

11 V10Choice needs to know the Count it is a choice object for and the choice items it provides.

12 V10Choice needs to request the Count to update its state in response to user choices.

13 An applet does not require an exit option because the application hosting the applet provides exit facilities, either by simply loading a new page in a browser or from a menu in an applet viewer.

14 CountAppletView only needs to know enough to add the choice and view objects to itself. As both of these need to know the Count they are dependent on, so does a CountAppletView object.

15 CountAppletView only needs add the choice and view objects to itself.

16 The answer depends on the environment used.

REVIEW QUESTIONS

Answers in Appendix A.

1 What are the main advantages of graphical user interfaces that make them so popular?

2 What does an object of the following classes need to know?
   (a) From the Java AWT – Choice, Panel, Applet, TextField.
   (b) General generic computing graphics classes – locator, pick, menu, point.
   (c) Real world classes – student, savings account, address.

3 What services could the objects above provide?

4 How would those requests alter the object state?

EXERCISES

Answers to exercises flagged with an asterisk appear in Appendix B.

1* List five logical input devices that could be used with a GUI.

2* What input can we request the devices listed in one above to provide?

3 How could those five logical input devices be provided by a low-cost personal computer?

4 How could those five logical input devices be provided by a high-cost personal graphics workstation used for computer-aided design and manufacturing (CAD/CAM)?

Specialization to aid reuse

Overview

The Count class is modified to be an abstract class capturing all that is common about counting classes. The first specialization of the abstract Count is for counting integers, additional specializations are for counting characters and dates. These reuse the ConsoleChoice class and each can be viewed using the same console human interaction components developed for the original Count class. Small changes in the test method main() are all that is required to reuse the GUI human interaction components developed for the original Count class. The storage and restoring of objects using serialization to achieve lightweight persistence is introduced. Extra functionality is added to the choice classes to demonstrate this serialization. Multiple objects of the CountViewContainer class are added to one application frame demonstrating the ease with which they can be reused.

Count as an abstract class

An abstract class is used to provide a class that can be specialized to create a number of subclasses. The first stage in changing Count from a concrete class to an abstract class is to identify the methods that every counting class will need to implement. These are declared as abstract methods (Figure 7.1).

7.1 What does every counting class need to do?

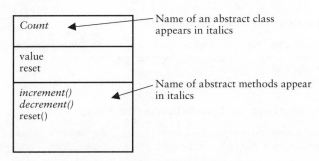

Figure 7.1 Diagram showing the abstract Count class.

133

Other methods that can be implemented in the abstract class will be inherited by all subclasses of Count.

The following source code shows Count as an abstract class.

```java
//: Count.java

package chap07;

import java.util.Observable;
import java.io.Serializable;

/** Implementation of <code>Count</code> as an abstract class
 * representing a generic Counting object.
 * Uses the fact that all objects have a string
 * representation so requires setValue(String) be overridden
 * by all Count subclasses
 * @author Stuart F Lewis
 * @version 1.00, 9/08/98
 */
public abstract class Count extends Observable implements Serializable {

// instance variables
/** Current <code>value</code> of this Count.
 * @serial Current <code>value</code> of this Count.
 */
private String value = " ";

/** Current <code>reset</code> value for this Count.
 * @serial Current <code>reset</code> value for this Count.
 */
private String reset = " ";

/** Superconstructor for all new Counts.
 * Reset value is always set.
 */
public Count() {
this.reset();
setResetValue(getValue());
}

/** Increases the value of this Count.
 */
public abstract void increment();

/** Decreases the value of this <code>Count</code>.
 */
public abstract void decrement();

/** Sets the current value of this <code>Count</code>.
 * Called by every subclass by the superconstructor
 * calling reset().
 * @param val the current value for this <code>Count</code>
 */
public abstract void setValue(String val);

/** Gets the current value of this <code>Count</code>.
 * @return the current value of this <code>Count</code>.
 */
public abstract String getValue();
```

```
/** Resets the value of this Count.
*/
public void reset() {
setValue(reset);
}

/** Sets the reset value of this Count.
* @param val the reset value for this <code>Count</code>
*/
public void setResetValue(String val) {
reset = val;
}

/** Gets the reset value of this Count.
* @return the reset value for this <code>Count</code>
*/
public String getResetValue() {
return reset;
}

/** Returns the current value of this Count as a String.
* @return a string representing the current value of this Count
*/
public String toString() {
return getValue()+"";
}

/** Compares this Count to the specified object.
* The result is <code>true</code> if and only if the argument is not
* <code>null</code> and is a <code>Count</code> object that has
* the same current value and reset value as this <code>Count</code>.
*
* @param  anObject  the object to compare this <code>Count</code> to.
* @return <code>true</code> if the <code>Counts </code>are equal;
*        <code>false</code> otherwise.
*/
public boolean equals(Object anObject) {
if ((anObject != null) && (anObject instanceof Count)) {
  Count anotherCount = (Count)anObject;
  if ((this.getValue().equals(anotherCount.getValue())) &&
     (reset.equals(anotherCount.reset))) {
     return true;
  }//if
}//if
return false;
}//method equals

/** Called whenever any instance variables are changed.
* Notifies all Observers of the change of state.
* see java.util.Observable
*/
protected void changed() {
setChanged();
notifyObservers();
}

} ///:~
```

Notice how similar this implementation is to the previously developed Count class. The methods that will need to be implemented by each Count subclass are declared as abstract and have no body. The compiler will insist that any class extending the abstract class Count must implement all of the abstract methods or be an abstract class itself. The changed() method visibility has been modified from private to protected so that subclasses will be able to access it.

An abstract class cannot be used to create objects, so this is the first class which does not have a main() method to test and demonstrate how the class can be used. The appropriate tests will be added to the first concrete specialization of this Count class. Count does have a constructor that is called by every subclass. The superconstructor ensures that the instance variables inherited by every subclass are initialized by calling the reset() method which then calls setValue().

Counting integers

To test the abstract class Count, start by implementing the simple integer count as a subclass.

Specialization of Count to count integers

This first specialization shows how the original Count class can be rewritten as CountInt, the first subclass of the abstract Count class (Figure 7.2). The functionality is the same as the previous Count but several methods are inherited from the superclass Count.

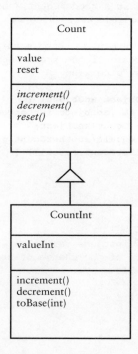

Figure 7.2   Diagram showing the abstract Count class extended to CountInt.

An additional method toBase is developed to display the value of CountInt in different bases. This is not a further specialization, just a difference in how the value is presented. This added presentation service does not involve a change in attributes or services.

Implementation of CountInt

To implement CountInt the four abstract methods declared in the superclass Count must be implemented. Using an int variable to store the current value of this CountInt means that the code for the increment and decrement methods is identical to the original Count class.

The additional method toBase(int) uses the static conversion methods from the Integer class to return a String representing the value in different bases. Check the API documentation to see the full specification of these static conversion methods from the class Integer.

7.2 Develop a method that uses a generalized routine to convert the value to other bases.

The fully commented source code for CountInt shows the abstract methods being implemented by overriding the inherited methods from Count.

```
//: CountInt.java
package chap07;

/** <code>CountInt</code>
 * representing a Counting object for integers extending
 * the general Count class.
 * Observable to inform any interested observers of
 * any change of state.
 * @see java.util.Observable
 * @author Stuart F Lewis
 * @version 2.00, 9/08/98
 */
public class CountInt extends Count {

/** This valueInt is an int and thus is different from the
 * superclass String instance variable value which is
 * private to the superclass and thus not accessible here.
 * However value is updated by calls to getValue().
 * @serial Current int <code>valueInt</code> of this Count.
 */
private int valueInt;

/** Constructs a new IntCount with initial value zero.
 * Reset value is also zero. Both are set by the super()
 * constructor Count() calling reset() which then calls
 * setValue(String reset)
 */
public CountInt() {
}
```

```
/** Constructs a new CountInt with initial value supplied.
* Reset value is the initial value.
* @param val the initial value for this <code>Count</code>
*/
public CountInt(int val) {
setValue(val);
setResetValue(getValue());
}

/** Increases the value of this Count.
*/
public void increment() {
valueInt++;
changed();
}

/** Decreases the value of this Count.
*/
public void decrement() {
valueInt--;
changed();
}

/** Sets the current value of this Count.
* try to set the value to the string parameter
* but if that is not possible, default to zero
*/
public void setValue(String val) {
int value = 0;
try {
  value = Integer.parseInt(val);
  }
catch( NumberFormatException e) {
    //System.out.println("Error in " + val);
    value = 0;
    }
setValue(value);
}

/** Sets the current value of this Count.
*/
public void setValue(int val) {
valueInt = val;
changed();
}

/**Gets the current value of this CountInt as a String.
* @return a string representing the current value of this CountInt
*/
public String getValue() {
return valueInt+"";
}

/**Creates a string representation of the current value of this
* CountInt as an unsigned integer in the specified base.
* The unsigned integer value is the argument plus 2^{32} if
* the argument is negative; otherwise it is equal to the argument.
* This value is converted to a string of ASCII digits in the
* specified base with no extra leading <code>0</code>s.
```

```
 * @param base int representing the base one of ;
 *      binary 2, octal 8, hex 16
 * @return a string representing the current unsigned integer ;
 *      value of this CountInt
 */
public String toBase(int base){
switch (base)
{
 case 2 :   return Integer.toBinaryString(valueInt);
 case 8 :   return Integer.toOctalString(valueInt);
 case 16 : return Integer.toHexString(valueInt);
}//switch
return valueInt+"";
}

/** testing code for CountInt.
 * If a is initialized as Count a = new CountInt()
 * a.setValue(int) and a.toBase(int) are
 * "No method found matching .." errors.
 * They are methods only available for the subclass CountInt
 * not for the superclass Count - in other words if you are calling
 * toBase() or setValue(int) with an int parameter
 * you must know you have a CountInt object.
 * b is initialized as Count a = new CountInt()
 * and only calls methods from the superclass Count
 */
public static void main(String args[]) {

CountInt a = new CountInt();

Count b = new CountInt(5);
 a.setValue(2);
 System.out.println("Start value for Count a " + a);
 System.out.println("Start value for Count b " + b);

 a.increment();
 b.increment();
 System.out.println("Value for Count a after one increment " + a);
 System.out.println("Value for Count b after one increment " + b);

 b.setValue("234");
 System.out.println("Value for Count b after setting is " + b);

 System.out.println("Reset value for Count a is " + a.getResetValue());
 System.out.println("Reset value for Count b is " + b.getResetValue());

 System.out.println("Integer value for Count a " + a +
              " expressed in base 2 is " + a.toBase(2));
 a.increment();
 System.out.println("Integer value for Count a " + a +
              " expressed in base 2 is " + a.toBase(2));

 a.setResetValue("14");
 a.reset();
 System.out.println("Integer value for Count a " + a +
              " expressed in base 16 is " + a.toBase(16));

 a.increment();
```

```
System.out.println("Integer value for Count a " + a +
          " expressed in base 16 is " + a.toBase(16));
a.increment();
System.out.println("Integer value for Count a " + a +
          " expressed in base 16 is " + a.toBase(16));
a.decrement();
System.out.println("Integer value for Count a " + a +
          " expressed in base 16 is " + a.toBase(16));
}//method main
} ///:~
```

?   **7.3** When the program is run what do you think it will display?

?   **7.4** Explain the difference between the two counts a and b.

This testing also serves to check that the superclass methods that were implemented in the abstract class Count work correctly.

Count on the console

Now the ConsoleChoice class developed earlier can be reused with CountInt. The only necessary changes are to import ConsoleChoice from package chap05 and change the new statement to create an instance of the CountInt class and not the abstract Count class as that cannot be instantiated. After recompiling with the abstract Count class and the CountInt class the CountConsoleChoice class works exactly as before.

Serialization of the Count

This is an ideal opportunity to introduce some extra functionality into CountConsoleChoice. The abstract Count class was defined as implementing the Serializable interface. The means that all the subclasses of Count are also Serializable. Serialization is used for lightweight persistence enabling objects to be written to and read from disk storage. Check the API documentation for a full specification of the serialization process.

There are several options when considering whose task it is to store and restore objects within an application. Some objects may need to be able to store themselves, others will be stored as part of a more complex object. Storing the complete state of an application may be achieved by storing all of the objects in a collection, then serializing the whole collection.

In this introduction to serialization, the task of saving or restoring a Count will be added to CountConsoleChoice. After all, CountConsoleChoice offers the user opportunities to control the Count in several ways so it is an ideal place to add serialization. First two additional options are added to the constructor for CountConsoleChoice.

```
this.addItem("Save");
this.addItem("Restore");
```

Now two additional cases are added to the switch statement in executeChoice() to call two private helper methods that actually perform the serialization.

```
case 4 : save();
         break;
case 5 : load();
         break;
```

To transfer information from an external source a program opens a sequential stream along which the data flows. The external information source may be a file, network socket, another program or in memory. The stream is connected to a disk file named "t.ser" using a FileOutputStream (Figure 7.3).

The method save() that writes the Count out to disk starts by creating a new FileOutputStream, to receive the object as bytes. Then an ObjectOutputStream is created that writes to the FileOutputStream. The Count c is written and the stream is flushed and closed.

```
/** Store the Count c using serialization
*/
private void save() throws IOException{
FileOutputStream ostream = new FileOutputStream("t.ser");
ObjectOutputStream p = new ObjectOutputStream(ostream);
p.writeObject(c);
p.flush();
ostream.close();
}
```

7.5 How could this be improved to store a number of different Counts in different files?

To transfer information to an external source a program now opens a sequential stream along which the data flows. The external information source may be a file, network socket, another program or in memory. The stream is connected to a disk file named "t.ser" using a FileInputStream.

The method load() that reads the Count back from the disk contains several statements to display the Count c before and after it is reloaded.

```
//** Restore the Count c from file using serialization
*/
private void load() throws IOException {
FileInputStream istream = new FileInputStream("t.ser");
ObjectInputStream o = new ObjectInputStream(istream);
 try {
 Count tempObj= (Count)o.readObject();
 System.out.println("This count is " + c + " " +
 c.getClass().getName()+ "@" + c.hashCode());
 if (c.getClass().getName().equals(tempObj.getClass().getName())) {
   c.setValue(tempObj.getValue());
   c.setResetValue(tempObj.getResetValue());
   System.out.println("Loaded count is " + tempObj+ " " +
      tempObj.getClass().getName()+ "@" + tempObj.hashCode());
```

```
}//same subclass
  else {
  throw new InvalidClassException("not the same class");
}//not the same class
}//try
catch (ClassNotFoundException e) {
System.out.println (" Class of a serialized object " +
 " cannot be found.");
}//catch
catch (InvalidClassException e) {
System.out.println (" Something is wrong with a class " +
                    " used by serialization.");
}//catch
istream.close();
}/:~
```

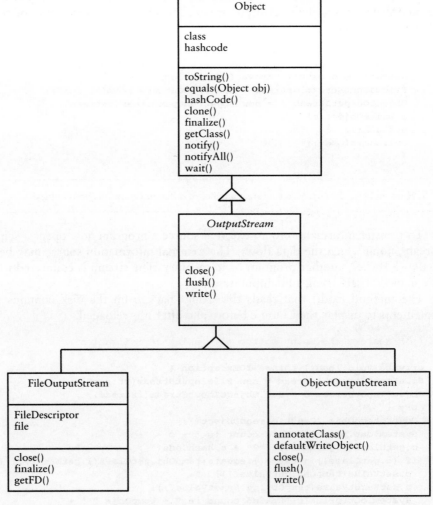

Figure 7.3   Diagram showing the Java class *OutputStream*.

? **7.6** How could this be improved to read a number of different Counts in different files?

The FileInputStream is connected from the same physical file. Then an ObjectInputStream is created that reads from the FileInputStream. The Count c is read and the stream is closed. As readObject() returns an object it must be cast to a Count; this may throw a ClassNotFoundException. If the two Count objects, the current one for this CountConsoleChoice and the one retrieved from the file, are the same subclass then the values are transferred from the tempObj to the current count.

? **7.7** Why are methods used to transfer the values rather than the assignment operator = ?

If the subclasses are different, an InvalidClassException is thrown.

The main method for testing the CountConsoleChoice (Figure 7.4) is modified as described above to instantiate a CountInt object and test the toBase() method recently added to CountInt.

```
public static void main(String args[]) throws IOException {
CountInt ic = new CountInt();
CountConsoleChoice ccm = new CountConsoleChoice(ic);
  while (ccm.getChoice() < ccm.getItemCount()){
   ccm.executeChoice();
   System.out.println("Current a count is " + ic.toBase(2) + " " +
          ic.getClass().getName()+ "@" + ic.hashCode());
  }//while
 }
```

? **7.8** Combine the methods above with the CountConsoleChoice class developed earlier and test the serialization process.

? **7.9** What will the program display if the CountInt decrements below zero and becomes negative? Why ?

When running the code try changing the value, saving it, resetting it and then loading it back from file. This first concrete specialization of a Count class demonstrates reusing the console interaction class developed earlier and object serialization.

? **7.10** Describe what has happened in the screen display of the CountConsoleChoice class being used to test the serialization process.

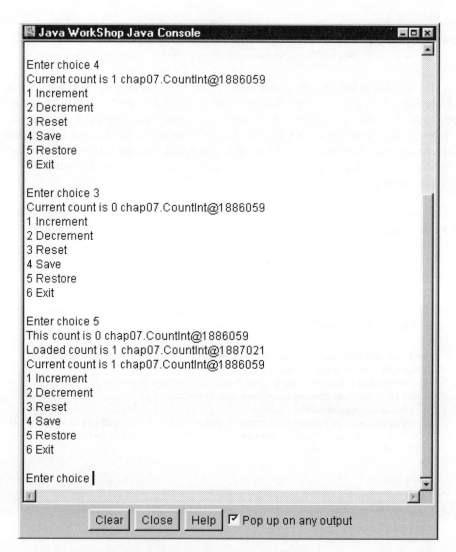

Figure 7.4   CountConsoleChoice.

Counting dates

To further reuse our developed classes consider the problem of counting dates. In an application that needs to manage dates, this is an important activity. Unfortunately, as there are seven days of the week, twelve months of the year with a variable number of days and leap years to consider a sequence of dates is a non-trivial problem.

Fortunately, the API includes three classes that know about dates (Figure 7.5). The Date class represents a specific instant in time, with millisecond precision. The Calendar class is an abstract base class for converting between a Date object and a set of integer fields such as YEAR, MONTH, DAY, HOUR, and so on. It represents a

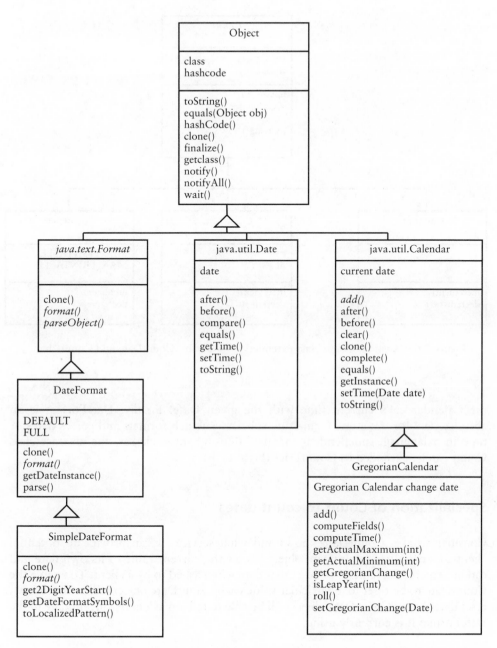

Figure 7.5 Java date classes.

sequence of dates. Like other locale-sensitive classes, Calendar provides a class method, getInstance, for getting a generally useful object of this type. Calendar's getInstance method returns a GregorianCalendar object whose time fields have been initialized with the current date and time. The cal.setTime(Date date) method sets

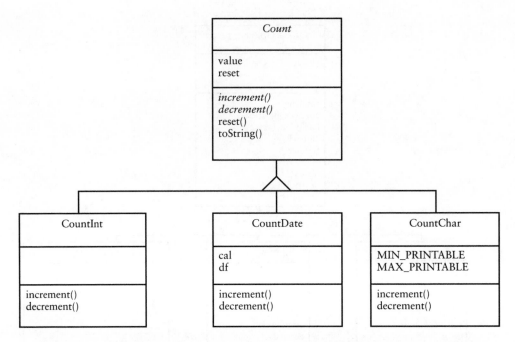

Figure 7.6   Abstract Count class extended to CountInt, CountDate and CountChar.

the Calendar cal's current time with the given Date. Finally, DateFormat is an abstract class for date/time formatting subclasses which formats and parses dates or time in a language-independent manner. Reusing three classes, the abstract class Count can be extended to CountDate (Figure 7.6).

Specialization of Count to count dates

Consider what a CountDate knows and what services it can provide to potential clients. Essentially a CountDate object knows the current value of its own date and can increment, decrement, or reset that date when asked to by a client. To enable the CountDate to be reset to a particular value each CountDate object will know its own reset date. Every CountDate object will be able to tell any client its current date in the DateFormat it is currently using.

Implementation of CountDate

The classes Date and Calendar must be imported from java.util and DateFormat from java.text. Read the API documentation for the full specification of these classes. The state of a CountDate object is stored in two instance variables of the classes Calendar and DateFormat.

Three constructors are provided: a no argument constructor, one that accepts a Date and one that accepts a String that is parsed for a valid date. The increment and decrement methods use the method add() from the Calendar class that adds the specified (signed) amount of time to the given time field, based on the calendar's rules. Here one day is added to or subtracted from the current calendar date.

The setValue() method is used by both the super() class constructor and the String argument constructor to parse a Date from the given String. If this fails, today's date is returned.

```
//: CountDate.java
package chap07;
import java.util.*;
import java.text.*;

/** <code>CountDate</code>
 * representing a Counting object for dates extending
 * the general Count class.
 * Observable to inform any interested observers of
 * any change of state.
 * @see java.util.Observable
 * @author Stuart F Lewis
 * @version 2.00, 9/08/98
 */
public class CountDate extends Count {

/** A Calender to give the sequence of dates.
 * Current <code>value</code> of this CountDate is
 * returned by cal.getTime().
 * @see java.util.Calendar
 */
private Calendar cal;

/**A date formatter which formats and parses dates or time
 * in a language-independent manner.
 * Initialized to format a date with the default formatting
 * style for the default locale.
 * because setValue may be called by the
 * no argument constructor we must initialize the date format.
 * it is also more efficient to get the format and use it
 * multiple times so that the system doesn't have to fetch
 * the information about the
 * local language and country conventions multiple times.
 * use this DateFormat to parse in constructor and setValue.
 * @see java.text.DateFormat
 */
private DateFormat df
  = DateFormat.getDateInstance(DateFormat.FULL);

/** Constructs a new CountDate with initial value today.
 * Reset value is also today. The super() constructor calls
 * reset() which then calls
 * setValue() with an empty String so default is today.
 */
public CountDate() {
}
```

```
/** Constructs a new CountDate with initial Date supplied.
 * Reset value is the initial value.
 * @param val the initial Date for this <code>Count</code>
 */
public CountDate(Date val) {
setValue(val);
setResetValue(getValue());
}

/** Constructs a new CountDate with initial value supplied.
 * value is converted from the string supplied.
 * Reset value is the initial value too.
 * @param val String representing the initial value for this
 *        <code>Count</code>
 */
public CountDate(String val) {
setValue(val);
setResetValue(getValue());
}

/** Increases the value of this Count.
 */
public void increment() {
cal.add(cal.DATE,1);
changed();
}

/** Decreases the value of this Count.
 */
public void decrement() {
cal.add(cal.DATE,-1);
changed();
}

/** Sets the current value of this Count.
 * Because setValue will be called by the
 * no-argument constructor of the superclass Count
 * if the date format or calendar have not been initialized
 * do that now.
 * Try to set the value to the string parameter
 * but if that is not possible, default to today's date
 */
public void setValue(String val) {

if (df==null) {
  df = DateFormat.getDateInstance();
}//if

Date dateVal = new Date();
try {
   dateVal = df.parse(val);
   }
catch( ParseException e) {
   //System.out.println("Error in " + val);
   dateVal = new Date();
   }
if (cal ==null) {
   cal = Calendar.getInstance();
}
setValue(dateVal);
//System.out.println("Date set to " + df.format(value));
}
```

```
/** Sets the current Date of this Count.
*/
public void setValue(Date val) {
cal.setTime(val);
changed();
}

/** Sets the current DateFormat of this CountDate.
*/
public void setDateFormat(DateFormat d) {
df = d;
changed();
}

/** Gets the current DateFormat of this CountDate.
*/
public DateFormat getDateFormat() {
return df;
}

/**Gets the current value of this CountDate as a String.
* @return a string representing the current Date of this CountDate
*/
public String getValue(){
return df.format(cal.getTime());
}

/** testing code for CountDate.
* Creates a new CountDate using each constructor.
* Demonstrates incrementing and decrementing over a century
* boundary and the end of February in a leap year.
* Shows how the DateFormat used can be changed to present
* the Date in different ways.
*/
public static void main(String args[]) {

//test with no argument constructor
 System.out.println("No argument constructor");
 CountDate a = new CountDate();
 System.out.println(a);
 a.setValue("Thursday, 30 December 1999");
 System.out.println(a);
 a.increment();
 a.increment();
 System.out.println(a);
 a.decrement();
 a.decrement();
 a.decrement();
 a.decrement();
 System.out.println(a);
 a.setDateFormat(DateFormat.getDateInstance());
 System.out.println(a);
 a.reset();
 System.out.println(a);
 System.out.println();

//test with Date argument constructor
 System.out.println("Date argument constructor");
 a = new CountDate(new Date());
 System.out.println(a);
 System.out.println();
```

```
//test with String argument constructor
System.out.println("String argument constructor");
a = new CountDate("Monday, 28 February 2000");
System.out.println(a);
a.increment();
System.out.println(a);
a.increment();
System.out.println(a);
a.decrement();
a.decrement();
a.decrement();
a.decrement();
a.setDateFormat(DateFormat.getDateInstance(DateFormat.LONG));
System.out.println(a);
a.reset();
System.out.println(a);
}//method main
} ///:~
```

7.11 What will the program display when it is run?

7.12 What can you learn from this?

7.13 Where is the current value of CountDate stored?

Adding the second test below to CountConsoleChoice main demonstrates that it can be reused with this second subclass without change.

```
Count c = new CountDate();
ccm = new CountConsoleChoice(c);
  while (ccm.getChoice() < ccm.getItemCount()) {
   ccm.executeChoice();
   System.out.println("Current count is " + c + " " +
          c.getClass().getName()+ "@" + c.hashCode());
  }//while
```

All of the choices work including the save and restore.

7.14 What will happen if a CountInt object is restored from the file when a CountDate object is expected?

Counting characters

Count can be specialized to move through any sequence of values where each value has a known predecessor and successor. The char primitive data type is just such a sequence but with the special feature that it can wrap around to the beginning at the end. Certain char values are unprintable, in particular the control codes at the low end of the ASCII set. As Java supports the Unicode character set it is possible to imagine Count classes for each alphabet within the Unicode set.

Specialization of Count to count characters

Consider what a CountChar knows and what services it can provide to potential clients. Essentially a CountChar object knows the current value of its own character, the start and end of the sequence. CountChar can increment, decrement, or reset that character when asked to by a client. To enable the CountChar to be reset to a particular value each CountChar object will know its own reset character. Every CountChar object will be able to tell any client its current character.

Implementation of CountChar

To achieve the wrap around effect for the ASCII set define two constant values for the maximum and minimum printable characters.

```java
//: CountChar.java
package chap07;

/** <code>CountChar</code>
 * representing a Counting object for characters extending
 * the general Count class.
 * Observable to inform any interested observers of
 * any change of state.
 * @see java.util.Observable
 * @author Stuart F Lewis
 * @version 2.00, 9/09/98
 */

public class CountChar extends Count{
/** Current <code>value</code> of this Count.
 */
char valueChar;

/** Constant for the minimum displayable value of this Count.
 */
static final char MIN_PRINTABLE = ' ';
/** Constant for the maximum displayable value of this Count.
 */
static final char MAX_PRINTABLE = '|';

/** Constructs a new CountChar with initial value of
 * <code>MIN_PRINTABLE</code>.
 * Reset value is also <code>MIN_PRINTABLE</code>.
 */
public CountChar(){
}
```

```
/** Constructs a new CountChar with initial value supplied.
 * Reset value is the initial value.
 * @param val the initial value for this <code>Count</code>
 */
public CountChar(char val) {
setValue(val);
setResetValue(getValue());
}


/** Increase the value of this Count.
 * Wraparound if the <code>MAX_PRINTABLE</code> is passed
 */
public void increment() {
valueChar++;
if (valueChar > MAX_PRINTABLE) {
  valueChar = MIN_PRINTABLE;
}//if
changed();
}


/** Decrease the value of this Count.
 * Wraparound if the <code>MIN_PRINTABLE</code> is passed
 */
public void decrement() {
valueChar—;
if (valueChar < MIN_PRINTABLE) {
    valueChar = MAX_PRINTABLE;
}//if
changed();
}


/** Sets the current value of this Count.
 * try to set the value to the string parameter
 * but if that is not possible, default to <code>MIN_PRINTABLE</code>
 */
public void setValue(String val) {
if (val.length() > 0) {
    char valueIn = val.charAt(0);
    setValue(valueIn);
}//if
}


/** Sets the current value of this Count.
 * try to set the value to the char parameter
 * but if that is not possible, default to <code>MIN_PRINTABLE</code>
 * @param val for this CountChar
 */
public void setValue(char val) {
valueChar = val;
if ((valueChar > MAX_PRINTABLE) || (valueChar < MIN_PRINTABLE)) {
    valueChar = MIN_PRINTABLE;
}//if
changed();
}
/**Gets the current value of this CountChar as a String.
 * @return a string representing the current char of this CountChar
```

```
*/
public String getValue() {
return valueChar+"";
}

/** testing code for CountChar
*
*/
public static void main(String args[]) {

  Count a = new CountChar();
  //a.setValue('a');
  System.out.println(a);
  a.increment();
  a.increment();
  System.out.println(a);
  a.decrement();
  System.out.println(a);
  a.setResetValue("a");
  a.reset();
  System.out.println(a);
}//method main
} ///:~
```

7.15 When the program is run what do you think it will display?

7.16 How could CountChar be modified to count over a different range of characters?

This class can be tested by running the main() method from CountChar as above. Alternatively, by adding a third test to CountConsoleChoice main.

```
c = new CountChar();
ccm = new CountConsoleChoice(c);
  while (ccm.getChoice() < ccm.getItemCount()) {
    ccm.executeChoice();
    System.out.println("Current a count is " + c + " " +
            c.getClass().getName()+ "@" + c.hashCode());
  }//while
```

Again all of the choices work, without changing any other code in CountConsoleChoice.

Count on the application GUI

To provide a GUI interface to each of the subclasses of the abstract Count there are several choices.

Reusing CountViewContainer

Reusing the CountViewContainer class and associated classes CountGuiChoice and CountGuiDisplay developed earlier in package chap06 will work with minimal changes (Figure 7.7). Change the package statements to chap07 to recompile with the abstract class Count. Change the new statement to create an instance of one of the concrete subclasses CountInt, CountDate or CountChar and not the abstract Count class as that cannot be instantiated.

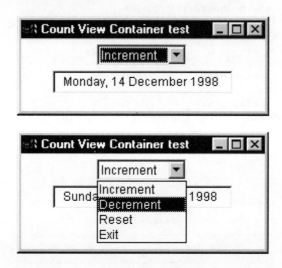

Figure 7.7   Count View Container test reused.

Enhancing CountGuiChoice

Alternatively CountGuiChoice can be re-implemented as CountGuiChoice2 with added functionality similar to CountConsoleChoice and be used to demonstrate a slightly different way of handling ItemEvents by overriding processItemEvent from the superclass Choice. As CountGuiChoice listens to itself and is the only listener defined, the ItemListener interface is more complex than is necessary. The change from implementing the ItemListener interface to enabling ItemEvents on CountGuiChoice2 is similar to the 1.0 event-handling model used in V10Choice.

```
//: CountGuiChoice2.java
package chap07;
import java.awt.*;
import java.awt.event.*;
import java.io.*;

/** Count Gui Choice menu implementation
* showing the use of extends to inherit
* from the Choice superclass and an alternative to
* implementing the ItemListener interface.
* @see java.awt.Panel
```

```
 * @see java.awt.Choice
 * @see chap07.Count
 * @author Stuart F Lewis
 * @version 1.00, 29/08/98
 */

public class CountGuiChoice2 extends Choice {

/** Count for which this is the Gui Choice interface.
 * @see chap07.Count
 */
private Count c;

/** Constructs a new <code>CountGuiChoice2</code>
 * as interface to Count countObject
 * with an initial menu of four items.
 * Enables item Events on this <code>CountGuiChoice2</code> as
 * processItemEvent will process any events generated by the
 * user on this Choice
 * @param countObject Count for which this is the Gui Choice
 * interface.
 */

public CountGuiChoice2(Count countObject) {
c = countObject;
this.add("Increment");
this.add("Decrement");
this.add("Reset");
this.add("Save");
this.add("Restore");
this.add("Exit");
enableEvents(AWTEvent.ITEM_EVENT_MASK);
}//constructor

/** Processes item events occurring on this
 * <code>CountGuiChoice2</code>
 * menu by requesting the Count c to perform appropriate method.
 * Called when user generates an ItemEvent by selecting
 * from this Choice.
 * Overrides superclass processItemEvent.
 * But is NOT called unless item events are
 * enabled for this component. Item events are enabled
 * when one of the following occurs:
 * <p><ul>
 * <li>An <code>ItemListener</code> object is registered
 * via <code>addItemListener</code>.
 * <li>Item events are enabled via <code>enableEvents</code>.
 * </ul>
 * @param e the item event generated by selecting a choice.
 * @see    java.awt.event.ItemEvent
 * @see    java.awt.event.ItemListener
 * @see    java.awt.Choice#addItemListener
 * @see    java.awt.Component#enableEvents
 */
public void processItemEvent(ItemEvent e) {
Frame f = new Frame();
FileDialog fd = new FileDialog(f);
```

```
switch (getSelectedIndex())
{
 case 0 : c.increment();
          break;
 case 1 : c.decrement();
          break;
 case 2 : c.reset();
          break;
 case 3 : fd.setTitle("Select file to save to");
          fd.setMode(FileDialog.SAVE);
          fd.pack();
          fd.show();
          save(fd.getFile());
          break;
 case 4 : fd.setTitle("Select file to restore from");
          fd.setMode(FileDialog.LOAD);
          fd.pack();
          fd.show();
          load(fd.getFile());
          break;
 case 5 : System.exit(0);
}//switch
}//processItemEvent

/** Store the Count c using serialization
* @param String fileName to store in (.ser extension preferred).
*/
private void save(String fileName) {
try {
  FileOutputStream ostream = new FileOutputStream(fileName);
  ObjectOutputStream p = new ObjectOutputStream(ostream);
  p.writeObject(c);
  p.flush();
  ostream.close();
}
catch (IOException e) {
  System.out.println(e);
}
}

/** Restore the Count c from file using serialization
* @param String fileName stored in (.ser extension preferred).
*/
private void load(String fileName) {
try {
 FileInputStream istream = new FileInputStream(fileName);
 ObjectInputStream o = new ObjectInputStream(istream);
 Count tempObj= (Count)o.readObject();
 istream.close();
 System.out.println("This count is " + c + " " +
 c.getClass().getName()+ "@" + c.hashCode());
 if (c.getClass().getName().equals(tempObj.getClass().getName())) {
  c.setValue(tempObj.getValue());
  c.setResetValue(tempObj.getResetValue());
  System.out.println("Loaded count is " + tempObj+ " " +
    tempObj.getClass().getName()+ "@" + tempObj.hashCode());
 }//same subclass
```

```
      else {
      throw new InvalidClassException("not the same class");
}//not the same class
}//try
catch (ClassNotFoundException e) {
System.out.println (" Class of a serialized object " +
 " cannot be found.");
}//catch
catch (InvalidClassException e) {
System.out.println (" Something is wrong with a class " +
          " used by serialization.");
}//catch
catch (IOException e) {
  System.out.println(e);
}//catch
}//method restore

/** Test data for the file CountGuiChoice2.
* Creates a new Count and an interface to it using CountGuiChoice2.
* Adds the CountGuiChoice2 to a frame and shows it
* make a choice, the only one working should be exit.
*/

public static void main(String args[]) {
Count ic = new CountDate();
Frame f = new Frame("Count Gui Choice test");
Panel p = new Panel();
Choice CountActionChooser = new CountGuiChoice2(ic);
p.add(CountActionChooser);
TextField t = new CountGuiDisplay(ic);
p.add(t);
f.add(p);
f.setLocation(100,100);
f.pack();
f.show();
}//method main

} ///:~
```

The FileDialog class allows the user to choose the file where the Count is saved or restored from. The addition of a CountGuiDisplay to the main method allows the value of the count to be viewed and means that this test itself is a CountViewContainer (Figure 7.8).

7.17 How does the implementation of save() and load() differ in CountGuiChoice2 to that used in CountConsoleChoice? Why must it be changed?

Adding inner classes as Listeners

The best way to design classes using the new Java 1.1 event model is to use an inner eventListener.class that implements ActionListener for each different ActionEvent generating AWT component. This maximises flexibility and modularity and fully utilises the java.awt.event.ActionListener interface. This is demonstrated by a CountGuiChoicePanel that uses buttons on a panel each with their own listener

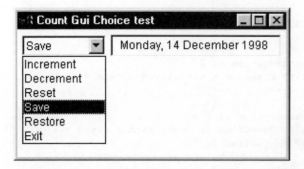

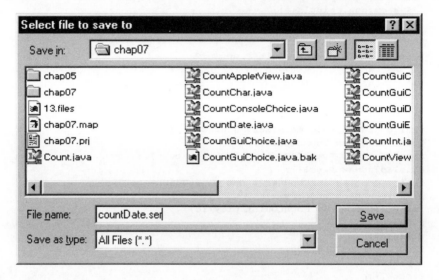

Figure 7.8   CountGuiChoice2 test.

classes that implement the ActionListener interface to handle any events generated by that button.

```
//: CountGuiChoicePanel.java
package chap07;
import java.awt.*;
import java.awt.event.*;

/** Count Gui Choice menu implementation
 * showing the use of extends to inherit
 * from the Panel superclass and an alternative to
 * using the AWT Choice class.
 * @see java.awt.Panel
 * @see java.awt.Choice
 * @see chap07.Count
 * @author Stuart F Lewis
 * @version 1.00, 09/09/98
 */
public class CountGuiChoicePanel extends Panel {
```

```
/** Count for which this is the Gui Choice interface.
 * @see chap07.Count
 */
private Count c;

/** Button for the increment choice.
 * @see chap07.Count
 */
Button increment = new Button("Increment");

/** Button for the decrement choice.
 * @see chap07.Count
 */
Button decrement = new Button("Decrement");

/** Button for the reset choice.
 * @see chap07.Count
 */
Button reset = new Button("Reset");

/** Button for the exit choice. Does a System.exit(0).
 * @see java.lang.System
 */
Button exit = new Button("Exit");

/** Constructs a new <code>CountGuiChoicePanel</code>
 * as interface to Count countObject
 * with an initial choice of four buttons. Each has their own
 * ActionListener inner class which will process any action events
 * generated by the user pressing the buttons on this Choice Panel
 * @param countObject Count for which this is the Gui Choice ;
 *        Panel interface.
 */

public CountGuiChoicePanel(Count countObject) {
c = countObject;
increment.addActionListener(new incrementListener());
decrement.addActionListener(new decrementListener());
reset.addActionListener(new resetListener());
exit.addActionListener(new exitListener());
this.add(increment);
this.add(decrement);
this.add(reset);
this.add(exit);
}//constructor

/** Processes increment events occurring on this
 * <code>CountGuiChoicePanel</code>
 * menu by requesting the Count c to perform appropriate method.
 * Called when user generates an increment by pressing the increment
 * button on this Count Gui Choice Panel.
 * @see java.awt.event.ActionEvent
 * @see java.awt.event.ActionListener
 * @see java.awt.Button#addActionListener
 * @see chap07.Count
 */
public class incrementListener implements ActionListener {
  public void actionPerformed(ActionEvent e) {
```

```
      c.increment();
  }
}

/** Processes decrement events occurring on this
* <code>CountGuiChoicePanel</code>
* menu by requesting the Count c to perform appropriate method.
* Called when user generates a decrement by pressing the decrement
* button on this Count Gui Choice Panel.
* @see java.awt.event.ActionEvent
* @see java.awt.event.ActionListener
* @see java.awt.Button#addActionListener
* @see chap07.Count
*/
public class decrementListener implements ActionListener {
 public void actionPerformed(ActionEvent e) {
    c.decrement();
  }
}

/** Processes reset events occurring on this
* <code>CountGuiChoicePanel</code>
* menu by requesting the Count c to perform appropriate method.
* Called when user generates a reset by pressing the reset
* button on this Count Gui Choice Panel.
* @see java.awt.event.ActionEvent
* @see java.awt.event.ActionListener
* @see java.awt.Button#addActionListener
* @see chap07.Count
*/
public class resetListener implements ActionListener {
 public void actionPerformed(ActionEvent e) {
    c.reset();
  }
}

/** Processes exit events occurring on this
* <code>CountGuiChoicePanel</code>
* menu by doing a System.exit(0).
* Called when user generates an exit by pressing the exit
* button on this Count Gui Choice Panel.
* @see java.awt.event.ActionEvent
* @see java.awt.event.ActionListener
* @see java.awt.Button#addActionListener
* @see java.lang.System
*/
public class exitListener implements ActionListener {
 public void actionPerformed(ActionEvent e) {
    System.exit(0);
  }
}

/** Test data for the file CountGuiChoicePanel.
* Creates a new Count and an interface to it using
* CountGuiChoicePanel.
* Adds the CountGuiChoicePanel to a frame and shows it
* make a choice, the only one working should be exit.
*/
public static void main(String args[]) {
Count ic = new CountDate();
Frame f = new Frame("Count Gui Choice test");
```

```
Panel p = new Panel();
Panel CountActionChooser = new CountGuiChoicePanel(ic);
p.add(CountActionChooser);
TextField t = new CountGuiDisplay(ic);
p.add(t);
f.add(p);
f.setLocation(100,100);
f.pack();
f.show();
}//method main
} ///:~
```

Each listener class implements the ActionListener interface in one method actionPerformed that requests the Count to perform the appropriate method (Figure 7.9).

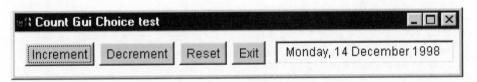

Figure 7.9   CountGuiChoice Panel test.

7.18 How could a similar functionality to save and restore Count objects be added to this interface?

Generating and handling events from other GUI components

Apart from the Choice and Button classes, many of the other AWT components can generate different events including TextField. Every time the user types a key in the text field, two action events are sent to the text field. The first one represents the key press and the second one, the key release. These events are passed by processEvent along to processActionEvent, which then redirects the event to any listener objects that have registered an interest in events generated by this text field. Other objects may listen for different kinds of semantic events such as ActionEvent or TextEvent and are spared the details of processing individual key presses.

An editable TextField can be used to provide input to directly alter the value of the Count.

Implementation for the CountGuiEdit class

To implement an editable TextField using the 1.1 event model either the ActionListener or TextListener interface can be used. The ActionEvent has two advantages. The value of the text field is available using the getActionCommand() method and the event is generated only when the user presses return. A TextEvent occurs if the text item is changed in any way without needing to press <return>.

Both are included in the source code but the addTextListener() is commented out.

```java
//: CountGuiEdit.java
package chap07;
import java.util.*;
import java.awt.*;
import java.awt.event.*;

/** Count Gui Edit implementation
 * showing the use of extends to inherit
 * from the TextField superclass and implements to
 * implement the Observer interface allowing this
 * TextField to watch for and be notified of any change
 * in the state of the related Count.
 * Now able to change the model Count by editing its view value.
 * Must press <enter> to take the action of changing the
 * current value of the Count c.
 * @see java.util.Observer
 * @see java.awt.TextField
 * @see java.awt.event.ActionEvent
 * @see java.awt.event.ActionListener
 * @see java.awt.TextField#addActionListener
 * @see java.awt.event.TextEvent
 * @see java.awt.event.TextListener
 * @see java.awt.TextComponent#addTextListener
 * @see chap07.Count
 * @author Stuart F Lewis
 * @version 1.00, 02/09/98
 */
public class CountGuiEdit extends TextField
        implements Observer, ActionListener, TextListener {

/** Count for which this is the CountGuiEdit interface.
 * @see chap07.Count
 */
private Count c;

/** Constructs a new <code>CountGuiEdit</code>
 * as interface to Count countObject.
 * blanks the display field.
 * Registers this <code>CountGuiEdit</code> as
 * an Observer for any changes generated by countObject
 * gets and displays the initial value of countObject.
 * sets this <code>CountGuiEdit</code> as not editable.
 * @param countObject Count for which this is the CountGuiEdit
 * interface.
 * @see java.util.Observer
 * @see java.awt.TextField
 */
public CountGuiEdit(Count countObject) {
c = countObject;
c.addObserver(this);
setText(c+"");
//Listen for  <return>
this.addActionListener(this);
//Listen to changes
//this.addTextListener(this);
}//constructor
/** Performs an action with the newly changed text item.
 * Requests the Count c to set the current value to the view value.
```

```
* Called when user generates an ActionEvent by changing this text item
* and pressing <return> to generate the ActionEvent.
* @param e ActionEvent generated by CountGuiEdit.
*/
public void actionPerformed(ActionEvent e) {
//c.setValue(getText());
//Not required as the text value is available from e
c.setValue(e.getActionCommand());
}//actionPerformed

/** Performs an action with the newly changed text item.
* Requests the Count c to set the current value to the view value.
* Called when user generates a TextEvent by changing this text item
* in any way without needing to press <return>.
* @param e TextEvent generated by CountGuiEdit.
*/
public void textValueChanged(TextEvent e) {
if (!(getText().equals(c.getValue()))) {
    c.setValue(getText());
}
}// textValueChanged

/**
* @return the value of CountGuiEdit as a string*/
public String toString() {
return getText();
}

/** Displays the new Count state.
* Called when the Count c being observed notifies
* observers of a state change.
* @param Observable o the observable object ie. the Count.
* @param Object arg an optional argument passed to the ;
*            notifyObservers method, always null in this case.
*/
public void update(Observable o,Object arg) {
setText(o+"");
}

/** Test data for the file CountGuiEdit.
* Creates a new Count ic and a view tv on to it using CountGuiEdit.
* Creates another new Count ic2 with a value 12345
* and a view tv2 on to it using CountGuiEdit.
* Adds tv and tv2 to a Panel p.
* Adds the panel p to a frame and shows it.
* @see java.awt.Panel
* @see java.awt.Frame
* @see java.awt.TextField
*/
public static void main(String args[]) {
Count ic = new CountDate();
TextField tv = new CountGuiEdit(ic);
Count ic2 = new CountInt(12345);
TextField tv2 = new CountGuiEdit(ic2);
Frame f = new Frame("Count Gui Edit test");
Panel p = new Panel();
p.add(tv);
p.add(tv2);
```

```
f.add(p);
f.setLocation(100,100);
f.pack();
f.show();
}//method main
} ///:~
```

7.19 How will the interaction with the user change if the //this.addTextListener(this); line is uncommented?

7.20 Why would some subclasses of Count prefer to respond to ActionEvent rather than TextEvent?

Now all of the GUI components have been implemented there remains only the final stage of implementing the GUI adding the components to a container. This version of the CountViewContainer uses CountGuiChoicePanel and CountGuiEdit (Figures 7.10 and 7.11).

```
//: CountViewContainer.java
package chap07;
import java.awt.*;

/** Count ViewContainer implementation
 * showing the use of extends to inherit
 * from the Panel superclass.
 * Knows nothing about the state, methods, or interface
 * of a Count apart from the existence of the CountGui
 * Choice panel and editable Display classes.
 * @see java.awt.Panel
 * @author Stuart F Lewis
 * @version 1.00, 29/09/98
 */
public class CountViewContainer extends Panel {
```

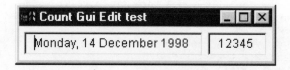

Figure 7.10   CountGuiEdit test.

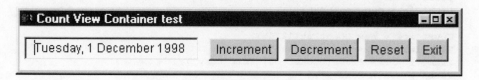

Figure 7.11   CountViewContainer test.

```
/** Constructs a new <code>CountViewContainer</code>
 * as interface to Count countObject.
 * with initial menu of four buttons provided by CountGuiChoicePanel
 * and an editable display field provided by CountGuiEdit.
 * Adds both the menu and display field to this Panel.
 * @param countObject Count for which this is the Gui ViewContainer.
 * @see java.awt.Choice
 * @see java.awt.TextField
 * @see chap07.CountGuiChoicePanel
 * @see chap07.CountGuiEdit
 */
public CountViewContainer(Count countObject) {
Panel c = new CountGuiChoicePanel(countObject);
TextField t = new CountGuiEdit(countObject);
this.add(t);
this.add(c);
}//constructor
/** Test data for the file CountViewContainer.
 * Creates a new Count and a container to view it using
 * CountViewContainer.
 * Adds the CountViewContainer to a frame and shows it
 */
public static void main(String args[]) {
Count ic = new CountDate();
Panel p = new CountViewContainer(ic);
Frame f = new Frame("Count View Container test");
f.add(p);
f.setLocation(100,100);
f.pack();
f.show();
}//method main
} ///:~
```

Any number of CountViewContainer panels can be added to a frame providing views on to one or more Count objects, as is demonstrated in this source code:

```
//: Test1.java
package chap07;
import java.awt.*;

/** A test class for
 * the CountViewContainer implementation.
 * showing multiple Count objects and their views
 * Knows nothing about the state, methods, or interface
 * of a Count apart from the existence of the CountViewContainer class
 * @see chap07.CountViewContainer
 * @author Stuart F Lewis
 * @version 1.00, 21/09/98
 */
public class Test1 {
/**
 * Test data for the CountViewContainer class.
 * Creates three new Count objects and six containers to view them
 * using CountViewContainer.
 * Adds these CountViewContainers to a frame and shows it
 */
public static void main(String args[]) {
```

```
Count ic = new CountDate();
Count ic2 = new CountInt();
Count ic3 = new CountChar();
Frame f = new Frame("Multiple Count View Containers test");
f.setLayout(new GridLayout(3,1));
Panel p = new CountViewContainer(ic);
Panel p2 = new CountViewContainer(ic2);
Panel p3 = new CountViewContainer(ic3);
f.add(p);
f.add(p2);
f.add(p3);
Panel p4 = new CountViewContainer(ic);
Panel p5 = new CountViewContainer(ic2);
Panel p6 = new CountViewContainer(ic3);
f.add(p4);
f.add(p5);
f.add(p6);
f.setLocation(100,100);
f.pack();
f.show();
}//method main
} ///:~
```

?   **7.21** What is the problem with having multiple CountViewContainer panels in the same frame? (Figure 7.12.) How could it be solved?

Count on the applet GUI

To provide a similar interface using a browser a V10ChoicePanel must be developed.

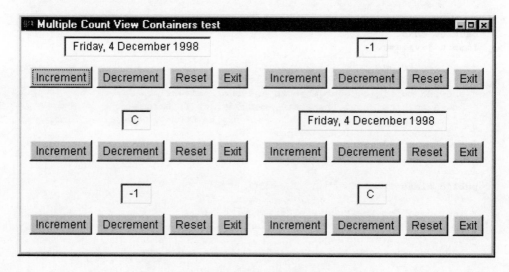

Figure 7.12   Multiple Count View Containers.

This is the same as CountGuiChoicePanel but using the simpler v1.0 event model and with no exit button being required by the applet.

```
//: V10ChoicePanel.java
package chap07;
import java.awt.*;

/** Count V10ChoicePanel using Version 1.0 event handling model
 * showing the use of extends to inherit
 * from the Panel superclass and an alternative to
 * using the AWT Choice class.
 * @see java.awt.Panel
 * @see java.awt.Choice
 * @see chap07.Count
 * @author Stuart F Lewis
 * @version 1.00, 09/05/98
 */
public class V10ChoicePanel extends Panel {

/** Count for which this is the Gui Choice interface.
 * @see chap07.Count
 */
private Count c;
/** Button for the increment choice.
 * @see chap07.Count
 */
Button increment = new Button("Increment");
/** Button for the decrement choice.
 * @see chap07.Count
 */
Button decrement = new Button("Decrement");
/** Button for the reset choice.
 * @see chap07.Count
 */
Button reset = new Button("Reset");

/** Constructs a new <code>V10ChoicePanel</code>
 * as interface to Count countObject
 * with initial choice of three buttons.
 * An applet does not need an exit option.
 * @param countObject Count for which this is the Gui Choice
 * interface.
 */

public V10ChoicePanel(Count countObject) {
c = countObject;
this.add(increment);
this.add(decrement);
this.add(reset);
}//constructor

/** Executes the newly selected Choice item.
 * Requests the Count c to perform appropriate method.
 * Called when user generates an ActionEvent
 * by selecting from this Choice
```

```
* @param e ActionEvent generated by V10ChoicePanel.
* @param o Object generated by V10ChoicePanel.
* @return a boolean indicating that the event has been handled
* @deprecated As of JDK version 1.1,
*             should register this component as ItemListener
*             on the Choice component which fires Item events.
* @see chap06.CountGuiChoice
*/
public boolean action(Event e, Object o) {
if (o.equals("Increment")) {c.increment();}
if (o.equals("Decrement")) {c.decrement();}
if (o.equals("Reset")) {c.reset();}
return true;
}//action

/**Test data for the file V10ChoicePanel.
* Creates a new Count and an interface to it using V10ChoicePanel.
* Adds the V10ChoicePanel to a panel.
* Adds a view onto the Count using CountGuiDisplay to the panel.
* Adds the panel to a frame and shows it
* make a choice, see the view change.
* The only problem is that the exit choice
* has been removed because an applet does not need it so
* this test cannot be exited from.
*/
public static void main(String args[]) {
Count ic = new CountDate();
Frame f = new Frame("Count version 1.0 Choice test");
Panel p = new Panel();
Panel CountActionChooser = new V10ChoicePanel(ic);
p.add(CountActionChooser);
TextField t = new CountGuiDisplay(ic);
p.add(t);
f.add(p);
f.setLocation(100,100);
f.pack();
f.show();
}//method main
} ///:~
```

Again, a V10GuiEdit class must be developed because the 1.1 ActionListener event model will not work.

```
//: V10GuiEdit.java
package chap07;
import java.util.*;
import java.awt.*;

/** Count Gui Edit implementation
* showing the use of extends to inherit
* from the TextField superclass and implements to
* implement the Observer interface allowing this
* TextField to watch for and be notified of any change
* in the state of the related Count.
* Now able to change the model Count by editing its view value.
* Must press <enter> to take the action of changing the
* current value of the Count c.
* @see java.util.Observer
* @see java.awt.TextField
```

```
* @see chap07.Count
* @author Stuart F Lewis
* @version 1.00, 22/09/98
*/
public class V10GuiEdit extends TextField implements Observer {

/** Count for which this is the Gui Display interface.
* @see chap07.Count
*/
private Count c;

/** Constructs a new <code>V10GuiEdit</code>
* as interface to Count countObject.
* Blanks the display field.
* Registers this <code>V10GuiEdit</code> as
* an Observer for any changes generated by countObject.
* Gets and displays the initial value of countObject.
* Sets this <code>V10GuiEdit</code> as not editable.
* @param countObject Count for which this is the GuiEdit interface.
* @see java.util.Observer
* @see java.awt.TextField
*/
public V10GuiEdit(Count countObject) {
c = countObject;
c.addObserver(this);
setText(c+"");
}//constructor

/** Performs an action with the newly changed text item.
* Requests the Count c to set the current value to the view value.
* Called when user generates an ActionEvent by changing this text item
* and pressing <return> to generate the ActionEvent.
* @param e ActionEvent generated by V10GuiEdit.
* @param o Object generated by V10GuiEdit.
* @return a boolean indicating that the event has been handled
* @deprecated as of JDK version 1.1,
*             should register this component as ActionListener
*             on the TextField component which fires Action events.
* @see chap07.CountGuiEdit
*/
public boolean action(Event e, Object o) {
c.setValue(getText());
return true;
}//action

/** Displays the new Count state.
* Called when the Count c being observed notifies
* observers of a state change.
* @param Observable o the observable object ie. the Count.
* @param Object arg an optional argument passed to the ;
*             notifyObservers method, always null in this case.
*/
public void update(Observable o,Object arg) {
setText(o+"");
}
/** Test data for the file V10GuiEdit.
* Creates a new Count ic and a view tv on to it using V10GuiEdit.
* Creates another new Count ic2 with a value 12345
* and a view tv2 on to it using V10GuiEdit.
* Adds tv and tv2 to a Panel p.
* Adds the panel p to a frame and shows it.
```

```
* @see java.awt.Panel
* @see java.awt.Frame
* @see java.awt.TextField
*/
public static void main(String args[]) {
Count ic = new CountDate();
TextField tv = new V10GuiEdit(ic);
Count ic2 = new CountInt(12345);
TextField tv2 = new V10GuiEdit(ic2);
Frame f = new Frame("Count Gui Edit test");
Panel p = new Panel();
p.add(tv);
p.add(tv2);
f.add(p);
f.setLocation(100,100);
f.pack();
f.show();
}//method main
} ///:~
```

Now CountAppletView can be implemented using a V10ChoicePanel and V10GuiEdit. Again, a start value for the Count will be passed as the first parameter but now another parameter is needed to say what to count, integers or characters.

```
//: CountAppletView.java
package chap07;
import java.applet.Applet;
import java.awt.*;
/** A test class for
* the CountAppletView implementation.
* showing how a CountAppletView extends Applet.
* Uses V10Choice class using version 1.0 events and CountGuiDisplay.
* Knows nothing about the state, methods, or interface
* of a Count apart from the existence of the V10Choice and
* the CountGuiDisplay classes
* @see chap06.CountGuiDisplay
* @see chap06.V10Choice
* @author Stuart F Lewis
* @version 1.00, 19/09/98
*/

public class CountAppletView extends Applet {

/** Initializes the applet. You never need to call this directly; it
* is called automatically by the system once the applet is created.
* Test data for the CountAppletView class.
* Tries to get a Count class and start value
* for the count from the parameters.
* If that is not possible, defaults to a CountInt starting at zero.
* Creates a new Count and a CountGuiDisplay to view it.
* Uses V10Choice to make the Choice with version 1.0 events.
* Adds these Count Views to a frame and shows it
*/
public void init() {
String countType = getParameter("countType");
Count ic = new CountInt();
```

```
   if (countType!=null) {
     if (countType.equals("Int")) {
      ic.setValue(getParameter("countStart"));
     }//if
     if (countType.equals("Date")) {
      ic = new CountDate(getParameter("countStart"));
     }//if
     if (countType.equals("Char")) {
      ic = new CountChar();
      ic.setValue(getParameter("countStart"));
     }//if
   }//if
   Panel c = new V10ChoicePanel(ic);
   TextField t = new V10GuiEdit(ic);
   add(c);
   add(t);
   }

   /** Called to start the applet.
   * You never need to call this directly;
   * it is called when the applet's document is visited.
   */
   public void start() {
   }

   /** Called to stop the applet. This is called when the applet's
   * document is no longer on the screen. It is guaranteed to be
   * called before destroy() is called. You never need to call
   * this method directly
   */
   public void stop() {
   }

   /** Cleans up whatever resources are being held.
   * If the applet is active, it is stopped.
   */
   public void destroy() {
   }

   /**
   * Returns information about this applet. This applet overrides
   * this method to return a <code>String</code> containing information
   * about the author, version, and copyright of the applet.
   * <p>
   * The implementation of this method provided by the
   * <code>Applet</code> class returns <code>null</code>.
   *
   * @return a string containing information about ;
   *         the author, version, and copyright of the applet.
   */
   public String getAppletInfo() {
   return "Written by Stuart F Lewis. Version 1.00, 19/09/98\n" +
       " (c) 1998 Stuart F Lewis All Rights Reserved.";
   }

   /**
   * Returns information about the parameters that are understood by
   * this applet. This applet overrides this method to return an
   * array of <code>Strings</code> describing these parameters.
```

```
 *  <p>
 *  Each element of the array is a set of three
 *  <code>Strings</code> containing the name, the type, and a
 *  description. For example:
 *  <p><blockquote><pre>
 *  String pinfo[][] = {
 *  {"name",          "range and type",          "description"},
 *  {"countStart",    "any value of right type", "start value "},
 *  {"countType",     "one of Count classes",    "Int, Char"}
 *  };
 *  </pre></blockquote>
 *  <p>
 *  The implementation of this method provided by the
 *  <code>Applet</code> class returns <code>null</code>.
 *
 *  @return an array describing the parameters this applet looks for.
 */
public String[][] getParameterInfo() {
String pinfo[][] = {
  {"name",          "range and type",          "description"},
  {"countStart",    "any value of right type", "start value "},
  {"countType",     "one of Count classes",    "Int, Char"}
};
return pinfo;
}
} ///:~
```

7.22 Even though the GUI components have been re-implemented to use version 1.0 event handling, why may there still be problems running this CountAppletView (Figure 7.13) with all subclasses of Count?

The principles of extending an abstract class and then using the same user interface classes for the console and GUI to the different subclasses can be used with

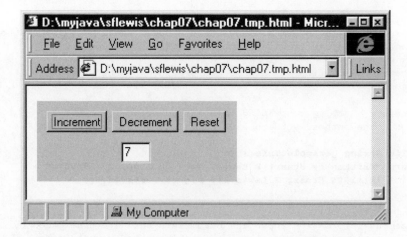

Figure 7.13   Diagram showing the CountAppletView.

any class. The clear separation of the problem solution classes from the interface classes enables those interfaces to be reused.

Summary

When designing an abstract class, consider what is common about all possible subclasses of that class in terms of what they all know and what services they could all provide to potential clients. An abstract class is a generalization that captures the common attributes and methods of the subclasses. As an abstract class cannot be instantiated, test code should be added to the main() method of the first concrete subclass. For each specialization of the abstract class consider what is the same and what is different about the specialized class compared to the generalization. Serialization provides a facility to save and restore objects from backing storage. Using the facilities of the API can help develop more sophisticated solutions to common problems in handling dates or providing GUI interfaces. There are several different approaches to handling events generated by GUI interfaces; choose the most appropriate for the complexity of the interface. This choice is currently restricted when writing applets to run with browsers that only support the 1.0 event-handling model. The clear separation of the problem solution classes from the interface classes enables different interface classes to be replaced without changing the problem solution classes.

Answers to in-text questions

1 Every counting class needs to increment, decrement, reset, set and get its value.

2 A method similar to the one below.

```
/**
 * Convert the integer to an unsigned number.
 */
private static String toUnsignedString(int i, int shift) {
    char[] buf = new char[32];
    int charPos = 32;
    int radix = 1 << shift;
    int mask = radix - 1;
    do {
        buf[--charPos] = digits[i & mask];
        i >>>= shift;
    } while (i != 0);
    return new String(buf, charPos, (32 - charPos));
}
```

3 When the program is run it will display.

```
Start value for Count a 2
Start value for Count b 5
Value for Count a after one increment 3
Value for Count b after one increment 6
Value for Count b after setting is 234
```

```
Reset value for Count a is 0
Reset value for Count b is 5
Integer value for Count a 3 expressed in base 2 is 11
Integer value for Count a 4 expressed in base 2 is 100
Integer value for Count a 14 expressed in base 16 is e
Integer value for Count a 15 expressed in base 16 is f
Integer value for Count a 16 expressed in base 16 is 10
Integer value for Count a 15 expressed in base 16 is f
/:~
```

4 The first count a is an object of class CountInt whereas the second count b is an object of class Count constructed using the constructor for class CountInt. Therefore, b cannot provide methods only implemented for class CountInt.

5 The file name or the ObjectOutputStream could be passed as a parameter to the method.

6 The file name or the ObjectInputStream could be passed as a parameter to the method

7 The values are private and so can only be accessed via their get and set methods.

8 The full source for the enhanced CountConsoleChoice class is:

```java
//: CountConsoleChoice.java
package chap07;
import java.io.*;
import chap05.ConsoleChoice;

/** A CountConsoleChoice menu class.
 * showing the use of extends to inherit
 * from the ConsoleChoice superclass
 * @see java.io.IOException
 * @author Stuart F Lewis
 * @version 1.00, 12/03/98
 */

public class CountConsoleChoice extends ConsoleChoice {
/** Count for which this is the Console Choice interface.
 * @see chap07.Count
 */
private Count c;

/** Constructs a new <code>CountConsoleChoice</code>
 * as interface to Count c
 * with initial menu of four items and prompt.
 * @param c Count for which this is the Console Choice interface.
 */
public CountConsoleChoice(Count c) {
this.c = c;
this.addItem("Increment");
this.addItem("Decrement");
this.addItem("Reset");
this.addItem("Save");
this.addItem("Restore");
this.addItem("Exit");
this.addPrompt("Enter choice");
}
```

```
/** Executes the currently chosen Choice item.
* Requests the Count c to perform appropriate method.
*/
void executeChoice() throws IOException {
switch (choice)
{
 case 1 :   c.increment();
    break;
 case 2 :   c.decrement();
    break;
 case 3 :   c.reset();
    break;
 case 4 :   save();
    break;
 case 5 :   load();
    break;
}//switch
}//executeChoice

/** Store the Count c using serialization
*/
private void save() throws IOException {
FileOutputStream ostream = new FileOutputStream("t.tmp");
ObjectOutputStream p = new ObjectOutputStream(ostream);
p.writeObject(c);
p.flush();
ostream.close();
}

/** Retrieve the Count c using serialization
*/
private void load() throws IOException {
FileInputStream istream = new FileInputStream("t.tmp");
ObjectInputStream o = new ObjectInputStream(istream);
 try {
    Count tempObj = (Count)o.readObject();
   System.out.println("This count is " + c + " " +
        c.getClass().getName()+ "@" + c.hashCode());
   if (c.getClass().getName().equals
        (tempObj.getClass().getName())) {
        c.setValue(tempObj.getValue());
        c.setResetValue(tempObj.getResetValue());
        System.out.println("Loaded count is " + tempObj + " " +
        tempObj.getClass().getName()+ "@" + tempObj.hashCode());
 }//same subclass
    else {
    throw new InvalidClassException("not the same class");
 }//not the same class
 }
 catch (ClassNotFoundException e) {
 System.out.println( "Class of serialized object not found.");
 }
 catch (InvalidClassException e) {
 System.out.println (" Something is wrong with a class " +
                        " used by serialization.");
 }
     istream.close();
}
```

```
/** Test data for the file CountConsoleChoice.
 * For each of the concrete subclasses
 * CountInt, CountDate and CountChar
 * Creates a new Count and CountConsoleChoice.
 * While not exit option, executes choice.
 * Display a view of the Count.
 */
public static void main(String args[]) throws IOException {

CountInt ic = new CountInt();
CountConsoleChoice ccm = new CountConsoleChoice(ic);
  while (ccm.getChoice() < ccm.getItemCount()) {
    ccm.executeChoice();
    System.out.println("Current count is " + ic.toBase(2) + " " +
          ic.getClass().getName()+ "@" + ic.hashCode());
  }//while

Count c = new CountDate();
ccm = new CountConsoleChoice(c);
  while (ccm.getChoice() < ccm.getItemCount()) {
    ccm.executeChoice();
    System.out.println("Current count is " + c + " " +
          c.getClass().getName()+ "@" + c.hashCode());
  }//while

c = new CountChar();
ccm = new CountConsoleChoice(c);
  while (ccm.getChoice() < ccm.getItemCount()) {
    ccm.executeChoice();
    System.out.println("Current a count is " + c + " " +
          c.getClass().getName()+ "@" + c.hashCode());
  }//while

}//method main
} ///:~
```

9 1111111111111111111111111111111111. Because this is the unsigned binary representation of –1.

10 A CountInt is stored with a current value of one. After resetting this CountInt has a value of zero. Restoring the CountInt returns the value to one.

11 The program display is similar to

```
No argument constructor
Tuesday, 22 September 1998
Thursday, 30 December 1999
Saturday, 1 January 2000
Tuesday, 28 December 1999
28-Dec-99
22-Sep-98

Date argument constructor
Tuesday, 22 September 1998

String argument constructor
Monday, 28 February 2000
Tuesday, 29 February 2000
Wednesday, 1 March 2000
```

```
26 February, 2000
22 September, 1998
```

12 Java is year 2000 compliant.

13 In the cal object and it can be returned as a Date by cal.getTime()

14 If the class restored from the file is a different class from that which was expected the boolean expression

```
(c.getClass().getName().equals(tempObj.getClass().getName()))
```

would evaluate to false and an InvalidClassException will be thrown.

15 The program displays

```
"

!

a
```

16 Add instance variables to store the maximum and minimum values for this CountChar and use in a similar way to the constants MAX_PRINTABLE and MIN_PRINTABLE are currently used. Accessor methods to set and get these instance variables would also be needed.

17 Both accept a file name as a String parameter. Both catch any IOException generated. The second change must be made because the method processItemEvent overrides the one inherited from java.awt.Choice and cannot throw any exceptions because its signature must match that of the overridden method.

18 Add an extra button and associated inner listener class to perform the action required.

19 The user will not need to press return to update the count with the value in the text field, the update will be perform after any single key is entered.

20 TextEvent is more useful for the single character CountChar and CountInt. ActionEvent is more appropriate for CountDate where the user will want to enter a sequence of characters before the Count is updated.

21 Each CountGuiChoicePanel has an exit option. Use the close window (frame) event to exit from the GUI.

22 If any subclasses use any 1.1 classes, they will not work with 1.0 browsers. For example, there is parseException used by CountDate and other problems with Date model used being from 1.1.

REVIEW QUESTIONS

Answers in Appendix A.

1 What does an object of the following classes need to know?

(a) From the Java API – Date, Calendar, DateFormat.

(b) General generic computing classes – file, directory, text.

(c) Real world classes – date, calendar, appointment book.

2   What services could the objects above provide?

3   How would those requests alter the object state?

EXERCISES

Answers to exercises flagged with an asterisk appear in Appendix B.

1* What does an abstract class have to include?

2   What services could an abstract class provide?

3* How does an abstract class store the object state?

4   For any abstract class from the API investigate the differences between the direct known subclasses.

8

Providing objects with more significant functionality

Overview

In the context of developing a simple guessing game, a more complex object is designed. A skeleton game is used to implement and test both the console and GUI interface for playing the game before the game is completed. Several more API classes are introduced from the AWT and other packages. The game is completed with some more functionality being added. Interfaces to customize the game are added for the console and GUI.

Description of the MasterMindGame

The aim of the game is to guess a sequence of numbers or characters hidden from the player. Consider a simple version in which only the digits zero through to nine are used and the length of the sequence is four digits. The player is allowed a maximum of ten guesses before the correct answer is revealed. After each incorrect guess, the player receives some feedback to help improve their chances of guessing correctly the next time.

8.1 What does a MasterMindGame need to know?

8.2 What does a MasterMindGame need to do?

8.3 Draw a UML class diagram showing the MasterMindGame class.

Proceeding in a similar style to that used with the Count, a MasterMindGame will be Observable and implement Serializable. This will simplify the process of updating the GUI and enable games to be stored.

179

8.4 Should the answer be stored as part of the game state?

Having decided that the game may be stored introduces further possibilities. The game could be improved to allow different ranges of characters to be used, to have answers of different lengths, and allow more or fewer guesses. This suggests two separate activities. Firstly, playing the game. A repeated process of guess, check the answer, and guess again. Secondly, changing the game attributes to provide a similar but slightly different game.

Implementing MasterMindGame play

The MasterMindGame class will be fully designed and developed later. To develop and test the game play interface a skeleton MasterMindGame will be used. This demonstrates the power of separating the interface from the problem domain. The skeleton provides only enough functionality to test the interface. This abstraction and postponement of the details of implementing the game will provide a rapid interface prototype that could be adapted for reuse with any similar game.

```java
//: MasterMindGame.java
package chap08;
import java.util.Observable;
import java.io.Serializable;

/** <code>MasterMindGame</code>
* a skeleton guessing game
* Observable to inform any interested observers of
* any change of state.
* @see java.util.Observable
* @author Stuart F Lewis
* @version 1.00, 15/09/98
*/
class MasterMindGame extends Observable implements Serializable {

/** Current <code>answer</code> for this MasterMindGame.
* @serial Current <code>answer</code> for this MasterMindGame.
*/
private String answer;

/** Current <code>noCharactersInAnswer</code> for this MasterMindGame.
* @serial <code>noCharactersInAnswer</code> for this MasterMindGame.
*/
private int noCharactersInAnswer = 4;

/** Current <code>maxGuesses</code> limit for this MasterMindGame.
* @serial <code>maxGuesses</code> limit for this MasterMindGame.
*/
private int maxGuesses = 10;

/** Current <code>guessesSoFar</code> used for this MasterMindGame.
* @serial <code>maxGuesses</code> limit for this MasterMindGame.
*/
private int guessesSoFar = 0;
```

```
/** Constructs a new MasterMindGame with initial answer randomised.
*/
public MasterMindGame() {
answer = makeRandomAnswer();
}// Constructor

/** Makes a new random answer to use in a MasterMindGame.
*/
private String makeRandomAnswer() {
return "random answer";
}

/** Set the answer for this MasterMindGame to a new random value.
*/
public void setAnswer() {
answer = makeRandomAnswer();
changed();
}

/** Get the current answer for this MasterMindGame.
* @return a string representing
* the current answer for this MasterMindGame
*/
private String getAnswer() {
return answer;
}//method answer

/** Check if there are any guesses left for this MasterMindGame.
* @return boolean true if there is at least
* one guess left for this MasterMindGame
*/
public boolean isGuessLeft() {
return (guessesSoFar < maxGuesses);
}

/** Checks the guess against the answer for this MasterMindGame.
* @param guess a string representing a guess for this MasterMindGame.
* @return boolean true if the guess is correct for this MasterMindGame
*/
public boolean isCorrect(String guess) {
return (guess.equals(answer));
}//method isCorrect

/** Get the <code>noCharactersInAnswer</code> for this
*    MasterMindGame.
* @return the <code>noCharactersInAnswer</code> for this
* MasterMindGame
*/
public int getNoCharactersInAnswer() {
return noCharactersInAnswer;
}

/** Get the <code>maxGuesses</code> limit for this MasterMindGame.
* @return the <code>maxGuesses</code> limit for this
* MasterMindGame.
*/
public int getMaxGuesses() {
return maxGuesses;
}
```

```
/** Returns the current state of this MasterMindGame as a String.
* @return a string representing the state of this MasterMindGame ;
*   showing the number of characters in answer,
*   number of guesses so far, maximum, and the answer too.
*/
public String toString() {
return "Number of characters in answer is " + noCharactersInAnswer +
 ".\n Guesses so far " + guessesSoFar +
 ".\n Maximum allowed "+ maxGuesses +
 ".\n The answer is " + answer + ".\n ";
}

/** Returns feedback about a guess as a String.
* @param guess a string representing a guess for this MasterMindGame.
* @return a string representing feedback about a guess ;
*/
public String getFeedback(String guess) {
return toString();
}

/** Called whenever any instance variables are changed.
* Notifies all Observers of the change of state.
* @see java.util.Observable
*/
public void changed() {
setChanged();
notifyObservers();
}

/**Test data for MasterMindGame.
* Creates a new MasterMindGame.
* Displays the initial state of MasterMindGame g
*/
public static void main(String args[]) {
MasterMindGame g = new MasterMindGame();
System.out.println(g);
String myGuess = "abc";
System.out.println(g.getFeedback(myGuess));
}//method main
} ///:~
```

Adding a console interface

The console interaction involved in playing the game can be expressed in this pseudo code.

```
guess
WHILE (not correct and guesses left) DO
  get some feedback
  guess again
ENDWHILE
IF (not correct) display the answer.
```

Alternatively, it may be shown as a diagram based on Jackson Structured Programming and Structured Systems Analysis Design Method Entity Life History diagramming notation (Figure 8.1).

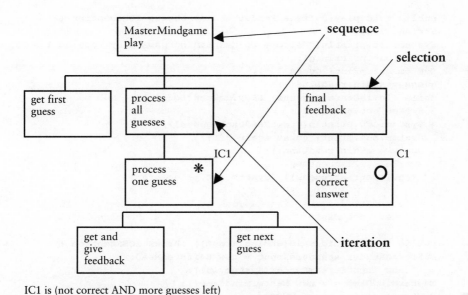

IC1 is (not correct AND more guesses left)
C1 is (not correct)

Figure 8.1   MasterMindGame play.

Implementation is straightforward.

```
//: MMGConsole.java
package chap08;
import java.io.*;

/** A MasterMindGame Console class.
 * @see java.io.IOException
 * @author Stuart F Lewis
 * @version 1.00, 12/09/98
 */
public class MMGConsole {

/** MasterMindGame for which this is the Console interface.
 * @see chap08.MasterMindGame
 */
private MasterMindGame g;

/** Constructs a new <code>MMGConsole</code>
 * as interface to MasterMindGame g
 * @param g MasterMindGame for which this is the Console interface.
 */
public MMGConsole(MasterMindGame g) {
this.g = g;
}

/** Play the MasterMindGame on the console.
 * Display a view of the MasterMindGame.
 * Guess. While not exit option, get feedback, keep guessing.
 */
```

```
public void play(BufferedReader stdin) throws IOException {
String guess;
System.out.println("Welcome to MasterMind game play version 1.0 ");
System.out.println(g);
System.out.print("guess ? ");
guess = stdin.readLine();
while (!g.isCorrect(guess) && g.isGuessLeft()) {
  System.out.println();
  System.out.println(g.getFeedback(guess));
  System.out.print("guess again ? ");
  guess = stdin.readLine();
}//while still guessing
if (!g.isCorrect(guess)) {System.out.println(g);};
}
/** Test data for the file MMGConsole.
 * Create a new MasterMindGame and play it on the console.
 */
public static void main(String args[]) throws IOException {
BufferedReader standardInput = new BufferedReader
    (new InputStreamReader(System.in));
MasterMindGame g = new MasterMindGame();
MMGConsole mmgc = new MMGConsole(g);
mmgc.play(standardInput);
}//method main
} ///:~
```

8.5 When the program is run with the skeleton class above what will be displayed?

8.6 What value entered as a guess will cause the program to end before the maximum number of guesses is reached?

Adding a GUI interface

The same skeleton game class can be used to implement the GUI interface. The ActionListener interface is most suitable on this occasion as the pressing of return in a TextField containing the guess will constitute a guess attempt. The ActionEvent generated will be used to send the guess on to the MasterMindGame to obtain the feedback. The new guess could also be read from the TextField. Two more AWT classes are used on this GUI (Figure 8.2).

Label displays a single line of read-only text. The string "Guess" labels the editable input field for the player's guess. TextArea is a multiple line region that displays text. The initial state of the game is displayed and the feedback is appended as each guess is made.

8.7 What is the immediate common superclass of TextField and TextArea?

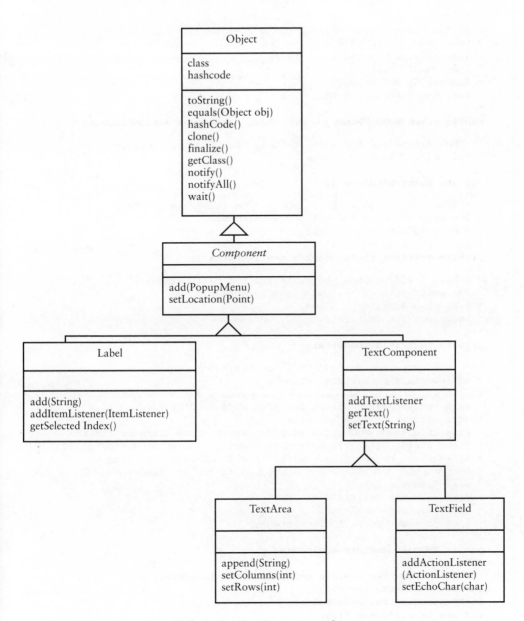

Figure 8.2 TextComponent class.

```
//: MMGGuiGuess.java
package chap08;
import java.awt.*;
import java.awt.event.*;
/** MasterMindGame Gui Guess entry implementation
 * showing the use of extends to inherit
 * from the Panel superclass and implements to
 * implement the ActionListener interface allowing this
 * Panel to receive and act on any change
```

```
* in the value of the related guess field.
* @see java.awt.TextField
* @see java.awt.TextArea
* @see chap08.MasterMindGame
* @author Stuart F Lewis
* @version 1.00, 14/09/98
*/
public class MMGGuiGuess extends Panel implements ActionListener {

/** MasterMindGame for which this is the Gui guess interface.
* @see chap08.MasterMindGame
*/
private MasterMindGame g;

/** Text area to show the feedback from the MasterMindGame
* for which this is the Gui guess interface.
* @see chap08.MasterMindGame
* @see java.awt.TextArea*/
private TextArea theFeedback = new TextArea();

/** Text field to show the Guess for the MasterMindGame
* for which this is the Gui guess interface.
* @see chap08.MasterMindGame
* @see java.awt.TextField
*/
private TextField theGuess;

/** Constructs a new <code>MMGGuiGuess</code>
* as interface to MasterMindGame g.
* gets and displays the initial state from g in the feedback area.
* sets <code>theFeedback</code> area as not editable.
* adds <code>theFeedback</code>.
* adds this <code>MMGGuiGuess</code> as an actionlistener for the
* guess field. Will call actionPerformed when user generates an
* ActionEvent by changing the text field <code>theGuess</code>.
* @param g MasterMindGame for which this is the Gui guess interface.
* @see java.awt.Label
* @see java.awt.TextField
* @see java.awt.TextArea
* @see java.awt.event.ActionListener
*/
public MMGGuiGuess(MasterMindGame g) {
this.g = g;
theGuess = new TextField(g.getNoCharactersInAnswer());
theFeedback.setText(g+"");
theFeedback.setEditable(false);
add(new Label("Guess "));
add(theGuess);
add(theFeedback);
theGuess.addActionListener(this);
}//constructor

/** Performs an action with the newly changed text item.
* Requests the MasterMindGame g to check the current guess on the view.
* Called when user generates an ActionEvent by changing this text item
* and pressing <return> to generate the ActionEvent.
* @param e ActionEvent generated by MMGGuiGuess.
*/
public void actionPerformed(ActionEvent e) {
```

```
//Could either use cmd field from event e using getActionCommand()
theFeedback.append(g.getFeedback(e.getActionCommand())+"");
//Or get the text from theGuess display - both are the new guess
//theFeedback.append(g.getFeedback(theGuess.getText())+"");
}

/** Test data for the file MMGGuiGuess.
* Creates a new MasterMindGame g.
* Creates a view gv on to g using MMGGuiGuess.
* Adds gv to a Panel p.
* Adds the panel p to a frame and shows it.
* @see java.awt.Panel
* @see java.awt.Frame
*/
public static void main(String args[]) {
MasterMindGame g = new MasterMindGame();
Panel gv = new MMGGuiGuess(g);
Frame f = new Frame("MasterMindGame Gui Guess test");
Panel p = new Panel();
p.add(gv);
f.add(p);
f.setLocation(100,100);
f.pack();
f.show();
}//method main
} ///:~
```

Now both the console and GUI (Figure 8.3) interfaces for the game play have been developed and tested using only a skeleton game class.

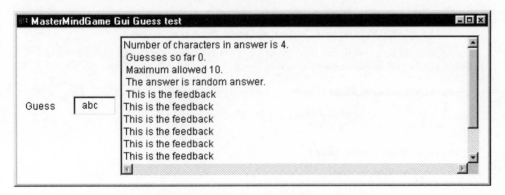

Figure 8.3   Master Mind GUI Guess test.

Improving MasterMindGame

The game could be improved to allow different ranges of characters to be used, to have answers of different lengths, and allow more or fewer guesses. Allowing the game attributes to be changed will provide several similar but slightly different games.

Adding a console choice interface to customize MasterMindGame

The process of choosing which attributes to alter is an ideal task for a Choice class. Again the generalized ConsoleChoice class can be reused to provide a MMGConsoleChoice (Master Mind Game ConsoleChoice).

8.8 What more than a ConsoleChoice class does a MMGConsoleChoice need to know?

8.9 What more than a ConsoleChoice class does a MMGConsoleChoice need to do?

Implementing a console choice interface MMGConsoleChoice for MasterMindGame

```
//: MMGConsoleChoice.java
package chap08;
import java.io.*;
import chap05.ConsoleChoice;
/** A MasterMindGame ConsoleChoice menu class.
* showing the use of extends to inherit
* from the ConsoleChoice superclass
* @see chap05.ConsoleChoice
* @see java.io.IOException
* @author Stuart F Lewis
* @version 1.00, 12/09/98
*/
public class MMGConsoleChoice extends ConsoleChoice {

/** MasterMindGame for which this is the Console Choice interface.
* @see chap08.MasterMindGame
*/
private MasterMindGame g;

/** MMGConsole used to play this game.
* @see chap08.MMGConsole
*/
private MMGConsole mmgc;

BufferedReader stdin;

/** Constructs a new <code>MasterMindGameConsoleChoice</code>
* as interface to MasterMindGame g
* with initial menu of six items and prompt.
* @param g MasterMindGame for which this is the
* Console Choice interface.
*/
public MMGConsoleChoice(MasterMindGame g) {
this.g = g;
mmgc = new MMGConsole(g);
this.addItem("Play");
this.addItem("Set maximum number of guesses");
this.addItem("Set minimum character");
this.addItem("Set maximum character");
```

```
this.addItem("See game state");
this.addItem("Save game state");
this.addItem("Restore game state");
this.addItem("Exit");
this.addPrompt("Enter choice");
stdin = new BufferedReader
    (new InputStreamReader(System.in));
}

/** Executes the currently chosen Choice item.
* Request the MMGConsole to play the game.
* Requests the MasterMindGame g to perform appropriate method to
* customize the game.
*/
void executeChoice() throws IOException {
switch (choice){
 case 1 :  mmgc.play(stdin);
           break;
 case 2 :  System.out.print("Maximum number of guesses? ");
           int guesses = 10;
           try {
               guesses = Integer.parseInt(stdin.readLine());
           }
           catch (NumberFormatException e) {
               guesses = 10;
           }
           g.setMaxGuesses(guesses);
           break;
 case 3 :  System.out.print("minimum character? ");
           g.setMinChar(stdin.readLine().charAt(0));
           break;
 case 4 :  System.out.print("maximum character? ");
           g.setMaxChar(stdin.readLine().charAt(0));
           break;
 case 5 :  System.out.print(g);
           break;
 case 6 :  save();
           break;
 case 7 :  load();
           break;
 case 8 :  System.out.println(g);
           break;
}//switch
}//executeChoice

/** Store the MasterMindGame g using serialization*/
private void save() throws IOException {
FileOutputStream ostream = new FileOutputStream("mmg.ser");
ObjectOutputStream p = new ObjectOutputStream(ostream);
p.writeObject(g);
p.flush();
ostream.close();
}
/** Restore the MasterMindGame g from file using serialization*/
private void load() throws IOException {
FileInputStream istream = new FileInputStream("mmg.ser");
ObjectInputStream o = new ObjectInputStream(istream);
```

```
try {
MasterMindGame tempObj= (MasterMindGame)o.readObject();
 g = tempObj;
}//try
catch (ClassNotFoundException e) {
System.out.println (" Class of a serialized object " +
" cannot be found.");
}//catch
catch (InvalidClassException e) {
System.out.println (" Something is wrong with a class " +
 " used by serialization.");
}//catch
istream.close();
}

/** Test data for the file MasterMindGame MMGConsoleChoice.
* Creates a new MasterMindGame and MasterMindGameConsoleChoice.
* While not exit option, executes choice.
* Display a view of the MasterMindGame.
*/
public static void main(String args[]) throws IOException {
MasterMindGame g = new MasterMindGame();
MMGConsoleChoice mmc = new MMGConsoleChoice(g);
System.out.println("Welcome to MasterMind version 2.0 ");
System.out.println(g);
while (mmc.getChoice() < mmc.getItemCount()){
  mmc.executeChoice();
 }//while
}//method main
} ///:~
```

Before this will compile the extra methods must be added to the MasterMindGame skeleton either as stubs to be implemented later or as fully implemented methods.

8.10 What methods must be added?

Now the two distinct activities, playing the game and setting the game attributes by making a choice then editing the chosen attribute, can be clearly seen separated between MMGConsole and MMGConsoleChoice. This is an ideal time to fully implement MasterMindGame. There are certain problems in allowing the user to customize the game. If the game is set up so that each character can only appear in the answer once, then what should be done if the user requests an answer length longer than the number of characters in the sequence?

8.11 How does this code overcome that problem?

In choosing the maximum and minimum character, it is difficult to prevent the user from choosing a minimum character that is greater than the current maximum.

8.12 How could this problem be overcome?

Implementing the improved MasterMindGame

Some of the methods required for the fully functional MasterMindGame need designing using either pseudo code or structure diagrams. An additional utility class Random is used to generate a sequence of random values used to create the answer. Nested for loops are used to check the guess against the answer and supply some feedback. Here is the pseudo code for three of the more complex methods.

```
BEGIN makeRandomAnswer
get a new sequence of random integers
work out the range of character values
WHILE (answer not generated)
   get the next random number from the sequence
   convert it to a character in the range
   IF (character not already used in answer)
      add to answer
   ENDIF
ENDWHILE
set guesses so far to zero
END


BEGIN getNumberInCorrectPosition
FOR (all characters in the answer)
   IF (character in the guess is the same as in answer)
      add one to NumberInCorrectPosition
   ENDIF
ENDFOR
END getNumberInCorrectPosition


BEGIN getNumberCorrect
FOR (all characters in the answer)
 FOR (all characters in the guess)
   IF (character in the guess is the same as in answer)
      AND (not at the same position)
         add one to NumberCorrect
   ENDIF
 ENDFOR
ENDFOR
END getNumberCorrect
```

8.13 Draw structure charts to show these methods.

```
//: MasterMindGame.java
package chap08;
import java.util.Observable;
import java.util.Random;
import java.io.*;
/** <code>MasterMindGame</code>
 * a guessing game for a character string
 * Observable to inform any interested observers of
 * any change of state.
 * @see java.util.Observable
 * @author Stuart F Lewis
 * @version 2.00, 25/09/98
 */
class MasterMindGame extends Observable implements Serializable {

/** Current <code>answer</code> for this MasterMindGame.
 * @serial Current <code>answer</code> for this MasterMindGame.
 */
private String answer;

/** Current <code>noCharactersInAnswer</code> for this MasterMindGame.
 * @serial <code>noCharactersInAnswer</code> for this MasterMindGame.
 */
private int noCharactersInAnswer = 4 ;

/** Current <code>maxGuesses</code> limit for this MasterMindGame.
 * @serial <code>maxGuesses</code> limit for this MasterMindGame.
 */
private int maxGuesses = 10;

/** Current <code>guessesSoFar</code> used for this MasterMindGame.
 * @serial <code>maxGuesses</code> limit for this MasterMindGame.
 */
private int guessesSoFar = 0;

/** Constant for the minimum displayable value for this MasterMindGame.
 */
static final char MIN_PRINTABLE = ' ';
/** Constant for the maximum displayable value for this MasterMindGame.
 */
static final char MAX_PRINTABLE = '|';

/** Current <code>minChar</code> for the minimum character value
 * used in this MasterMindGame.
 */
private char minChar = '0';
/** Current <code>maxChar</code> for the maximum character value
 * used in this MasterMindGame.
 */
private char maxChar = '9';

/** Private constructor for a new MasterMindGame
 * with initial answer set. Useful for testing.
 * @param ans a string representing the answer for this MasterMindGame.
 */
private MasterMindGame (String ans) {
answer = ans;
noCharactersInAnswer = answer.length();
}// Constructor

/** Constructs a new MasterMindGame with initial answer randomised.
 * Uses a random number sequence to append random characters in the
 * range <code>minChar</code> to <code>maxChar</code> inclusive
```

```java
*/
public MasterMindGame () {
answer = makeRandomAnswer();
}// Constructor

/** Makes a new random answer to use in a MasterMindGame.
 * Uses a random number sequence to append random characters in the
 * range <code>minChar</code> to <code>maxChar</code> inclusive.
 * does not allow duplicate characters in the answer.
 * sets guesses at this answer so far to zero.
 * @return a string representing a new random answer for this
 * MasterMindGame
 * @see java.util.Random
 * @see java.lang.Math
 * @see java.lang.StringBuffer
 * @see java.lang.String
 */
private String makeRandomAnswer() {
Random r = new Random();
int range = maxChar - minChar + 1;
StringBuffer randomAnswer = new StringBuffer(noCharactersInAnswer);
int j =0 ;
while (j < noCharactersInAnswer) {
   int i = r.nextInt();
   char c = (char)(Math.abs((i%range)) + (int)minChar);
   if (randomAnswer.toString().indexOf(c)<0) { // not already used
      randomAnswer.append(c);
      j++;
   }
}
guessesSoFar = 0;
changed();
return randomAnswer.toString();
}

/** Set the current answer for this MasterMindGame to a new random
value.
 */
public void setAnswer() {
answer = makeRandomAnswer();
changed();
}

/** Get the current answer for this MasterMindGame.
 * @return a string representing the current answer
 * for this MasterMindGame
 */
private String getAnswer() {
return answer;
}//method getAnswer

/** Check if there are any guesses left for this MasterMindGame.
 * @return boolean true if there is at least one guess
 * left for this MasterMindGame
 */
public boolean isGuessLeft() {
return (guessesSoFar < maxGuesses);
}
/** Checks the guess against the answer for this MasterMindGame.
 * @param guess a string representing a guess for this MasterMindGame.
 * @return int number of characters in the correct position for this
```

```
*         MasterMindGame
*/
private int getNumberInCorrectPosition(String guess) {
int numberInCorrectPosition = 0;
for (int i = 0; (i < answer.length() && i < guess.length() ); i++) {
  if (answer.charAt(i) == guess.charAt(i)) {
    numberInCorrectPosition++;
  }//if
}//for
return numberInCorrectPosition;
}//method getNumberInCorrectPosition


/** Checks the guess against the answer for this MasterMindGame.
* @param guess a string representing a guess for this MasterMindGame.
* @return int number of characters that are correct for this
*         MasterMindGame
*/
private int getNumberCorrect(String guess) {
int numberCorrect = 0;
for (int i = 0; i < answer.length() ; i++) {
  for (int j =0 ; j < guess.length() ; j++) {
     if ((answer.charAt(i) == guess.charAt(j))
             && (i != j)) {
                     numberCorrect++;
                     }//if
  }//inner for
}//outer for
return numberCorrect;
}//method getNumberCorrect

/** Checks the guess against the answer for this MasterMindGame.
* @param guess a string representing a guess for this MasterMindGame.
* @return boolean true if the guess is correct for this MasterMindGame
*/
public boolean isCorrect(String guess) {
return (guess.equals(answer));
}//method isCorrect

/** Set the <code>maxGuesses</code> limit for this MasterMindGame.
*/
public void setMaxGuesses(int n) {
maxGuesses = n;
changed();
}

/** Set the <code>noCharactersInAnswer</code> for this MasterMindGame.
* If the number of characters in the answer is less than the range
* between the minChar and maxChar set it to the parameter.
*/
public void setNoCharactersInAnswer(int n) {
if (n < (maxChar-minChar)) {noCharactersInAnswer = n;};
answer = makeRandomAnswer();
changed();
}
/** Set the <code>minChar</code> for the minimum character value
* used in this MasterMindGame.
*/
```

```
public void setMinChar(char c) {
if (c >= MIN_PRINTABLE) {
  minChar = c;
  answer = makeRandomAnswer();
  changed();
}
}

/** Set the <code>maxChar</code> for the maximum character value
* used in this MasterMindGame.
*/
public void setMaxChar(char c) {
if (c <= MAX_PRINTABLE) {
  maxChar = c;
  answer = makeRandomAnswer();
  changed();
}
}

/** Get the <code>noCharactersInAnswer</code> for this MasterMindGame.
* @return the <code>noCharactersInAnswer</code> for this MasterMindGame
*/
public int getNoCharactersInAnswer() {
return noCharactersInAnswer;
}

/** Get the <code>maxGuesses</code> limit for this MasterMindGame.
* @return the <code>maxGuesses</code> limit for this MasterMindGame.
*/
public int getMaxGuesses() {
return maxGuesses;
}

/** Get the <code>minChar</code> for the minimum character value
* used in this MasterMindGame.
* @return the <code>minChar</code> for the minimum character value
*/
public char getMinChar() {
return minChar ;
}

/** Get the <code>maxChar</code> for the maximum character value
* used in this MasterMindGame.
* @return the <code>maxChar</code> for the maximum character value
*/
public char getMaxChar() {
return maxChar ;
}

/** Returns the current state of this MasterMindGame as a String.
* @return a string representing the state of this MasterMindGame ;
*      showing the number of guesses so far, left, and if all ;
*      the guesses have been used, the answer too.
*/
public String toString() {
StringBuffer returnAnswer = new StringBuffer(answer);
if (isGuessLeft()) {
```

```
    for (int j =0 ; j < returnAnswer.length() ; j++) {
        returnAnswer.setCharAt(j,'?');
    }
}
return "Number of characters in answer is " + noCharactersInAnswer +
    ".\n Guesses so far " + guessesSoFar +
    ".\n Maximum allowed "+ maxGuesses +
    ".\n The answer is " + returnAnswer +
    ".\n minimum character is " + minChar +
    ".\n maximum character is " + maxChar + ".\n";
}

/** Returns feedback about a guess as a String.
* @see toString()
* @param guess a string representing a guess for this MasterMindGame.
* @return a string representing feedback about a guess ;
*     either saying that it is correct ;
*     or showing the number of characters that are correct ;
*      and the number of characters in the correct position.;
*     or saying that the maximum number of guesses has been reached ;
*         followed by the current state using toString().
*/
public String getFeedback(String guess) {
if (isGuessLeft()) {
  guessesSoFar++;
  changed();
  if (getNumberInCorrectPosition(guess)==getNoCharactersInAnswer()) {
   return("Guess " + guess + " is correct.\n");
  }
  return("Guess " + guess + "\n has " +
      getNumberInCorrectPosition(guess) +
      " correct in the right position\n plus " +
      getNumberCorrect(guess) +
      " more correct in the wrong position.\n");
}
return "Maximum number of guesses reached \n" + toString();
}

/** Called whenever any instance variables are changed.
* Notifies all Observers of the change of state.
* @see java.util.Observable
*/
public void changed() {
setChanged();
notifyObservers();
}

/**Test data for MasterMindGame.
* Creates a new MasterMindGame g with a known answer.
* Displays the initial state of MasterMindGame g and
* the result of a guess. Makes several guesses,
* one correct, displaying the feedback each time.
*/
public static void main(String args[]) {
MasterMindGame g = new MasterMindGame("1245");
//MasterMindGame g = new MasterMindGame();
System.out.println(g + " " + g.isCorrect("6789"));
System.out.println(g.getFeedback("6789"));
System.out.println(g.getFeedback("1234"));
```

```
System.out.println(g.getFeedback("1243"));
System.out.println(g.getFeedback("1235"));
System.out.println(g.getFeedback("1245"));
System.out.println(g.isCorrect("1245"));

System.out.println(g.getFeedback("0123"));
System.out.println(g.getFeedback("4567"));
System.out.println(g.getFeedback("1111"));
System.out.println(g.getFeedback("6666"));

g.setNoCharactersInAnswer(10);
System.out.println(g.getAnswer());
g.setMaxGuesses(50);
System.out.println(g.getAnswer());
g.setMinChar('A');
System.out.println(g.getAnswer());
g.setMaxChar('Z');
System.out.println(g.getAnswer());
System.out.println(g);
}//method main
} ///:~
```

The program displays this output when run:

```
Number of characters in answer is 4.
 Guesses so far 0.
 Maximum allowed 10.
 The answer is ????.
 minimum character is 0.
 maximum character is 9.
 false

Guess 6789
 has 0 correct in the right position
 plus 0 more correct in the wrong position.

Guess 1234
 has 2 correct in the right position
 plus 1 more correct in the wrong position.

Guess 1243
 has 3 correct in the right position
 plus 0 more correct in the wrong position.

Guess 1235
 has 3 correct in the right position
 plus 0 more correct in the wrong position.

Guess 1245 is correct.

true
Guess 0123
 has 0 correct in the right position
 plus 2 more correct in the wrong position.
Guess 4567
 has 0 correct in the right position
 plus 2 more correct in the wrong position.

Guess 1111
 has 1 correct in the right position
```

```
    plus 3 more correct in the wrong position.
Guess 6666
    has 0 correct in the right position
    plus 0 more correct in the wrong position.
7492
7492
BECD
BAVP
Number of characters in answer is 4.
    Guesses so far 0.
    Maximum allowed 50.
    The answer is ????.
    minimum character is A.
    maximum character is Z.
```

Several private helper methods implement the functionality keeping the interface to other classes to a minimum although they are available to test the class in the main() method. Particularly useful in this respect is the private constructor for a new MasterMindGame with initial answer set and getAnswer() to return the answer.

? **8.14** Why are these methods not available from outside the class?

Adding a more sophisticated GUI

The initial GUI for playing the game will work with the completed game. However, to provide a display and editing facility for the game attributes a slightly more sophisticated GUI is required.

To display a view of the current attribute values use a MMGGuiDisplay (Figure 8.4) extending Panel to show the state of a game.

```java
//: MMGGuiDisplay.java
package chap08;
import java.util.*;
import java.awt.*;

/** MasterMindGame Gui Display implementation
 * showing the use of extends to inherit
 * from the Panel superclass and implements to
 * implement the Observer interface allowing this
 * Panel to watch for and be notified of any change
 * in the state of the related MasterMindGame.
 * @see java.util.Observer
 * @see java.awt.TextField
 * @see chap08.MasterMindGame
 * @author Stuart F Lewis
 * @version 1.00, 14/09/98
 */
public class MMGGuiDisplay extends Panel implements Observer {
/** MasterMindGame for which this is the Gui Display interface.
 * @see chap08.MasterMindGame
 */
private MasterMindGame g;
```

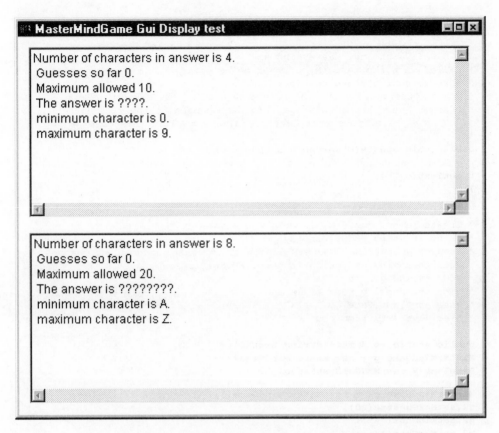

Figure 8.4   MasterMindGame Gui Display test showing two games.

```
/** Text area to show the state of the MasterMindGame
 * for which this is the Gui Display interface.
 * @see chap08.MasterMindGame
 * @see java.awt.TextField*/
private TextArea t = new TextArea();

/** Constructs a new <code>MMGGuiDisplay</code>
 * as interface to MasterMindGame g.
 * blanks the display field.
 * Registers this <code>MMGGuiDisplay</code> as
 * an Observer for any changes generated by g
 * gets and displays the initial value of g.
 * sets this <code>MMGGuiDisplay</code> as not editable.
 * @param g MasterMindGame for which this is the Gui Display
 * interface.
 * @see java.util.Observer
 * @see java.awt.TextField
 */
public MMGGuiDisplay(MasterMindGame g) {
this.g = g;
g.addObserver(this);add(t);
t.setText(g+"");
```

```
      t.setEditable(false);
      }//constructor

      /** Displays the new MasterMindGame state.
       * Called when the MasterMindGame c being observed notifies
       * observers of a state change.
       * @param Observable o the observable object ie. the MasterMindGame.
       * @param Object arg an optional argument passed to the ;
       *              notifyObservers method, always null in this case.
       */
      public void update(Observable o,Object arg) {
      //get the value and display it. Not necessary as toString() works.
      t.setText(o+"");
      }

      /** Test data for the file MMGGuiDisplay.
       * Creates a new MasterMindGame g and a view gv
       * on to it using MMGGuiDisplay.
       * Creates another new MasterMindGame g2 and makes some state changes
       * Creates a view gv2 on to it using MMGGuiDisplay.
       * Adds gv and gv2 to a Panel p.
       * Adds the panel p to a frame and shows it.
       * @see java.awt.Panel
       * @see java.awt.Frame
       */
      public static void main(String args[]) {
      MasterMindGame g = new MasterMindGame();
      Panel gv = new MMGGuiDisplay(g);

      MasterMindGame g2 = new MasterMindGame();
      g2.setMaxGuesses(20);
      g2.setMinChar('A');
      g2.setMaxChar('Z');
      g2.setNoCharactersInAnswer(8);
      Panel gv2 = new MMGGuiDisplay(g2);
      Frame f = new Frame("MasterMindGame Gui Display test");
      Panel p = new Panel();
      p.add(gv);
      p.add(gv2);
      f.add(p);
      f.setLocation(100,100);
      f.pack();
      f.show();
      }//method main
      } ///:~
```

To edit the attribute values use a MMGGuiEdit extending Panel using labels and inner classes and reusing MMGGuiDisplay. This gives two views onto the same model game. One is editable and the other is not; it does however reflect any changes made to the model game, whilst MMGGuiDisplay must be an observer watching for changes in the model. The view MMGGuiEdit updates the model when an ActionEvent is generated by the user pressing enter. This satisfies the activity of setting the game attributes, the choice and editing functions being combined on the GUI. This also combines the view and controller classes from the MVC pattern into the MMGGuiEdit class also known as a 'delegate'.

```
//: MMGGuiEdit.java
package chap08;
import java.awt.*;
import java.awt.event.*;

/** MasterMindGame Gui Edit entry implementation
 * showing the use of extends to inherit
 * from the Panel superclass and implements to
 * implement the ActionListener interface allowing this
 * Panel to receive and act on any change
 * in the value of the related editable fields showing the state
 * of the MasterMindGame for which this is the Gui Edit interface.
 * @see java.awt.TextField
 * @see java.awt.TextArea
 * @see chap08.MasterMindGame
 * @author Stuart F Lewis
 * @version 1.00, 14/05/98
 */
public class MMGGuiEdit extends Panel {

/** MasterMindGame for which this is the Gui Edit interface.
 * @see chap08.MasterMindGame
 */
private MasterMindGame g;

/** Text field to show the maximum number of guesses for the
 * MasterMindGame for which this is the Gui Edit interface.
 * @see chap08.MasterMindGame
 * @see java.awt.TextField*/
private TextField maxGuesses = new TextField();

/** Text field to show the minimum character for the
 * MasterMindGame for which this is the Gui Edit interface.
 * @see chap08.MasterMindGame
 * @see java.awt.TextField*/
private TextField minChar = new TextField(1);

/** Text field to show the maximum character for the
 * MasterMindGame for which this is the Gui Edit interface.
 * @see chap08.MasterMindGame
 * @see java.awt.TextField*/
private TextField maxChar = new TextField(1);

/** Text field to show the number of characters in an answer
 * for the MasterMindGame for which this is the Gui Edit interface.
 * @see chap08.MasterMindGame
 * @see java.awt.TextField*/
private TextField noCharactersInAnswer = new TextField(1);

/** Constructs a new <code>MMGGuiEdit</code>
 * as interface to MasterMindGame g.
 * sets up the editable fields showing the current state.
 * Each has their own ActionListener inner class which will
 * process any action events when user generates an ActionEvent
 * by changing any editable text field.
 * Generated by the user.
 * @param g MasterMindGame for which this is the Gui Edit
 * interface.
 * @see java.awt.TextField
 * @see java.awt.TextArea* @see java.awt.event.ActionListener
 */
```

```java
public MMGGuiEdit(MasterMindGame g) {
this.g = g;
noCharactersInAnswer.setText(g.getNoCharactersInAnswer()+"");
maxGuesses.setText(g.getMaxGuesses()+"");
minChar.setText(g.getMinChar()+"");
maxChar.setText(g.getMaxChar()+"");
noCharactersInAnswer.addActionListener(new
            noCharactersInAnswerListener());
maxGuesses.addActionListener(new
     maxGuessesListener());
minChar.addActionListener(new minCharListener());
maxChar.addActionListener(new maxCharListener());
setLayout(new GridLayout(4,2));
add(new Label("Number of characters"));
add(noCharactersInAnswer);
add(new Label("Maximum guesses allowed"));
add(maxGuesses);
add(new Label("Minimum character"));
add(minChar);
add(new Label("Maximum character"));
add(maxChar);
}//constructor

/** Processes change NoCharactersInAnswer events occurring on this
* <code>MMGGuiEdit</code> menu by requesting the
* MasterMindGame g to perform appropriate method.
* Called when user generates change noCharactersInAnswer
* by editing the text field on this MMGGuiEdit Panel.
* @see java.awt.event.ActionEvent
* @see java.awt.event.ActionListener
* @see java.awt.TextField#addActionListener
* @see chap08.MasterMindGame
*/
public class noCharactersInAnswerListener implements ActionListener {
 public void actionPerformed(ActionEvent ae) {
 int answerLength = g.getNoCharactersInAnswer();
 try {
  answerLength = Integer.parseInt(noCharactersInAnswer.getText());
 }
 catch (NumberFormatException e) {
  answerLength = g.getNoCharactersInAnswer();
 }
 g.setNoCharactersInAnswer(answerLength);
 }//end actionPerformed
}

/** Processes change maxGuesses events occurring on this
* <code>MMGGuiEdit</code> menu by requesting the
* MasterMindGame g to perform appropriate method.
* Called when user generates change maxGuesses by editing the text
* field on this MMGGuiEdit Panel.
* @see java.awt.event.ActionEvent
* @see java.awt.event.ActionListener
* @see java.awt.TextField#addActionListener
* @see chap08.MasterMindGame
*/
public class maxGuessesListener implements ActionListener {
```

```
   public void actionPerformed(ActionEvent ae) {
   int guesses = g.getMaxGuesses();
   try {
    guesses = Integer.parseInt(maxGuesses.getText());
   }
   catch (NumberFormatException e) {
    guesses = g.getMaxGuesses();
   }
   g.setMaxGuesses(guesses);
   }//end actionPerformed
 }

 /** Processes change minChar events occurring on this
 * <code>MMGGuiEdit</code> menu by requesting the
 * MasterMindGame g to perform appropriate method.
 * Called when user generates change minChar by editing the text
 * field on this MMGGuiEdit Panel.
 * @see java.awt.event.ActionEvent
 * @see java.awt.event.ActionListener
 * @see java.awt.TextField#addActionListener
 * @see chap08.MasterMindGame
 */
 public class minCharListener implements ActionListener {
  public void actionPerformed(ActionEvent ae) {
  g.setMinChar(minChar.getText().charAt(0));
  g.setMaxChar(maxChar.getText().charAt(0));
  }//end actionPerformed
 }

 /** Processes change maxChar events occurring on this
 * <code>MMGGuiEdit</code> menu by requesting the
 * MasterMindGame g to perform appropriate method.
 * Called when user generates change maxChar by editing the text
 * field on this MMGGuiEdit Panel.
 * @see java.awt.event.ActionEvent
 * @see java.awt.event.ActionListener
 * @see java.awt.TextField#addActionListener
 * @see chap08.MasterMindGame
 */
 public class maxCharListener implements ActionListener {
  public void actionPerformed(ActionEvent ae) {
  g.setMinChar(minChar.getText().charAt(0));
  g.setMaxChar(maxChar.getText().charAt(0));
  }//end actionPerformed
 }

 /** Test data for the file MMGGuiEdit.
 * Creates a new MasterMindGame g and a view gv
 * on to it using MMGGuiEdit.
 * Creates another view of the state gs on
 * to MasterMindGame g using MMGGuiDisplay.
 * Adds gv to a Panel p.
 * Adds the panel p to a frame and shows it.
 * @see java.awt.Panel
 * @see java.awt.Frame
 */
 public static void main(String args[]) {
 MasterMindGame g = new MasterMindGame();
```

```
Panel gv = new MMGGuiEdit(g);
Panel gs = new MMGGuiDisplay(g);
Frame f = new Frame("MasterMindGame Gui Edit test");
Panel p = new Panel();
p.add(gv);p.add(gs);f.add(p);
f.setLocation(100,100);
f.pack();
f.show();
}//method main
} ///:~
```

MMGGuiGuess will still satisfy the other activity of playing the game. Now all of the GUI classes can be combined in a MMGViewContainer composed of three panels, MMGGuiEdit, MMGGuiDisplay, and MMGGuiGuess (Figure 8.5), all providing views onto the same model MasterMindGame g.

```
//: MMGViewContainer.java
package chap08;
import java.awt.*;

/** MasterMindGame ViewContainer implementation
 * showing the use of extends to inherit
 * from the Panel superclass.
```

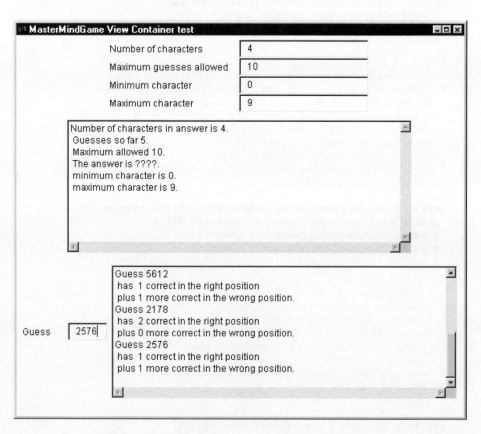

Figure 8.5   MasterMindGame View Container test.

```
* Knows nothing about the state, methods, or interface
* of a MasterMindGame apart from the existence of the MMGGui
* Edit, Guess and Display classes.
* @see java.awt.Panel
* @author Stuart F Lewis
* @version 1.00, 14/05/98
*/
public class MMGViewContainer extends Panel {

/** Constructs a new <code>MMGViewContainer</code>
* as interface to MasterMindGame g
* with an edit panel provided by MMGGuiEdit,
* a display state area provided by MMGGuiDisplay,
* a guess entry and feedback panel provided by MMGGuiGuess.
* Adds them all to this Panel.
*
* @param g MasterMindGame for which this is the Gui ViewContainer.
* @see java.awt.TextField
*/
public MMGViewContainer(MasterMindGame g) {
Panel ep = new MMGGuiEdit(g);
Panel vs = new MMGGuiDisplay(g);
Panel gf = new MMGGuiGuess(g);
add(ep);
add(vs);
add(gf);
}//constructor

/** Test data for the file MMGViewContainer.
* Creates a new MasterMindGame and a container to view it using
* MMGViewContainer.
* Adds the MMGViewContainer to a frame and shows it
*/
public static void main(String args[]) {
MasterMindGame g = new MasterMindGame();
Panel p = new MMGViewContainer(g);
Frame f = new Frame("MasterMindGame View Container test");
f.add(p);
f.setLocation(100,100);
//fix the width so the panels show
Dimension d = new Dimension();
d = f.getSize();
d.width = 800;
d.height = 500;
f.setSize(d);
f.show();
}//method main
} ///:~
```

Classes involved in MasterMindGame

All of the classes used in building the MasterMindGame can be summarised on a single UML diagram showing the console interface classes at the top and the GUI classes at the bottom. The same central MasterMindGame class is used by both. This diagram (Figure 8.6) shows more detail about each attribute and method. The + or − indicates the visibility as either public or private. As UML class diagrams can be used throughout the lifecycle from analysis to implementation the amount of detail can vary according to the stage at which the class has reached.

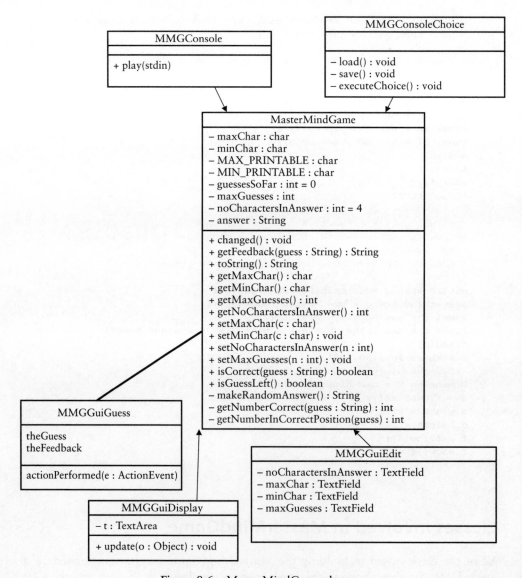

Figure 8.6   MasterMindGame classes.

Summary

In the context of developing a simple guessing game, a more complex object was designed. A skeleton game was used to implement and test both the console and GUI interface for playing the game before the game was completed. Several more API classes were introduced from the AWT and other packages. The game was completed with some more functionality being added. Interfaces to customize the game were added for the console and GUI. Several views were added to the model, some of which combined controller functions to provide delegate classes.

Answers to in-text questions

1 A MasterMindGame needs to know the answer, the number of characters in that answer, the maximum number of guesses allowed, and the number of guesses made so far.

2 A MasterMindGame needs to provide methods to make a new random answer, to check if a given answer is correct, to check if the player has guesses left, and to give some feedback about incorrect guesses.

3 See Figure 8.7.

4 For a simple game, storing the answer would be quite acceptable. However, if the game was developed further two other choices could be considered. Firstly the answer could be encrypted, stored, and decrypted on restore. Secondly the answer could be declared as transient and not stored but a new one could be generated on restore.

5 When the program is run with the skeleton class above it will display:

```
Welcome to MasterMind version 1.0
Number of characters in answer is 4.
 Guesses so far 0.
 Maximum allowed 10.
 The answer is random answer
guess ?
```

6 random answer.

7 java.awt.TextComponent.

8 MMGConsoleChoice needs to know the MasterMindGame to which it is an interface, the MMGConsole used to play the game and the other choices available to customize the game.

9 MMGConsoleChoice needs to request the MMGConsole to play the game. Request the MasterMindGame g to perform appropriate methods to customize the game. Provide methods to implement any other functionality required.

10 setMaxGuesses, setMinChar and setMaxChar.

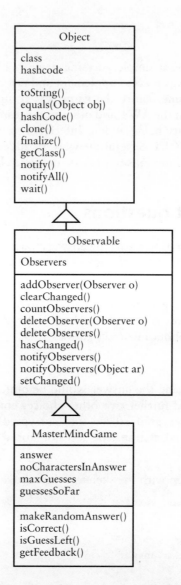

Figure 8.7   MasterMindGame class extended from Observable.

11 By only setting the number of characters in the answer to be equal to the parameter if it is less than the length of the sequence between the minimum and maximum character.

12 By checking both the maximum and minimum characters as a pair if either of them is changed.

13 Left as an exercise.

14 These methods are not available from outside the class because their visibility modifier is private.

REVIEW QUESTIONS

Answers in Appendix A.

1 What problems can arise when serializing the state of an object?

2 What are the advantages of developing a skeleton problem domain class?

3 Describe the stages in developing a GUI interface.

4 How do simple structure charts and pseudo code help in developing classes?

5 What other services does the Random class provide?

EXERCISES

Answers to exercises flagged with an asterisk appear in Appendix B.

1   Develop a hangman game to guess a hidden word.

2   What other games could use a similar interface?

3* Why is there a method random() in the Math class in the Java API?

4* How does the Random class differ from the method in the Math class?

9

Communication between objects

Overview

A general approach to building systems from multiple objects is described through a case study based on the fictitious Java Car Insurance Company (JCIC). Several problem domain classes are developed and prototyped using console input and output. The serialization process is used to store all the problem domain objects. Several additional AWT classes are introduced to help format output. Some reusable graphical user interface components are developed using other AWT facilities. These are used to complete the graphical user interface to the system. As the number of components increase, different layout managers are used to organise their relative position on the interface. The ease with which further changes or enhancements to the system could be made is considered.

Case study for the Java Car Insurance Company (JCIC)

The main task of the system required by JCIC is to determine the type and cost of motor insurance for different customers with different cars. The input for each customer applying for insurance with UCIC will consist of age of customer and the number of years no claims bonus. The input for each car will consist of a code to indicate whether it is a UK or foreign car and the value of the car. The output for each quote will consist of the type of cover, the excess payable on a claim, and the amount of premium.

Assume that if a customer has more than three years no claims, the accident record is good. The rules for determining the type and cost of a policy for each quote are as follows:

- If the age of the customer is 25 or over, the car is manufactured in the UK, and the accident record is good, the premium is 6% of the value of the car and a comprehensive policy is issued. If the accident record is bad, the premium is 7% of the value of the car, the customer pays the first £100 of any claim and a comprehensive policy is issued.

- If the age of the customer is 25 or over, the car is not manufactured in the UK, and the accident record is good, the premium is 6% of the value of the car, the customer pays the first £100 of any claim and a comprehensive policy is issued. If the accident record is bad, the premium is 7% of the value of the car, the customer pays the first £100 of any claim and a third-party-only policy is issued.
- If the age of the customer is under 25, the car is manufactured in the UK, and the accident record is good, the premium is 8% of the value of the car, the customer pays the first £200 of any claim and a comprehensive policy is issued. If the accident record is bad then the risk is declined.
- If the age of the customer is under 25, the car is not manufactured in the UK, and the accident record is good, the premium is 9% of the value of the car, the customer pays the first £250 of any claim and a comprehensive policy is issued. If the accident record is bad then the risk is declined.

9.1 Summarise the possible cases for each combination of customer and car.

Three problem domain classes can quickly be identified from the major nouns in the description above Customer, Car, and Quote.

9.2 For each of these classes, what attributes need to be stored?

These three classes can each be implemented as a Java class extending Observable and implementing Serializable as they represent the problem domain model. This will allow both the interface classes developed later and any other interested observers to watch for changes in the model. In particular the Quote will observe changes to the associated Customer or Car then update the calculated Quote values.

An editable view will be required for both the Customer and Car classes. Editable views combine the view and controller functions from the MVC pattern as a delegate. Combining these delegate classes with an output only view of the Quote will make up the system. As previously, these problem domain classes can be developed with a console interface for testing with a GUI being added later.

9.3 Draw a UML diagram for the Car class.

Implementation for the Customer class

In a real-world system many additional attributes are captured and stored by insurance companies about their customers, but here only those required for producing the Quote will be stored (Figure 9.1). The methods setAge() and setYearsNoClaims() are both overloaded to accept either a String parameter or an integer parameter.

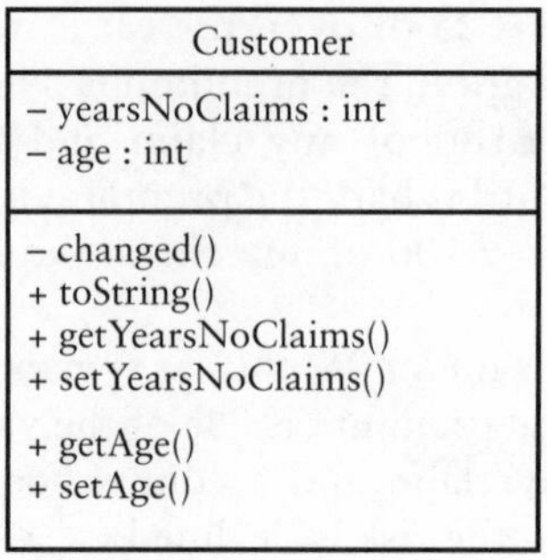

Figure 9.1   UML diagram for the Customer.

```
//: Customer.java
package chap09;

import java.util.Observable;
import java.io.Serializable;

/** <b>Customer</b> stores
* the details required for a Customer.
* @see java.util.Observable;
* @author Stuart F Lewis
* @version 2.00, 25/09/98
*/
public class Customer extends Observable implements Serializable {

/** Customer's age
* @serial age of this Customer.
*/
private int age;

/** Customer's driving record
* @serial driving record of this Customer.
*/
private int yearsNoClaims;

/** Constructor for Customer.
*/
public Customer() {
this(25,0);
}

/** Constructor for Customer.
* @param age of Customer
* @param years no claims
*/
public Customer(int a, int nc) {
age = a;
yearsNoClaims = nc;
}

/** Sets the age of this Customer.
* @param age of Customer
*/
public void setAge(int ageOfCustomer) {
age = ageOfCustomer;
changed();
}
```

```java
/** Sets the current age of this Customer.
* try to set the age to the string parameter
* but if that is not possible, default to 25
*/
public void setAge(String val) {
int ageInt;
try {
  ageInt = Integer.parseInt(val);
  }
catch( NumberFormatException e) {
   //System.out.println("Error in " + val);
   ageInt = 25;
   }
setAge(ageInt);
changed();
}


/** Gets the age of this Customer.
* @return the age of this Customer.*/
public int getAge() {
return age ;
}


/** Sets the current yearsNoClaims of this Customer.
* @param years no claims
*/
public void setYearsNoClaims(int val) {
yearsNoClaims = val;
changed();
}


/** Sets the current yearsNoClaims of this Customer.
* try to set the yearsNoClaims to the string parameter
* but if that is not possible, default to zero
* @param years no claims
*/
public void setYearsNoClaims(String val) {
int yearsNoClaimsInt;
try {
  yearsNoClaimsInt = Integer.parseInt(val);
  }
catch( NumberFormatException e) {
   //System.out.println("Error in " + val);
   yearsNoClaimsInt = 0;
   }
setYearsNoClaims(yearsNoClaimsInt);
changed();
}


/** Gets the current yearsNoClaims of this Customer.
* @return the current number of years No Claims of this Customer.
*/
public int getYearsNoClaims() {
return yearsNoClaims;
}
```

```java
/** Returns the Customer as a String.
 * @return a string representing the Customer
 */
public String toString() {
return " Age " + age + " years no claims " + yearsNoClaims;
}

/** Called whenever any instance variables are changed.
 * Notifies all Observers of the change of state.
 * @see java.util.Observable
 */
public void changed() {
setChanged();
notifyObservers();
}

/** Test routine for the class Customer.
 */
public static void main(String[] args) {
Customer myCustomer = new Customer();
System.out.println(myCustomer);
myCustomer = new Customer(30,5);
System.out.println(myCustomer);
}
} ///:~
```

? **9.4** When the program is run what will be displayed?

? **9.5** Write a Java implementation for the Car class described above.

These two classes are used to capture the input data that can be used to calculate the Quote.

Design for the Quote class

This third problem domain class relies on attributes from the other two classes Car and Customer to perform the calculation that is central to solving the Car Insurance Company problem. The design can be captured in the UML diagram for the Quote class (Figure 9.2).

All of the attributes that make up the state of a Quote are encapsulated using the private visibility modifier. The Car and Customer attributes can be accessed using a pair of set and get accessor methods. The other three attributes cannot be set, only get accessor methods are provided. The values of policy, premium, and excess are set by the recalculate method. The recalculate method is called in two different circumstances, firstly, when the state of the Quote is changed by setting a new Customer or Car; secondly, if the current Customer or Car state is changed and the Quote is notified of the change. After recalculating the values of policy, premium, and excess, the Quote then notifies any observers that it has now changed.

```
                        ┌─────────────────────────────────────────┐
                        │                  Quote                  │
                        ├─────────────────────────────────────────┤
                        │ – excess : String = ""                  │
                        │                                         │
                        │ – premium : String = ""                 │
                        │ – policy : String = ""                  │
                        │                                         │
                        │ – customer : Customer                   │
                        │ – car : car                             │
                        ├─────────────────────────────────────────┤
                        │ + getCar() : Car                        │
                        │ + setCar(car : Car) : void              │
                        │ + getCustomer() : Customer              │
                        │ + setCustomer(customer : Customer) : void│
                        │                                         │
                        │ + update(o : Observable, arg : Object) :│
                        │                                         │
                        │ – changed() : void                      │
                        │ – reCalculate() : void                  │
                        │                                         │
                        │ + toString() : String                   │
                        │ + getPolicy() : String                  │
                        │ + getPremium() : String                 │
                        │ +getExcess() : String                   │
                        └─────────────────────────────────────────┘
```

Figure 9.2   Quote class.

Implementation for the Quote class

The Quote class is both an observer and observed. When either the customer or car associated with a quote is changed the quote is notified. The quote updates the calculated attributes and informs any observers that the quote has changed. The Quote class also implements Serializable to allow quotes to be stored and restored from disk.

```
//: Quote.java
package chap09;
import java.util.*;
import java.io.*;
import java.text.*;

/** Quote is the calculator for the Car insurance company
 * Uses classes Customer Car and Panel.
 * @see chap09.Customer
 * @see chap09.Car
 * @see java.awt.Panel
 * @author Stuart F Lewis
 * @version 2.00, 25/09/98
 */
public class Quote extends Observable
        implements Observer, Serializable {

/** Customer for this quote.
 * @serial customer for this quote.
 */
private Customer customer;

/** Car for this quote.
 * @serial car for this quote.
 */
private Car car;
```

```
/** Policy type for this quote.
* @serial Policy type for this quote.
*/
private String policy = "";

/** Premium for this quote.
* @serial Premium for this quote.
*/
private String premium = "";

/** Excess for this quote.
* @serial Excess for this quote.
*/
private String excess = "";

/** Constructs a new Quote
*/
public Quote(Customer customer, Car car) {
this.customer = customer;
this.car = car;
//watch for changes in the customer or car
customer.addObserver(this);
car.addObserver(this);
reCalculate();
}// constructor

/** Returns the result of the calculation in the form
* policy excess premium
*/
public String toString() {
    return (policy + " " + excess + " " + premium);
}//toString

/** calculates the policy based on the customer and car
*/
private void reCalculate() {
//initialize values
double premRate = 0;
int result = 0;
int Value = car.getValue();
//calculate policy, excess and premium
if (customer.getAge()>=25) {result = result + 4;}
if (customer.getYearsNoClaims()>3) {result = result + 2;}
if (car.getOrigin().equals("U.K.")) {result = result + 1;}
switch (result) {
    case 7 : {policy="Comprehensive";excess="£0";
  premRate=(0.06 * Value);
            break;}
    case 6 : {policy="Comprehensive";excess="£100";
            premRate=(0.06 * Value);
            break;}
    case 5 : {policy="Comprehensive";excess="£100";
            premRate=(0.07 * Value);
            break;}
    case 4 : {policy="3rd Party";excess="£100";
            premRate=(0.07 * Value);
            break;}
```

```
        case 3 : {policy="Comprehensive";excess="£200";
                  premRate=(0.08 * Value);
                  break;}
        case 2 : {policy="Comprehensive";excess="£250";
                  premRate=(0.09 * Value);
                  break;}
        case 1 : {policy="No Cover";excess="-";
                  premRate=0.00;
                  break;}
        case 0 : {policy="No Cover";excess="-";
                  premRate=0.00;
                  break;}
}//switch
//Format premium
NumberFormat Np = NumberFormat.getCurrencyInstance();
premium = (String.valueOf(Np.format(premRate)));
// notify change
changed();
}// reCalculate

/** Notifies Observers of a new calculation.
*/
public void changed() {
setChanged();
notifyObservers();
}//changed

/** Recalculate the new Quote value.
* Called when the customer or car being observed notifies
* observers of a state change. In both cases recalculate.
* @param Observable o the observable object ie. the customer or
* car.
* @param Object arg an optional argument passed to the ;
*           notifyObservers method, always null in this case.
*/
public void update(Observable o,Object arg) {
reCalculate();
}

/** Access to the result of Quote calculation.
* @return the description of the policy
*/
public String getPolicy() {
return policy;
}

/** Access to the result of Quote calculation.
* @return the amount of excess payable for the policy
*/
public String getExcess() {
return excess;
}

/** Access to the result of Quote calculation.
* @return the amount of premium payable for the policy
*/
public String getPremium() {
return premium;
}
```

```java
/** Access to set the Customer for this Quote. Adds this
 * Quote as an observer of the Customer. If the state of the
 * Customer changes the quote will be updated
 * @param the Customer for this Quote
 */
public void setCustomer(Customer customer) {
this.customer = customer;
customer.addObserver(this);
reCalculate();
}

/** Access to the Customer for this Quote.
 * @return the Customer for this Quote
 */
public Customer getCustomer() {
return customer;
}

/** Access to set the Car for this Quote. Adds this
 * Quote as an observer of the Car. If the state of the
 * Car changes the quote will be updated
 * @param the Car for this Quote
 */
public void setCar(Car car) {
this.car = car;
car.addObserver(this);
reCalculate();
}

/** Access to the Car for this Quote.
 * @return the Car for this Quote
 */
public Car getCar() {
return car;
}

/** Test routine for Quote. Prints out three Quote
 * calculations to screen
 */
public static void main(String[] args) throws IOException {
Customer myCustomer = new Customer();
Car myCar = new Car();
Quote newpolicy = new Quote(myCustomer,myCar);
System.out.println(newpolicy + " " + myCustomer + myCar);

myCar.setValue(1000);
myCustomer.setYearsNoClaims(4);
System.out.println(newpolicy + " " + myCustomer + myCar);
myCustomer.setAge(40);
System.out.println(newpolicy + " " + myCustomer + myCar);
}//main
} ///:~
```

9.6 What will the program display when it is run?

9.7 Why are there no matching set methods for the three get methods for the policy, excess, and premium?

The NumberFormat is the abstract base class for all number formats. The static method getCurrencyInstance is used to get the currency number format for the default locale. This is another of the Java API classes that mean code can be independent of the locale conventions for formatting currency.

Adding console input and output to Quote

A console interface to Customer, Car and Quote is developed for testing these classes and prototyping the user interaction. The ConsoleChoice class from an earlier chapter is reused.

9.8 What more than a ConsoleChoice class does a QuoteConsoleChoice need to know?

9.9 What more than a ConsoleChoice class does a QuoteConsoleChoice need to do?

The QuoteConsoleChoice class (Figure 9.3) is now interacting with the three problem domain classes. After requesting and accepting the input data for the customer and car, these are passed on to the quote. If the details are requested then

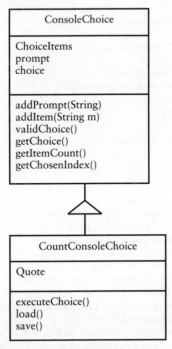

Figure 9.3   Diagram showing the QuoteConsoleChoice class.

the QuoteConsoleChoice asks the quote for them. The customer and car details are stored along with the quote by the process of serialization. The default serialization mechanism for an object writes the class of the object, the class signature, and the values of all non-transient and non-static fields. References to other objects cause those objects to be written also.

During deserialization, the customer and car will also be retrieved. This demonstrates the power of serialization as a method of persistent object storage.

```java
//: QuoteConsoleChoice.java
package chap09;
import java.io.*;
import chap05.ConsoleChoice;

/** A QuoteConsoleChoice menu class.
* showing the use of extends to inherit
* from the ConsoleChoice superclass
* @see java.io.IOException
* @author Stuart F Lewis
* @version 1.00, 12/09/98
*/
public class QuoteConsoleChoice extends ConsoleChoice {

/** Quote for which this is the Console Choice interface.
* @see chap09.Quote
*/
private Quote q;

/** Constructs a new <code>QuoteConsoleChoice</code>
* as interface to Quote q
* with initial menu of four items and prompt.
* @param q Quote for which this is the Console Choice interface.
*/
public QuoteConsoleChoice(Quote q) {
this.q = q;
this.addItem("Input details");
this.addItem("Display details and quote");
this.addItem("Save");
this.addItem("Restore");
this.addItem("Exit");
this.addPrompt("Enter choice");
}

/** Executes the currently chosen Choice item.
* Requests the Quote c to perform appropriate method.
*/
void executeChoice() throws IOException {
BufferedReader stdin = new BufferedReader
    (new InputStreamReader(System.in));
switch (choice)
{
  case 1 : Customer myCustomer = new Customer();
            System.out.print("Enter customer's age> ");
            myCustomer.setAge(stdin.readLine());
            System.out.println();
            System.out.print("Enter years no claims> ");
            myCustomer.setYearsNoClaims(stdin.readLine());
            System.out.println();
```

```
            Car myCar = new Car();
            System.out.print("Enter Car's origin> ");
            myCar.setOrigin(stdin.readLine());
            System.out.println();
            System.out.print("Enter Car's value> ");
            myCar.setValue(stdin.readLine());
            System.out.println();

            q.setCustomer(myCustomer);
            q.setCar(myCar);
            break;
  case 2 : System.out.println("Customer " + q.getCustomer());
            System.out.println("Car " + q.getCar());
            break;
  case 3 : save();
            break;
  case 4 : load();
            break;
}//switch
}//executeChoice

/** Store the Quote q using serialization
*/
private void save() throws IOException{
FileOutputStream ostream = new FileOutputStream("quote.ser");
ObjectOutputStream p = new ObjectOutputStream(ostream);
p.writeObject(q);
p.flush();
ostream.close();
}

/** Retrieve the Quote q using serialization
*/
private void load() throws IOException {
FileInputStream istream = new FileInputStream("quote.ser");
ObjectInputStream o = new ObjectInputStream(istream);
   try {
   Quote tempObj = (Quote)o.readObject();
   q.setCustomer(tempObj.getCustomer());
   q.setCar(tempObj.getCar());
   }
   catch (ClassNotFoundException e) {
   System.out.println (" Class of a serialized object cannot be
found.");
   }
   catch (InvalidClassException e) {
   System.out.println (" Something is wrong with a class " +
                           " used by serialization.");
   }
      istream.close();
}

/** Test data for the file QuoteConsoleChoice.
* Creates a new Quote and QuoteConsoleChoice.
* While not exit option, executes choice.
* Display a view of the Quote.
*/
```

```
public static void main(String args[]) throws IOException {
Customer myCustomer = new Customer();
Car myCar = new Car();
Quote q = new Quote(myCustomer,myCar);
QuoteConsoleChoice qcc = new QuoteConsoleChoice(q);
 while (qcc.getChoice() < qcc.getItemCount()){
  qcc.executeChoice();
  System.out.println("Current Quote is " + q);
 }//while

}//method main
} ///:~
```

? **9.10** What sequence of choices and input will test that serialization is working correctly?

Now the problem solution and the problem domain classes have been tested a GUI can be added.

Adding a GUI to input Car details

The simple input provided above allows any place of origin to be entered for the car. From the specification, only two possibilities are of interest in calculating a quote, either UK or not. This is another opportunity to develop a reusable GUI class allowing the choice between only two alternatives (Figure 9.4).

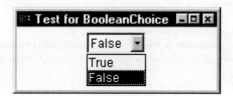

Figure 9.4   BooleanChoice test.

```
//: BooleanChoice.java
package chap09;

import java.awt.*;
import java.awt.event.*;
import java.io.*;
import java.util.Observable;

/** Boolean Chioce extends Choice and implements ItemListener.
 * Intended to only allow two choices.
 * @see java.awt.Choice
 * @see java.awt.event.ItemListener
 * @author Stuart F Lewis
 * @version 2.00, 25/09/98
 */
public class BooleanChoice extends Choice implements ItemListener {
```

```
/** state of this BooleanChoice
*/
private boolean state = true;
/** Constructs a new BooleanChoice
*/
public BooleanChoice(String TrueString, String FalseString) {
//add the true string
this.add(TrueString);
//add the false string
this.add(FalseString);
//Listen for change of state
this.addItemListener(this);
}//constructor
/**
*/
public void itemStateChanged(ItemEvent e) {
// Set state of Selection
if (this.getSelectedIndex() == 0) {
    state = true;
}
else {
    state = false;
}
}// itemStateChanged

/** Return the state as a boolean.
* @return true if the first item is selected, false otherwise
*/
public boolean getState() {
return state;
}

/** Return the state as a String
* @return the value of the box as a string
*/
public String toString() {
    return this.getSelectedItem();
}// toString

/**
* @return a boolean representation of the object.
*/
public boolean toBoolean() {
return state;
}// toBoolean

/** test routine for BooleanChoice.
* Displays a BooleanChoice box on the screen
*/
public static void main(String args[]) {
Frame f = new Frame("Test for BooleanChoice");
Panel p = new Panel();
Choice BooleanSelection = new BooleanChoice("True", "False");
p.add(BooleanSelection);
f.add(p);
f.pack();
f.show();
}// main
} ///:~
```

? **9.11** From the API which other AWT component could have been used for choosing between one of two possible choices?

One reusable class is ready to provide the input to a Car. The standard TextField can be specialized to allow only digits to be entered. The pseudo code to describe this process is:

```
IF there are characters THEN
   FOR all the characters DO
      IF the character is a digit THEN add it to the new contents
      ENDIF
   ENDFOR
   IF characters were removed THEN put the new contents in instead
   ENDIF
ENDIF
```

Fortunately, the API provides two useful classes to assist in this process. StringCharacterIterator implements the CharacterIterator interface. This allows each character in the String entered to be visited in turn. Using the static method isDigit(char) from the Character class the digits from the entered String are added to a new StringBuffer. A TextEvent is generated every time the user presses a key. To keep the cursor displayed at the end of the entered text it must be repositioned every time. This is achieved using setCaretPosition(int) inherited by DigitsOnlyTextField from java.awt.TextComponent. The position of the text insertion caret for the DigitsOnlyTextField always appears at the end of the number entered (Figure 9.5).

Figure 9.5   DigitsOnlyTextField Test.

? **9.12** What other facilities are provided by java.awt.TextComponent for controlling the user interaction with the text?

```
//: DigitsOnlyTextField.java
package chap09;

import java.awt.*;
import java.awt.event.*;
import java.text.*;

/** <b>DigitsOnlyTextField</b> extends TextField
 * and is designed to only allow Numeric characters to be entered.
 * @see java.awt.TextField
 * @see java.awt.event.TextListener
 * @see java.text.StringCharacterIterator;
```

```
* @see java.text.CharacterIterator;
* @author Stuart F Lewis
* @version 2.00, 25/09/98
*/
public class DigitsOnlyTextField extends TextField
                    implements TextListener {

/** Current <code>value</code> for this DigitsOnlyTextField.
*/
private String value;

/** constructor for a new DigitsOnlyTextField.
* Creates a new TextField that
* will only allow numeric characters to be entered.
* @param the number of columns wide for this TextField
*/
public DigitsOnlyTextField(int val) {
this.setColumns(val);
//Listen to changes
this.addTextListener(this);
}//DigitsOnlyTextField constructor

/** Gets the text from the box and checks it has no alpha characters.
* If it does it will remove them and put the updated value back
* in the box.
* @see java.lang.Character#isDigit
*/
public void textValueChanged(TextEvent e) {
//Get the text from box
String Contents = this.getText();
if (Contents.length()>0) {
  // remove non numeric characters
  StringBuffer numericContents = new StringBuffer();
  StringCharacterIterator iter =
          new StringCharacterIterator(Contents);
  for(char c = iter.first(); c != CharacterIterator.DONE;
                      c = iter.next()) {
      if (Character.isDigit(c)) {
        numericContents.append(c);
      }//if
      }//for
      String newContents = new String(numericContents);
      //put the cursor at the end of the number
      this.setCaretPosition(newContents.length()+1);
      // replace text if changed by removing some non digits
      if (!(Contents.equals(newContents))) {
          this.setText(newContents);
      }//if changed
}//if length greater than 0
}// textValueChanged

/**returns the value of the box as a string*/
public String toString() {
return getText();
}
```

```
/** test routine for DigitsOnlyTextField. Puts two boxes on a
* panel test by entering a mixture of numeric and non numeric
* characters.
*/
public static void main(String args[]) {
Frame f = new Frame("Test DigitsOnlyTextField");
Panel p = new Panel();
TextField CarValue = new DigitsOnlyTextField(8);
TextField CarValue2 = new DigitsOnlyTextField(12);
p.add(CarValue);
p.add(CarValue2);
f.add(p);
f.pack();
f.show();
CarValue.setText("123remove me456");
System.out.println(CarValue.getText());
System.out.println(CarValue);
}// main
} ///:~
```

9.13 How does the textValueChanged(TextEvent) method know where to position the text insertion cursor?

9.14 What will happen when the program is run?

Using these two specialized input components, the CarEdit panel can be constructed. The two input components generate different kinds of Event. CarEdit panel (Figure 9.6) will need to listen and respond to both by asking the associated car to update its state.

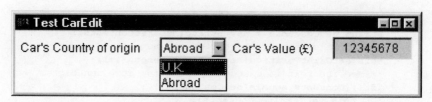

Figure 9.6 CarEdit using BooleanChoice and DigitsOnlyTextField.

```
//: CarEdit.java
package chap09;
import java.util.*;
import java.awt.*;
import java.awt.event.*;
```

```
/** <b>CarEdit</b> extends Panel and is designed to input
* the details required for a Car.
* Uses Car and Panel.
* @see chap09.Car
* @see java.awt.Panel
* @author Stuart F Lewis
* @version 2.00, 25/09/98
*/
public class CarEdit extends Panel
            implements Observer, ItemListener, TextListener {

/** Car for which this is the Gui editing interface.
* @see chap09.Car
*/
private Car c;

/** BooleanChoice input component for car origin
*/
BooleanChoice originOfCar = new BooleanChoice("U.K.","Abroad");

/** value input component
*/
DigitsOnlyTextField value = new DigitsOnlyTextField(8);

/** Constructor for CarEdit. Puts Car input classes on to a panel.
* @see chap09.CarEdit
*/
public CarEdit(Car c) {
this.c = c;
c.addObserver(this);
value.setBackground(Color.yellow);
add(new Label("Car's Country of origin"));
add(originOfCar);
add(new Label("Car's Value (£)"));
add(value);
//Listen for Choice selection
originOfCar.addItemListener(this);
//Listen to changes to value
value.addTextListener(this);
}

/** Performs an action with the newly changed text item.
* Requests the Count c to set the current value to the view value.
* Called when user generates an TextEvent by changing this text
* item in any way without needing to press <return>.
* @param e TextEvent generated by CountGuiEdit.
*/
public void textValueChanged(TextEvent e) {
if (!(value.getText().equals(String.valueOf(c.getValue())))) {
    c.setValue(value.getText());
}
}// textValueChanged

/** Displays the new Car state.
* Called when the Car c being observed notifies
* observers of a state change.
* @param Observable o the observable object ie. the Car.
```

```
 * @param Object arg an optional argument passed to the ;
 *    notifyObservers method, always null in this case.
 */
public void update(Observable o,Object arg) {
value.setText("""+c.getValue());
}

/** Executes the newly selected Choice item.
 * Requests the Count c to perform appropriate method.
 * Called when user generates an ItemEvent by selecting from this
 * Choice
 * @param e ItemEvent generated by CountActionChooser.
 */
public void itemStateChanged(ItemEvent e) {
c.setOrigin(originOfCar.getSelectedItem());
}//itemStateChanged
/** Test routine for the class CarEdit.
 */
public static void main(String[] args) {
Car myCar = new Car();
CarEdit CarEdit = new CarEdit(myCar);
Frame f = new Frame("Test CarEdit");
f.add(CarEdit);
f.pack();
f.show();
}
} ///:~
```

9.15 Write an implementation for the Customer class graphical user interface to allow a customer's age and years no claims to be entered.

The next stage is to add the editing components to a container to build up the graphical user interface. Here BorderLayout is used to organise the components (Figure 9.7).

```
//: InputDetails.java
package chap09;

import java.awt.*;
import java.awt.event.*;
```

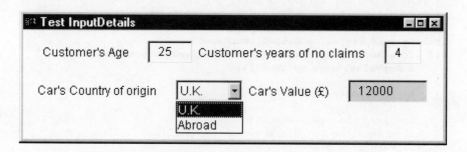

Figure 9.7   InputDetails using CustomerEdit and CarEdit.

```
/** <b>InputDetails</b> is designed to input
 * the details required for a quote.
 * @see chap09.CarEdit
 * @see chap09.CustomerEdit
 * @see chap09.Car
 * @see chap09.Customer
 * @see java.awt.Panel
 * @author Stuart F Lewis
 * @version 2.00, 25/09/98
 */
public class InputDetails extends Panel {

/** Constructor for InputDetails.
 * @see chap09.CarEdit
 * @see chap09.CustomerEdit
 */
public InputDetails(Customer customer, Car car) {
CustomerEdit cust = new CustomerEdit(customer);
CarEdit ce = new CarEdit(car);
setLayout(new BorderLayout());
add("North", cust);
add("South",ce);
}

/** Test routine for the class InputDetails.
 */
public static void main(String[] args) {
Customer myCustomer = new Customer();
Car myCar = new Car();
InputDetails inputDetails = new InputDetails(myCustomer,myCar);
Frame f = new Frame("Test InputDetails");
f.add(inputDetails);
f.pack();
f.show();
}
} ///:~
```

Adding a GUI to output Quote result

The final interface container brings together the input details panel and an output panel for the quote attributes. As the GUI becomes more crowded a layout manager is used to organise the relative position of the components. GridLayout organises components into a grid with a specified number of rows and columns, each element being the same size (Figure 9.8).

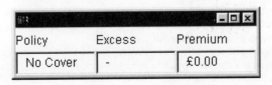

Figure 9.8 OutputQuote.

```java
//: OutputQuote.java
package chap09;
import java.awt.*;
import java.util.*;

/** <b>OutputQuote</b> displays
 * the results of the policy calculation.
 * @see java.awt.Panel
 * @author Stuart F Lewis
 * @version 2.00, 25/09/98
 */
public class OutputQuote extends Panel implements Observer {

/** Quote for which this is the Gui output interface.
 * @see chap09.Quote
 */
private Quote quote;
/** Three display only text fields to output the results
 * of the quote calculation that make up its state
 */
private TextField policy;
private TextField excess;
private TextField premium;

/** Constructor for OutputQuote.
 * @see chap09.Quote
 */
public OutputQuote(Quote q) {
quote = q;
quote.addObserver(this);
// create output boxes
policy = new TextField(quote.getPolicy());
excess = new TextField(quote.getExcess());
premium = new TextField(quote.getPremium());
policy.setEditable(false);
excess.setEditable(false);
premium.setEditable(false);
// set a grid to put them on
setLayout( new GridLayout(2,3));
// put labels on
add(new Label("Policy"));
add(new Label("Excess"));
add(new Label("Premium"));
// put display boxes on
add(policy);
add(excess);
add(premium);
}

/** Display the new Quote value.
 * Called when the Quote being observed notifies
 * observers of a state change.
 * @param Observable o the observable object ie. the Quote.
 * @param Object arg an optional argument passed to the ;
 *     notifyObservers method, always null in this case.
 */
public void update(Observable o,Object arg) {
```

```
policy.setText(quote.getPolicy());
excess.setText(quote.getExcess());
premium.setText(quote.getPremium());
}

/** test routine for the OutputQuote. Adds OutputQuote to
 * a Frame and displays the result of a calculation.
 */
public static void main(String[] args) {
Customer myCustomer = new Customer();
Car myCar = new Car();
Quote q = new Quote(myCustomer,myCar);
OutputQuote outputDetailPanel = new OutputQuote(q);
Frame f = new Frame();
f.add(outputDetailPanel);
f.pack();
f.show();
}
} ///:~
```

Combining the input and output GUI to process quotes

All of the components can now be added to the final interface (Figure 9.9). The input, process, and output elements of problem solving are combined to provide three problem domain objects communicating with four interface objects to present the quote (Figure 9.10). Here BorderLayout is used to organise the components.

```
//: CarInsViewContainer.java
package chap09;
import java.awt.*;
import java.awt.event.*;

/** <b>CarInsViewContainer</b> extends Frame
 * and is designed to enter Customer and Car details,
 * calculate the Quote and display it.
 * @see java.awt.Frame
 * @see java.awt.Button
 * @see java.awt.Panel
 * @author Stuart F Lewis
 * @version 2.00, 25/09/98
 */
public class CarInsViewContainer extends Frame
                implements ActionListener {

/** Contructs a new CarInsViewContainer.
 * Displays the InputDetails Panel and
 * OutputQuote and adds a Quit Button.
 */
public CarInsViewContainer(Quote q) {
setLayout(new BorderLayout());
//create Output Device
```

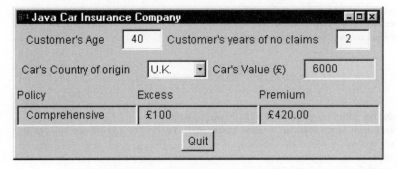

Figure 9.9   CarInsViewContainer.

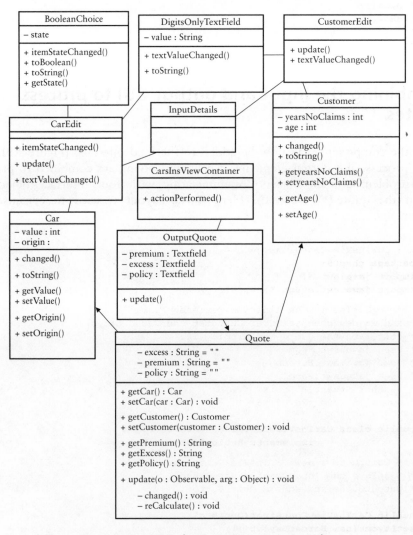

Figure 9.10   UML for CarInsViewContainer class.

```
OutputQuote out = new OutputQuote(q);
//create Input device
InputDetails in = new InputDetails(q.getCustomer(),q.getCar());
//create Quit button
Panel QuitPanel = new Panel();
Button QuitButton = new Button("Quit");
QuitPanel.add(QuitButton);
//Add Input device
add("North", in);
//Add Output Device
add("Center",out);
//Add Quit button
add("South",QuitPanel);
this.setBackground(Color.lightGray);
this.setTitle("Java Car Insurance Company");
//listen for quit button
QuitButton.addActionListener(this);
}

/** Quits the programme */
public void actionPerformed(ActionEvent e) {
System.exit(0);
}

/** Test CarInsViewContainer class. */
public static void main(String[] args) {
Customer myCustomer = new Customer();
Car myCar = new Car();
Quote newpolicy = new Quote(myCustomer,myCar);
Frame f = new CarInsViewContainer(newpolicy);
f.pack();
f.show();
}
} ///:~
```

9.16 What other facilities could be added to CarInsViewContainer?

One of the strengths of object orientation is the reduced impact of change on a system. If an additional field is required for one of the problem domain classes, only that class and its associated interfaces need to be changed.

9.17 JCIC require the year of manufacture of a car to be stored. Which classes must be altered?

The impact of change can severely affect the maintainability of a system.

Summary

A general approach to building systems from multiple objects was described through a case study based on the fictitious Java Car Insurance Company (JCIC). Several problem domain classes were developed and prototyped using console input and output. The serialization process was used to store all the problem domain objects. Several additional AWT classes were introduced to help format output. Some reusable graphical user interface components were developed using other AWT facilities. These were used to complete the graphical user interface to the system. As the number of components increased, different layout managers were used to organise their relative position on the interface. The ease with which further changes or enhancements to the system could be made was considered.

Answers to in-text questions

1   For a car value of £1000, the following quotes could be produced (Table 9.1).

Table 9.1   Quotes for a car value £1000.

Customer Age	No claims	Car Origin	Quote Type	Excess	Cost
25 plus	4 plus	UK	Comprehensive	0	60
25 plus	4 plus	not UK	Comprehensive	100	60
25 plus	0	UK	Comprehensive	100	70
25 plus	0	not UK	Third party	100	70
under 25	4 plus	UK	Comprehensive	200	80
under 25	4 plus	not UK	Comprehensive	250	90
under 25	0	UK	Declined	0	0
under 25	0	not UK	Declined	0	0

2   Customer attributes are age and years no claims. Car attributes are origin and value. Quote attributes are Customer and Car used to calculate policy type, excess and cost.

3   Left as an exercise.

4   When the program is run with the skeleton class above it will display:

```
Age 25 years no claims 0
Age 30 years no claims 5
```

5   A possible implementation for the Car class is

```
//: Car.java
package chap09;

import java.util.Observable;
import java.io.Serializable;

/** <b>Car</b> stores
 * the details required for a Car.
 * @see java.util.Observable;
 * @author Stuart F Lewis
 * @version 2.00, 25/09/98
 */
public class Car extends Observable implements Serializable {

/** Car's Country of origin
 * @serial Country of origin for this Car.
 */
private String origin;
```

```java
/** Car's value
* @serial value of this Car.
*/
private int value;

/** Constructor for Car.
*/
public Car() {
this("U.K.",0);
}

/** Constructor for Car.
*/
public Car(String originOfCar, int v) {
origin = originOfCar;
value = v;
}

/** Sets the origin of this Car.
*/
public void setOrigin(String originOfCar) {
origin = originOfCar;
changed();
}

/** Gets the origin of this Car.
* @return the origin value of this Car.
*/
public String getOrigin() {
return origin ;
}

/** Sets the current value of this Car.
*/
public void setValue(int val) {
value = val;
changed();
}

/** Sets the current value of this Car.
* try to set the value to the string parameter
* but if that is not possible, default to zero
*/
public void setValue(String val) {
int valueInt;
try {
    valueInt = Integer.parseInt(val);
  }
catch( NumberFormatException e) {
    //System.out.println("Error in " + val);
    valueInt = 0;
    }
setValue(valueInt);
}

/** Gets the current value of this Car.
* @return the current value of this Car.
*/
public int getValue() {
return value;
}
```

```
/** Returns the car as a String.
* @return a string representing the car
*/
public String toString() {
return " Country of origin " + origin + " value " + value;
}

/** Called whenever any instance variables are changed.
* Notifies all Observers of the change of state.
* @see java.util.Observable
*/
public void changed() {
setChanged();
notifyObservers();
}

/** Test routine for the class Car.
*/
public static void main(String[] args) {
Car myCar = new Car();
System.out.println(myCar);
myCar = new Car("Abroad",25000);
System.out.println(myCar);
}
} ///:~
```

6 The program displays each quote followed by the customer and car it is for:

```
Comprehensive £100 £0.00
Age 25 years no claims 0 Country of origin U.K. value 0
Comprehensive £200 £80.00
Age 25 years no claims 4 Country of origin U.K. value 1000
Comprehensive £0 £60.00
Age 40 years no claims 4 Country of origin U.K. value 1000
```

7 The attributes policy, excess, and premium are all calculated by Quote and should not be set by any other class

8 A QuoteConsoleChoice needs to know the Quote to which it is an interface and the choices available.

9 A QuoteConsoleChoice needs to request the Quote to satisfy those choices.

10 Choice one, to enter some details. Choice two to display the quote and details. Choice three to save to file. Choice one to change the details. Choice four to restore the first quote. Choice two to display the details which will be the same as first set of details entered if the serialization was successful.

11 Either java.awt.Checkbox or java.awt.CheckboxGroup.

12 The java.awt.TextComponent class defines methods that are used to maintain a current selection from the text. The text selection, a substring of the component's text, is the target of editing operations.

13 The text insertion cursor is positioned by asking the new String its length and adding one.

14 Two DigitsOnlyTextField boxes will appear on a frame. One will contain 123456 and the other will be empty. Both will only accept digits entered in them.

The standard console output will display the String before and after the alpha characters are removed.

```
123remove me456
123456
```

15 A possible implementation for the CustomerEdit class is

```java
//: CustomerEdit.java
package chap09;
import java.util.*;
import java.awt.*;
import java.awt.event.*;

/** <b>CustomerEdit</b> to input
 * the details required for a Customer.
 * @see chap09.Customer
 * @see java.awt.Panel
 * @author Stuart F Lewis
 * @version 2.00, 25/09/98
 */
public class CustomerEdit extends Panel
            implements Observer, TextListener {

/** Customer for which this is the Gui editing interface.
 * @see chap09.Customer
 */

private Customer c;

/** Customer age input component
 * @see chap09.DigitsOnlyTextField
 */
DigitsOnlyTextField age = new DigitsOnlyTextField(3);

/** yearsNoClaims input component
 * @see chap09.DigitsOnlyTextField
 */
DigitsOnlyTextField yearsNoClaims = new DigitsOnlyTextField(2);

/** Constructor for CustomerEdit. Puts Customer input classes
 * on to a panel.
 * @see chap09.CustomerEdit
 */
public CustomerEdit(Customer c) {
this.c = c;
c.addObserver(this);
add(new Label("Customer's Age"));
add(age);
add(new Label("Customer's years of no claims"));
add(yearsNoClaims);
//Listen to changes
age.addTextListener(this);
yearsNoClaims.addTextListener(this);
}

/** Performs an action with the newly changed text item.
 * Requests the Customer c to set the current value to the view
 * value.
 * Called when user generates a TextEvent by changing this text
```

```
 * item in any way without needing to press <return>.
 * @param e TextEvent generated by CustomerEdit.
 */
public void textValueChanged(TextEvent e) {
if (!(age.getText().equals(String.valueOf(c.getAge())))) {
    c.setAge(age.getText());
}
if (!(yearsNoClaims.getText().equals
    (String.valueOf(c.getYearsNoClaims()))))
    {c.setYearsNoClaims(yearsNoClaims.getText());
}
}// textValueChanged

/** Displays the new Customer state.
 * Called when the Customer c being observed notifies
 * observers of a state change.
 * @param Observable o the observable object ie. the Customer.
 * @param Object arg an optional argument passed to the ;
 *         notifyObservers method, always null in this case.
 */
public void update(Observable o,Object arg) {
age.setText(""+c.getAge());
yearsNoClaims.setText(""+c.getYearsNoClaims());
}

/** Test routine for the class CustomerEdit.
 */
public static void main(String[] args) {
Customer myCustomer = new Customer();
CustomerEdit testEdit = new CustomerEdit(myCustomer);
CustomerEdit testEdit2 = new CustomerEdit(myCustomer);
Frame f = new Frame("Test CustomerEdit");
f.add(testEdit);
f.add(testEdit2);
f.pack();
f.show();
}
} ///:~
```

16 Serialization of the quote, both save and restore. Extra fields for customer or car. Search facilities to retrieve particular quotes, customers or cars.

17 Only Car and CarEdit. If the year of manufacture were to affect the quote produced, the quote would also need to be changed to ask the car for the year of manufacture to use in the new quote calculation.

REVIEW QUESTIONS

Answers in Appendix A.

1 Why are truth tables or a summary of all possible combinations of input useful for testing classes?

2 What other locale-sensitive classes are provided by the API?

3 Why are locale-sensitive classes useful?

4 What are the advantages of subdividing the GUI into separate panels?

5 What other layout managers are available from the API?

EXERCISES

Answers to exercises flagged with an asterisk appear in Appendix B.

1   What other methods are used to select test data?

2   How can a GUI builder tool help in assembling an interface?

3* Some object-oriented design tools automatically generate code based on class specifications. Which methods are the most straightforward to generate?

4* What are the advantages of using layout managers?

10

Storing and retrieving data from multiple objects

Overview

The Collection class is described explaining why it is useful and what it can do. A case study for a general point-of-sale system is discussed. Several communicating classes are designed. Objects of these classes are stored using the Collection class from Java 2 (1.2). Various options for data management within Java 2 (1.2) are introduced. The graphical user interface is developed using javax.swing components from Java 2 (1.2).

Why use a Collection?

The Java classes developed so far have typically had only one instance or object of a particular class in existence at any one time. Where two or more objects of the same class have been used, each has been named separately. A Collection represents a group of objects, known as its elements. In the real world objects are often grouped together to form useful collections.

10.1 What real-world collections have you used?

Collection is the root interface in the collection hierarchy. This interface is implemented by the AbstractCollection class to provide a skeletal implementation of the Collection interface, to minimise the effort required implementing this interface. Java 2 (1.2) provides several general-purpose implementations of the collection interface. Each has a name of the form <Implementation><Interface>.

Collection interface

The interface refers to the kind of collection. A Set is an unordered Collection that contains no duplicate elements. A List may contain duplicates and multiple null elements and the elements can be accessed directly by their position in the List.

A Map is not a true collection but can be viewed as three separate collections. Each element of a Map is a pair consisting of a key and a value. Therefore, a Map can be viewed as a Set of keys, Collection of values, or Set of key-value mappings.

10.2 Why are the keys and key-value mappings a Set but the values are a Collection?

Collection implementation

The implementation refers to the class or data structure used to actually store the values in the Collection. A Hash table is the original mapping class from JDK 1.0 containing a pair of key and value for every object in the Hash table. A resizable Array (Vector) is an indexed storage area that can grow to contain more elements. A Tree is a hierarchical data structure, which provides a guaranteed access time for every element related to the number of elements. Linked Lists provide uniformly named methods to get, remove and insert an element at the beginning and end of the List. These operations allow LinkedList to be used as a stack, queue, or double-ended queue (deque).

The major advantage of using a Collection is that all Collections have a similar interface and can easily be converted between implementations. Polymorphic methods are specified by the Collection interface and implemented by every Collection subclass.

10.3 Refer to the API documentation and summarise the combinations of interfaces and implementations available as a table.

What a Collection can do

Every Collection provides methods to add and remove one or more elements. A Collection can also tell a client if it contains a particular object and provide an Iterator to deliver each element from the Collection to a client.

Each of the general-purpose implementations of the collection interface provides additional methods from both their interface and implementation.

10.4 What additional methods are provided by the TreeSet implementation?

Point Of Sale (POS) case study

A large out-of-town department store requires a POS system for special sales. Each sale consists of one or more items from the store. Each item is identified by a unique price lookup code (PLU). However, several PLU codes may be used for the same item. The price charged for an item depends on the date purchased and the quantity.

Some items have promotional prices effective from particular dates and others have discounted prices for bulk purchases. Every sale is made by a cashier during their session on a particular register. In addition to calculating the cost of every sale the system should provide useful reporting of sales over time.

One approach to deciding which classes to prototype first is to work through a key scenario for the system then build the classes in the reverse order. For example, consider the process of making a sale.

```
A cashier logs onto the system.
A new session is created for that cashier at that store.
A sale window is displayed.
FOR all the saleitems in a sale DO
        A PLU is entered (possibly by scanning an item or barcode).
        The item description is displayed.
        A quantity is entered.
        A price for that quantity is calculated.
ENDFOR
The total price is displayed.
The sale is completed.
The session is finished.
The cashier logs off.
```

How is that process supported by the classes? Take calculating the total price.

```
A sale needs its total price
 Ask each of the saleitems how much they are.
 Add up the total
A saleitem needs its price.
 Ask the item how much it is for a given quantity.
An item needs its price.
 Ask which price applies on this date.
A PLU code needs to find which item it applies to.
 Ask the store for the item that the PLU refers to.
```

The first stage in calculating the total price is to get the item for the scanned or entered PLU. So, starting with the PLU class, implement and test each in turn.

Implementing the PLU class

As with all problem domain or entity classes PLU needs to implement Serializable to support storage to disk. As the PLUs for an item will be stored in a Collection by each Item, consider at this stage which kind of Collection would be most suitable and use it to test the initial implementation. As every PLU must be unique a Set interface would seem most appropriate. This gives a choice between two possible implementations provided by the general-purpose Set implementations of the collection interface. HashSet makes no guarantees about the iteration order of the Set. TreeSet guarantees that the Set will be in ascending element order and sorted according to the natural order of the elements provided that the java.lang.Comparable interface is implemented by the elements of the Set.

To implement the java.lang.Comparable interface requires only one method, compareTo, that must return a negative integer, zero, or a positive integer if a PLU is less than, equal to, or greater than the given PLU. The benefit of implementing this interface is that any Collection of PLUs based on a TreeSet class will always appear in order without any sorting by the POS system.

10.5 Which exception may be thrown by the compareTo method?

For prototyping and testing purposes, a private static int nextPLU (Figure 10.1) is used to allocate the next value to any PLU created with the no argument constructor. The main method uses a Collection to store several PLUs and display them on the console output.

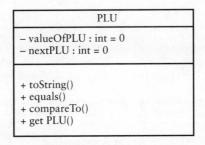

Figure 10.1   UML diagram for PLU class.

```
//: PLU.java
package chap10;

import java.util.*;
import java.io.*;
import javax.swing.*;

/** The class <code>PLU</code> represents a particular
 * Price LookUp code.
 * <pre>Instances of the class <code>Item</code> may have :
 *   Several different PLUs - Price LookUp codes
 *   (often linked to actual bar codes)
 * @see chap10.Item
 * @author Stuart F Lewis
 * @version 1.00, 20/10/98
 */
public class PLU implements Comparable, Serializable {

/** The next value for a PLU.
 */
private static int nextPLU = 0;

/** The value of this PLU.
 */
private int valueOfPLU = 0;
```

```
/** Constructs a new <code>PLU</code>
* with default code.
*/
public PLU() {
this(++nextPLU);
}//constructor

/** Constructs a new <code>PLU</code>
* with code supplied.
* @param plu int code supplied for this PLU.
*/
public PLU(int plu) {
this.valueOfPLU = plu;
}//constructor

/** Get the <code>PLU</code> for this PLU.
* @return the <code>PLU</code> for this PLU.
*/
public int getPLU() {
return valueOfPLU;
}//getNumber

/**
* Compares this <code>PLU</code> with the specified Object for
* order.
* Returns a negative integer, zero, or a positive integer
* if this <code>PLU</code>
* is less than, equal to, or greater than the given
* <code>PLU</code>.
*
* @param obj - the Object to be compared.
* @return a negative integer, zero, or a positive integer if this
*         <code>PLU</code> is less than, equal to,
*         or greater than the given Object.
* @throw ClassCastException - the specified Object's type
* prevents it from being compared to this <code>PLU</code>.
*/
public int compareTo(Object obj) {
 if ((obj != null) && (obj instanceof PLU)) {
            return valueOfPLU - ((PLU)obj).getPLU();
 }
 else{
 throw new ClassCastException("" + obj + " is not a PLU");
 }
}

/**
* Compares this object to the specified object.
* The result is <code>true</code> if and only if the argument is
* not <code>null</code> and is a <code>PLU</code> object that
* contains the same <code>int</code> value as this object.
* @param  obj  the object to compare with.
* @return <code>true</code> if the objects are the same;
*<code>false</code> otherwise.
*/
```

```java
public boolean equals(Object obj) {
  if ((obj != null) && (obj instanceof PLU)) {
          return valueOfPLU == ((PLU)obj).getPLU();
  }
return false;
}

/**
* Returns the current value of this PLU as a String.
* @return a string representing the current value of this PLU
*/
public String toString() {
return "" + getPLU();
}//method toString

/** Test data for the class <code>PLU</code>.
* Creates a new instance of an <code>PLU</code> collection.
*
*/
public static void main(String args[]) {

//Several different PLUs - Price LookUp codes
// (often linked to actual bar codes)
Collection pLUs = new TreeSet();

//add some PLUs to this collection
PLU plu = new PLU();
pLUs.add(plu);
plu = new PLU();
pLUs.add(plu);
//try to add duplicates
pLUs.add(plu);
pLUs.add(plu);
plu = new PLU();
pLUs.add(plu);
plu = new PLU();
pLUs.add(plu);
plu = new PLU();
pLUs.add(plu);

for (Iterator i = pLUs.iterator(); i.hasNext();){
    plu = (PLU)i.next();
    System.out.println(plu);
}

System.out.println(pLUs);

}//main

} ///:~
```

10.6 When the program is run what output will be displayed?

10.7 Why are there no duplicates in the PLUs listed?

Immediately the advantages of using a Collection are realised in being able to iterate over the elements using an Iterator and to print the entire Collection to the console in a single statement. To display a Collection using a graphical user interface sounds like a task for a reusable class similar to CountViewContainer but as it will display any Collection a more suitable name is CollectionViewContainer. The graphical components from the javax.swing package are all standard with Java 2 (1.2) and map closely to their AWT counterparts but often with added functionality. Here CollectionViewContainer extends JScrollPane and uses JList to display the Collection. Because JList currently does not have a constructor that accepts a Collection as a parameter, the Collection must be converted to an Array or Vector first. Here is an implementation of CollectionViewContainer.

```java
//: CollectionViewContainer.java
package chap10;

import java.util.*;
import java.awt.*;
import javax.swing.*;

/** Collection ViewContainer implementation
* showing the use of extends to inherit
* from the JScrollPane superclass.
* Knows nothing about the state, methods, or interface
* of the Collection of Objects
* @author Stuart F Lewis
* @version 1.00, 20/10/98
*/
public class CollectionViewContainer extends JScrollPane {

/** Constructs a new <code>CollectionViewContainer</code>
* as interface to Collection of Objects.
* @param Objects Collection for which this is the ViewContainer.
*/
public CollectionViewContainer(Collection Objects) {
Object [] ObjectsInArray = Objects.toArray();
JList dataList = new JList(ObjectsInArray);
this.getViewport().setView(dataList);
}//constructor

/** Test data for the file CollectionViewContainer.
* Creates a new Collection and a container to view it using
* CollectionViewContainer.
* Adds the CollectionViewContainer to a frame and shows it
*/
public static void main(String args[]) {
Collection ic = new TreeSet();

Integer val = new Integer(10);
for (int i = 0; i < 100; i++) {
        val = new Integer((int)(Math.random()*100));
        System.out.println(val);
        ic.add(val);
}
System.out.println();
System.out.println(ic);
```

```
JScrollPane scrollPane = new CollectionViewContainer(ic);
JFrame frame = new ClosableFrame("Collection View Container test");
frame.getContentPane().add(scrollPane);
frame.pack();
frame.setVisible(true);
}//method main
} ///:~
```

10.8 Why does the sequence of values displayed differ from the order in which they were generated?

Note that the testing method (Figure 10.2) uses a class ClosableFrame that has not yet been covered. This ClosableFrame inherits from the javax.swing.JFrame. There are two constructors, one with no arguments creates a Frame with no title, the other calls the superclass constructor to create a Frame with a title. A WindowListener created by the inner class FrameListener is added to this ClosableFrame. FrameListener inherits from the standard AWT WindowAdapter and only overrides the single method windowClosing to dispose of the Frame and exit. Here is the code:

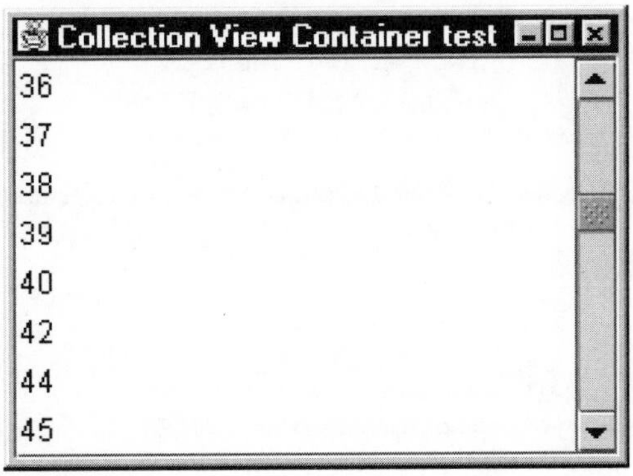

Figure 10.2   Collection View Container test.

```
//: ClosableFrame.java
package chap10;

import java.awt.*;
import java.awt.event.*;
import javax.swing.*;
/**
 * the public class ClosableFrame
 */
public class ClosableFrame extends JFrame {
/**
 * private variable frame to store the frame
 * so it can be disposed of later
 */
private ClosableFrame frame;
```

```
/**
 * Constructor for a new ClosableFrame.
 * creates a new FrameListener for this frame
 */
public ClosableFrame () {
this("");
}

/**
 * Constructor for a new ClosableFrame.
 * creates a new FrameListener for this frame
 * @param the title of the frame
 */
public ClosableFrame (String title) {
super(title);
WindowListener l = new FrameListener(this);
this.addWindowListener(l);
}// Constructor ClosableFrame

/**
 * inner class FrameListener extends WindowAdapter rather
 * than implementing
 * all the methods required by the public interface WindowListener
 */
private class FrameListener extends WindowAdapter {
/**
 * Constructor for a new FrameListener,
 * creates a new FrameListener for the frame
 * to be listened to, and stores the frame so
 * it can be disposed of later
 */
public FrameListener (ClosableFrame listenedToFrame) {
    frame = listenedToFrame;
}
//to finally get this to work I changed Event to WindowEvent !!!
// until then it had not been called because it did not
// exactly match the
// method defined in WindowListener
public void windowClosing(WindowEvent e) {
frame.dispose();
System.exit(0);
}
}//class

/**
 * main application test
 * creates a new frame
 * displays the frame
 */
public static void main(String args[]) {
ClosableFrame f = new ClosableFrame();
f.setSize(200,200);
f.setLocation(200,200);
f.show();
}// method main
} ///:~
```

? **10.9** How many methods are required to implement the public interface WindowListener?

An alternative approach to providing a closable Frame is to add an inner anonymous class to every frame that is created. Many example programs include this code:

```
frame.addWindowListener(new WindowAdapter() {
 public void windowClosing(WindowEvent e) {
   System.exit(0);
 }
});
```

The anonymous class also only overrides the single method windowClosing to exit when the Frame is closed.

10.10 What possible advantage may there be in using an inner anonymous class rather than specializing the JFrame class?

10.11 How could the PLU class use the CollectionViewContainer class to display the test PLU values?

Implementing the Price class

Apart from a number of possible PLU codes, an Item may also have a number of different prices that become effective after a particular date. This can be captured in a Price class (Figure 10.3).

```
//: Price.java
package chap10;
import java.util.*;
import java.io.*;
import java.text.DateFormat;
import javax.swing.*;
```

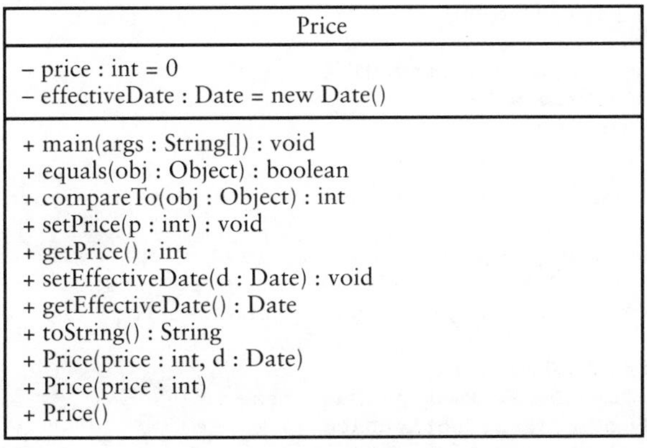

Price
– price : int = 0 – effectiveDate : Date = new Date()
+ main(args : String[]) : void + equals(obj : Object) : boolean + compareTo(obj : Object) : int + setPrice(p : int) : void + getPrice() : int + setEffectiveDate(d : Date) : void + getEffectiveDate() : Date + toString() : String + Price(price : int, d : Date) + Price(price : int) + Price()

Figure 10.3 Price UML.

```
/** The class <code>Price</code> represents the amount of money
 * charged for one of a particular item
 * effective from a particular date.
 * The Item may discount the Price for a bulk purchase
 * Observable to inform any interested observers of
 * any change of state.
 * @see java.util.Observable
 * @see java.util.Date
 * @see chap10.Item
 * @author Stuart F Lewis
 * @version 1.00, 19/10/98
 */
public class Price extends Observable
                   implements Comparable, Serializable {

/** Date this price is effective from.
 * @see java.util.Date
 */
private Date effectiveDate = new Date();

/** The amount of money (in pence) charged for one item
 * after the effective date.
 */
private int price = 0;

/** Constructs a new <code>Price</code>
 * with default effective date of today and default price
 */
public Price() {
this(500);
}//no argument constructor

/** Constructs a new <code>Price</code>
 * with default effective date of today and price supplied
 * @param price amount of money (in pence) charged for one item
 */
public Price(int price) {
this(price,new Date());
}

/** Constructs a new <code>Price</code>
 * with effective date  and price supplied.
 * @param price amount of money (in pence) charged for one item
 * @param d Date this price is effective from.
 * @see java.util.Date
 */
public Price(int price, Date d) {
this.effectiveDate = d;
this.price = price;
}

/** Returns the current state of this <code>Price</code> as a
 * String.
 * @return a string representing the current state of this ;
 *          <code>Price</code> showing the effective date and ;
 *     the amount of money (in pence) charged for one item
 */
public String toString() {
DateFormat df = DateFormat.getDateInstance();
return df.format(getEffectiveDate()) + '\t' +
Integer.toString(price);
}//method toString
```

```java
/** Get the <code>effectiveDate</code> for this price
* @return the <code>effectiveDate</code> for this price
*/
public Date getEffectiveDate() {
return effectiveDate;
}//getEffectiveDate

/** Set the <code>effectiveDate</code> for this price
* @param d Date this price is effective from.
*/
public void setEffectiveDate(Date d) {
this.effectiveDate = d;
}//setEffectiveDate

/** Get the <code>price</code> for this price
* @return the <code>price</code> for this price
*/
public int getPrice() {
return price;
}//getPrice

/** Set the <code>price</code> for this price
* @param price amount of money (in pence) charged for one item
*/
public void setPrice(int p) {
this.price = p;
}//setPrice

/**
* Compares this <code>price</code> with the specified
* Object for order.
* Returns a negative integer, zero, or a positive integer
* if this <code>price</code>
*      is less than, equal to, or greater than
* the given <code>PLU</code>.
*
* @param obj - the Object to be compared.
* @return a negative integer, zero, or a positive integer if this
*      <code>price</code> is less than, equal to,
*      or greater than the given Object.
* @throw ClassCastException - the specified Object's type
* prevents it
*      from being compared to this <code>Price</code>.
*/
public int compareTo(Object obj) {
 if ((obj != null) && (obj instanceof Price)) {
      Price p = (Price)obj;
      Date d = getEffectiveDate();
      Date d2 = p.getEffectiveDate();
      if (d.compareTo(d2) != 0) {
       return -(d.compareTo(d2)); //reverse date order - latest
       first
      }
      else {
          return getPrice() - p.getPrice();
      };
```

```
    }
    else {
    throw new ClassCastException("" + obj + " is not a Price");
    }
}

/**
* Compares this object to the specified object.
* The result is <code>true</code> if and only if the argument is
* not <code>null</code> and is a <code>Price</code> object that
* contains the same <code>int</code> value as this object.
*
* @param   obj  the object to compare with.
* @return <code>true</code> if the objects are the same;
*<code>false</code> otherwise.
*/
public boolean equals(Object obj) {
  if ((obj != null) && (obj instanceof Price)) {
      Date d = getEffectiveDate();
      Date d2 = ((Price)obj).getEffectiveDate();
      return d.equals(d2)
             && (getPrice() == ((Price)obj).getPrice());
  }
return false;
}

/** Test data for the class <code>Price</code>.
* Creates a new instance of an <code>Price</code>.
*
*/
public static void main(String args[]) {
Collection prices = new TreeSet();

Price p = new Price();
System.out.println(p);
prices.add(p);

DateFormat df = DateFormat.getDateInstance();
Date d = new Date();
try {
  d = df.parse("19-Oct-98");
}
catch (java.text.ParseException e) {};
p = new Price(500,d);
System.out.println(p);
prices.add(p);

try {
  d = df.parse("29-Oct-98");
}
catch (java.text.ParseException e) {};
p = new Price(300,d);
System.out.println(p);
prices.add(p);
p = new Price(200);
System.out.println(p);
prices.add(p);
```

```
System.out.println(prices);
JScrollPane scrollPane = new CollectionViewContainer(prices);
scrollPane.setColumnHeaderView(new JTextField("Date"+'
'+"Price"));
JFrame frame = new ClosableFrame("Prices Collection View
Container test");
frame.getContentPane().add(scrollPane);
frame.pack();
frame.setVisible(true);
}
} ///:~
```

10.12 When the program is run what will be displayed apart from the window shown in Figure 10.4?

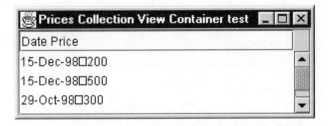

Figure 10.4   Price Collection View Container.

Implementing the Item class

Now that the PLU and Price classes have been implemented consider how an Item class will link to them both. Every Item may have many PLUs and Prices associated with the Item. Adding cardinality to the UML diagram can capture this relationship. The annotation 1..* indicates that each Item has one or more PLUs and Prices associated with it (Figure 10.5).

```
//: Item.java
package chap10;

import java.util.*;
import java.io.*;
import java.text.DateFormat;
import java.awt.*;
import javax.swing.*;
import javax.swing.text.AbstractWriter;
import javax.swing.tree.*;
```

```
/** The class <code>Item</code> represents a particular
* item.
* <pre>Which may have :
*    Several different PLUs - Price LookUp codes
*        (often linked to actual bar codes)
*    Several different prices effective from a particular dates.
* </pre>Observable to inform any interested observers of
```

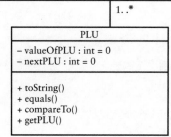

Price
– price : int = 0
– effectiveDate : Date = new Date()
+ main(args : String[]) : void
+ equals(obj : Object) : boolean
+ compareTo(obj : Object) : int
+ setPrice(p : int) : void
+ getPrice() : int
+ setEffectiveDate(d : Date) : void
+ getEffectiveDate() : Date
+ toString() : String
+ Price(price : int, d : Date)
+ Price(price : int)
+ Price()

1. .*

Item
– prices : Collection = new TreeSet()
– pLUs : Collection = new TreeSet()
– number : int = 0
– description : String =
– nextItemNumber : int = 0
+ compareTo(obj : Object) : int
+ howMuchForQty(qty : int, d : Date) : int
+ getPriceForDate(d : Date) : Price
– addPrice(p : Price) :
+ getPrices() : Collection
+ addPLU(u : PLU) : void
+ hasPLU(plu : PLU) : boolean
+ setPLUs(p : Collection) : void
+ getPLUs() : Collection
+ hasPLU(n : int) : boolean
+ getNumber() : int
+ getDescription() : String
+ toString() :

1. .*

PLU
– valueOfPLU : int = 0
– nextPLU : int = 0
+ toString()
+ equals()
+ compareTo()
+ getPLU()

Figure 10.5   Price UML.

```
 * any change of state.
 * @see java.util.Observable
 * @see chap10.PLU
 * @author Stuart F Lewis
 * @version 1.00, 23/05/98
 */
public class Item extends Observable implements Comparable,
Serializable {

/** The number of items.
 */
private static int nextItemNumber = 0;

/** The description of this item. Initialized to a default value.
 */
private String description = "description";

/** The number of this item.
 */
private int number = 0;

/** Several different PLUs - Price LookUp codes for this item.
 *   (often linked to actual bar codes)
 */
private Collection pLUs = new TreeSet();

/** Several different prices effective from a particular dates.
 */
private Collection prices = new TreeSet();

private static Price unknownPrice = new Price(0);
private static PLU unknownPLU = new PLU(0);

//constructor
public Item() {
this("The item's description");
}//constructor

//constructor
public Item(String description) {
this(description,unknownPrice);
}//constructor

//constructor
public Item(String description,Price price) {
this(description,unknownPLU,price);
}//constructor

//constructor
public Item(String description,PLU plu,Price price) {
this.description = description;
addPLU(plu);
addPrice(price);
this.number = ++nextItemNumber ;
}//constructor

public String toString() {
char newLine = (char)Character.LINE_SEPARATOR;
return number + " " + description;
}//method toString
```

```java
public String getDescription() {
return description;
}//getDescription

public int getNumber() {
return number;
}//getNumber

public boolean hasPLU(int n) {
 PLU plu = new PLU(n);
 return hasPLU(plu);
}

public Collection getPLUs() {
return pLUs;
}

public void setPLUs(Collection p) {
pLUs = p;
}

public boolean hasPLU( PLU plu) {
return pLUs.contains(plu);
}

public void addPLU(PLU u) {
pLUs.add(u);
}//addPLU

public Collection getPrices() {
return prices;
}

private void addPrice(Price p) {
prices.add(p);
}//addPrice

public Price getPriceForDate(Date d) {
Price price;
Collection thePrices = getPrices();
for (Iterator i = thePrices.iterator(); i.hasNext();) {
    price = (Price)i.next();
    System.out.println(" " + price + " "
    + price.getEffectiveDate());
    if (d.after(price.getEffectiveDate())) {
      return price;
    }//if
}//for
return unknownPrice;
}//method getPriceForDate

public int howMuchForQty(int qty , Date d) {
Price price = this.getPriceForDate(d);
int forQty = price.getPrice()*qty;
return forQty;
}//method howMuchForQty
```

```
/**
 * Compares this <code>Item</code> with the specified Object for
 * order.
 * Returns a negative integer, zero, or a positive integer
 * if this <code>Item</code> is less than, equal to, or greater
 * than the given <code>Item</code>.
 *
 * @param obj - the Object to be compared.
 * @return a negative integer, zero, or a positive integer if this
 *   <code>Item</code> is less than, equal to, or greater than the
 * given Object.
 * @throw ClassCastException - the specified Object's type
 * prevents it
 *   from being compared to this <code>Item</code>.
 */
public int compareTo(Object obj) {
  if ((obj != null) && (obj instanceof Item)) {
        Item i = (Item)obj;
        if (getDescription().compareTo(i.getDescription()) != 0) {
              return getDescription().compareTo(i.getDescription());
        }
        else {
              return getNumber() - i.getNumber();
        }
  }
  else {
  throw new ClassCastException("" + obj + " is not a Item");
  }
}

/** Test data for the class <code>Item</code>.
 * Creates a new instance of an <code>Item</code>.
 *
 */
public static void main(String args[]) {
Item anItem = new Item();
Collection theItems = new TreeSet();

//add some PLUs for this item
//Several different PLUs - Price LookUp codes
//     (often linked to actual bar codes)
 Collection thePLUs = new TreeSet();
// build the Collection of ThePLUs
//add some PLUs to this collection
PLU plu = new PLU();
thePLUs.add(plu);
plu = new PLU();
thePLUs.add(plu);
//try and add duplicates
thePLUs.add(plu);
thePLUs.add(plu);
plu = new PLU();
thePLUs.add(plu);
plu = new PLU();
thePLUs.add(plu);
plu = new PLU();
thePLUs.add(plu);
 anItem.setPLUs(thePLUs);
```

```
//add some prices for this item
Price price = new Price();
anItem.addPrice(price);
DateFormat df = DateFormat.getDateInstance();
Date d = new Date();
price = new Price(300,d);
anItem.addPrice(price);
try {
  d = df.parse("19-Oct-98");
}
catch (java.text.ParseException e) {};
price = new Price(300,d);
anItem.addPrice(price);
try {
  d = df.parse("02-Oct-98");
}
catch (java.text.ParseException e) {};
price = new Price(370,d);
anItem.addPrice(price);
price = new Price(37,d);
anItem.addPrice(price);

System.out.println(anItem);

theItems.add(anItem);

thePLUs = anItem.getPLUs();
Collection thePrices = anItem.getPrices();

for (Iterator i = thePLUs.iterator(); i.hasNext();) {
     System.out.println("A" + i.next());
}

System.out.println();
System.out.println(thePLUs.toString());
System.out.println(thePrices.toString());

for (Iterator i = thePrices.iterator(); i.hasNext();) {
     System.out.println("A " + i.next());
}

UIManager.LookAndFeelInfo[] uim =
       UIManager.getInstalledLookAndFeels();
for (int i = 0; i< uim.length; i++){
     System.out.println(uim[i].getClassName());
}

try {
 UIManager.setLookAndFeel(
"javax.swing.plaf.metal.MetalLookAndFeel");
}
catch (Exception e) {
     System.out.println("Can't change factories " + e);
}

JScrollPane scrollPLUs = new CollectionViewContainer(thePLUs);
scrollPLUs.setColumnHeaderView(new JTextField("the PLUs"));
Dimension dim = scrollPLUs.getPreferredSize();
System.out.println(dim);
dim.width = 20;
scrollPLUs.setPreferredSize(dim);
```

```
JScrollPane scrollPrices = new CollectionViewContainer(thePrices);
scrollPrices.setColumnHeaderView(new
JTextField("Date"+'\t'+"Price"));

JScrollPane scrollPane = new CollectionViewContainer(theItems);
scrollPane.setColumnHeaderView(new JTextField("Items"));

JFrame cframe = new ClosableFrame("Items Collection View Container
test");
Container contentPane = cframe.getContentPane();
contentPane.setLayout(new FlowLayout());
contentPane.add(scrollPane);
contentPane.add(scrollPLUs);
contentPane.add(scrollPrices);
cframe.pack();
cframe.setVisible(true);

//now view as a tree
JFrame frame = new ClosableFrame("Items Tree View Container test");
contentPane = frame.getContentPane();

//root node
DefaultMutableTreeNode top =
new DefaultMutableTreeNode("The items");

DefaultMutableTreeNode firstItem =
new DefaultMutableTreeNode(anItem);
top.add(firstItem);

//convert prices to sub tree
//add sub tree to root of price tree
//add price tree to item root
Object [] ModelObjectsInArray = thePrices.toArray();
JTree.DynamicUtilTreeNode jt =
 new JTree.DynamicUtilTreeNode("Date Price",ModelObjectsInArray);
firstItem.add(jt);

String pLUs = new String("Price Lookup codes");
ModelObjectsInArray = thePLUs.toArray();
jt = new JTree.DynamicUtilTreeNode(pLUs,ModelObjectsInArray);
firstItem.add(jt);

DefaultTreeModel treeModel = new DefaultTreeModel(top);
JTree tree = new JTree(treeModel);

System.out.println(tree);
System.out.println(treeModel);

//Create the scroll pane and add the tree to it.
JScrollPane scrPane = new JScrollPane(tree);

contentPane.add(scrPane);
frame.pack();
frame.setVisible(true);
//test serialization
 try {
    ObjectOutputStream out =
      new ObjectOutputStream(
        new FileOutputStream("Item.ser"));
```

```
        out.writeObject("Item storage");
        out.writeObject(anItem);
        out.close();
        // All output
    } catch(Exception e) {
        e.printStackTrace();
    }
}//method main
} ///:~
```

Changing the user interface look and feel is illustrated in Figures 10.6, 10.7 and 10.8.

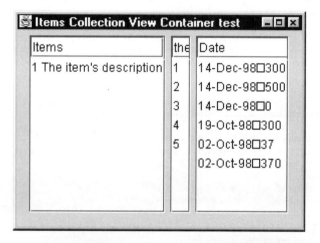

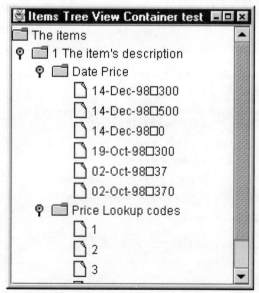

Figure 10.6   Item View Containers.

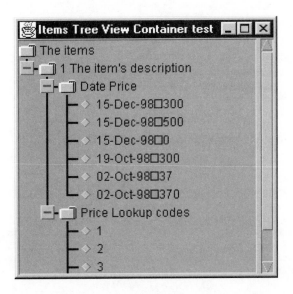

Figure 10.7   Item Tree View Container with MotifLookAndFeel.

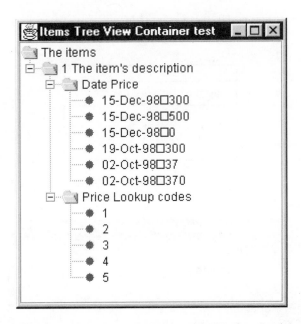

Figure 10.8   Item Tree View Container with WindowsLookAndFeel.

```
1 The item's description
A1
A2
A3
A4
A5
[1, 2, 3, 4, 5]
[13-Dec-98    300, 13-Dec-98 500, 13-Dec-98 0, 19-Oct-98    300, 02-Oct-98
37, 02-Oct-98        370]
A 13-Dec-98  300
A 13-Dec-98  500
A 13-Dec-98  0
A 19-Oct-98  300
A 02-Oct-98  37
A 02-Oct-98  370
javax.swing.plaf.metal.MetalLookAndFeel
com.sun.java.swing.plaf.motif.MotifLookAndFeel
com.sun.java.swing.plaf.windows.WindowsLookAndFeel
java.awt.Dimension[width=12,height=176]
javax.swing.JTree[,0,0,0x0,invalid,alignmentX=null,alignmentY=null,borde
r=,flags=32,maximumSize=,minimumSize=,preferredSize=,editable=false,invo
kesStopCellEditing=false,largeModel=false,rootVisible=true,rowHeight=0,s
crollsOnExpand=true,showsRootHandles=false,toggleClickCount=2,visibleRow
Count=20]
javax.swing.tree.DefaultTreeModel@84e94277
```

Implementing the SaleLineItem class

Every SaleLineItem (Figure 10.9) is a particular quantity of an Item sold as part of a Sale (Figure 10.10).

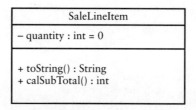

Figure 10.9   SaleLineItem.

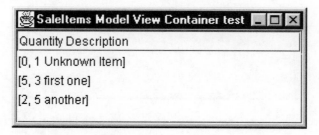

Figure 10.10   SaleLineItem View Container.

```java
//: SaleLineItem.java
package chap10;

import java.util.*;
import java.io.*;
import java.text.DateFormat;
import java.awt.*;
import javax.swing.*;

/** The class <code>SaleLineItem</code> represents a particular
 * SaleLineItem.
 * Observable to inform any interested observers of
 * any change of state.
 * @see java.util.Observable
 * @see chap10.PLU
 * @author Stuart F Lewis
 * @version 1.00, 23/05/98
 */
public class SaleLineItem extends Observable implements
Serializable {

private int quantity = 0;
private Item item = new Item("Unknown Item");

private static Item unknownItem = new Item("Unknown Item");

//constructor
public SaleLineItem() {
this(0);
}//constructor

//constructor
public SaleLineItem(int quantity) {
this(unknownItem,quantity);
}//constructor

//constructor
public SaleLineItem(Item item, int quantity) {
this.quantity = quantity;
this.item = item;
}//constructor

public int calcSubTotal() {
return item.howMuchForQty(quantity, new Date());
}

//toString
public String toString() {
StringBuffer buf = new StringBuffer();
buf.append("[");
buf.append(this.quantity);
buf.append(", ");
buf.append(this.item);
buf.append("]");
return buf.toString();
}//toString

/** Test data for the class <code>SaleLineItem</code>.
 * Creates a new instance of an <code>SaleLineItem</code>.
 *
 */
public static void main(String args[]) {
```

```
//For testing allow access to indexes
ArrayList saleItems = new ArrayList();
//normally Collection saleItems

//set up some SaleLineItem and add them to the collection
SaleLineItem s = new SaleLineItem();
saleItems.add(s);
System.out.println("" + s + s.calcSubTotal());

Price p = new Price(100);
Item i = new Item("first one",p);
s = new SaleLineItem(i,5);
saleItems.add(s);
System.out.println("" + s + s.calcSubTotal());

p = new Price(200);
i = new Item("another",p);
s = new SaleLineItem(i,2);
saleItems.add(s);
System.out.println("" + s + s.calcSubTotal());

System.out.println(saleItems);
s = (SaleLineItem)saleItems.get(1);
System.out.println("" + s + s.calcSubTotal());
s = (SaleLineItem)saleItems.get(2);
System.out.println("" + s + s.calcSubTotal());

JScrollPane scrollPane = new CollectionViewContainer(saleItems);
scrollPane.setColumnHeaderView(new JTextField("Quantity
Description"));
JFrame frame = new ClosableFrame("SaleItems Model View Container
test");
frame.getContentPane().add(scrollPane);
frame.pack();
frame.setVisible(true);
}

} ///:~
```

```
13-Dec-98 0 Sun Dec 13 15:45:29 GMT 1998
[0, 1 Unknown Item]0
  13-Dec-98     100 Sun Dec 13 15:45:41 GMT 1998
[5, 3 first one]0
  13-Dec-98     200 Sun Dec 13 15:45:41 GMT 1998
[2, 5 another]0
[[0, 1 Unknown Item], [5, 3 first one], [2, 5 another]]
  13-Dec-98     100 Sun Dec 13 15:45:41 GMT 1998
[5, 3 first one]500
  13-Dec-98     200 Sun Dec 13 15:45:41 GMT 1998
[2, 5 another]400
```

Implementing the Cashier class

Because these three classes are linked they may need to be compiled with the command:

javac Session.java Cashier.java Register.java

A Cashier (Figure 10.11) has a name and password for this example; the passwords are not encrypted.

```
                    ┌─────────────────────────────────────────┐
                    │                 Cashier                 │
                    ├─────────────────────────────────────────┤
                    │ – sessions : Collection = new TreeSet()  │
                    │ – number : int = 0                       │
                    │ – password : String = "password"         │
                    │ – name : String = "name"                 │
                    │ – nextCashierNumber : int = 0            │
                    ├─────────────────────────────────────────┤
                    │ + compareTo(obj : Object) : int          │
                    │ + addSession(s : Session) : void         │
                    │ + verifyPassword(password : String) : boolean │
                    │ + setNumber(n : int) : void              │
                    │ + getNumber() : int                      │
                    │ + toString() : String                    │
                    │ + setName(n : String) : void             │
                    │ + getName() : String                     │
                    └─────────────────────────────────────────┘
```

Figure 10.11   Cashier UML.

```java
//: Cashier.java
package chap10;

import java.util.*;
import java.io.*;
import java.text.DateFormat;

/** The class <code>Cashier</code> represents a particular
* Cashier.
* </pre>Observable to inform any interested observers of
* any change of state.
* @see java.util.Observable
* @see chap10.PLU
* @author Stuart F Lewis
* @version 1.00, 23/05/98
*/

public class Cashier extends Observable implements Comparable,
Serializable {

private static int nextCashierNumber = 0;

private String name = "name";
private String password = "password";
private int number = 0;

/** Several different sessions on a particular dates.
*/
private Collection sessions = new TreeSet();

//constructor
public Cashier() {
this("cashier's name","password");
}//constructor

//constructor
public Cashier(String name, String password) {
this.number = ++nextCashierNumber;
this.name = name;
this.password = password;
}//constructor
```

```java
public String getName() {
return name;
}//getName

public void setName(String n) {
name = n;
}//setName

public String toString() {
return name + "#" + number;
}//getName

public int getNumber() {
return number;
}//getNumber

public void setNumber(int n) {
number = n;
}//setNumber

public boolean verifyPassword(String password) {
if (this.password.equals(password)) {
    return true;
    }//if
return false;
}//verifyPassword

public void addSession(Session s) {
sessions.add(s);
}//addSession

/**
* Compares this <code>Cashier</code> with the specified Object
* for order.
* Returns a negative integer, zero, or a positive integer
* if this <code>Cashier</code> is less than, equal to, or greater
* than the given <code>Cashier</code>.
*
* @param obj - the Object to be compared.
* @return a negative integer, zero, or a positive integer if this
*           <code>Cashier</code> is less than, equal to, or greater
* than the given Object.
* @throw ClassCastException - the specified Object's type
* prevents it
*  from being compared to this <code>Cashier</code>.
*/
public int compareTo(Object obj) {
 if ((obj != null) && (obj instanceof Cashier)) {
      Cashier c = (Cashier)obj;
      if (getName().compareTo(c.getName()) != 0) {
           return getName().compareTo(c.getName());
      }
      else {
           return getNumber() - c.getNumber();
      }
 }
 else {
 throw new ClassCastException("" + obj + " is not a Cashier");
 }
}
```

```
/** Test data for the class <code>Cashier</code>.
 * Creates a new instance of a <code>Cashier</code>.
 *
 */
public static void main(String args[]) {

Collection cashiers = new TreeSet();

//set up some cashiers and add them to the collection
Cashier cashier = new Cashier("stuart","s");
cashiers.add(cashier);
cashier = new Cashier("three","stuart");
cashiers.add(cashier);
cashier = new Cashier("four","stuart");
cashiers.add(cashier);
cashier = new Cashier("five","stuart");
cashiers.add(cashier);

System.out.println(cashiers);
}
} ///:~

[five#4, four#3, stuart#1, three#2]
```

Implementing the Register class

A minimal class is left as an exercise to develop.

```
//: Register.java
package chap10;

/** The class <code>Register</code> represents a particular
 * Register.
 * @author Stuart F Lewis
 * @version 1.00, 23/05/98
 */
public class Register {

public void addSession(Session s) {
}//addSession

} ///:~
```

Implementing the Session class

A Session is a period of time that a particular Cashier is using a particular Register in a particular Store (Figure 10.12).

```
//: Session.java
package chap10;
import java.util.*;
import java.io.*;
import java.text.DateFormat;
```

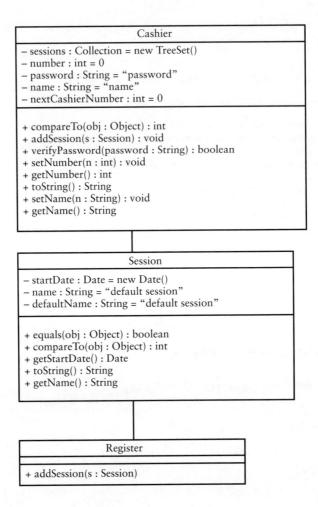

Figure 10.12   Session UML.

```
/** The class <code>Session</code> represents a particular
* item.
* <pre>Which may have :
*  a particular date.
* </pre>Observable to inform any interested observers of
* any change of state.
* @see java.util.Observable
* @see chap10.PLU
* @author Stuart F Lewis
* @version 1.00, 23/05/98
*/
public class Session extends Observable implements
Comparable, Serializable {

private static String defaultName = "default session";
```

```java
private String name = "default session";
private Date startDate = new Date();

//constructor
public Session() {
this(defaultName);
}//constructor

//constructor
public Session(Cashier c,Register r) {
this(defaultName);
}//constructor

//constructor
public Session(String name) {
this(name,new Date());
}//constructor

//constructor
public Session(Date d) {
this(defaultName,d);
}//constructor

//constructor
public Session(String name, Date d) {
this.name = name;
this.startDate = d;
}//constructor

public String getName() {
return name;
}//getName

public String toString() {
return name + " " " + startDate;
}//method toString

public Date getStartDate() {
return startDate;
}//getName
/**
 * Compares this <code>Session</code> with the specified Object
 * for order.
 * Returns a negative integer, zero, or a positive integer
 * if this <code>Session</code> is less than, equal to, or greater
 * than the given <code>Session</code>.
 *
 * @param obj - the Object to be compared.
 * @return a negative integer, zero, or a positive integer if this
 *      <code>Session</code> is less than, equal to, or greater than
 *        the given Session.
 * @throw ClassCastException - the specified Object's type prevents it
 *        from being compared to this <code>Session</code>.
 */
public int compareTo(Object obj) {
 if ((obj != null) && (obj instanceof Session)) {
        Session s = (Session)obj;
        Date d = getStartDate();
```

```
        Date d2 = s.getStartDate();
        if (d.compareTo(d2) != 0) {
              return d.compareTo(d2);
        }
        else {
              return getName().compareTo(s.getName());
        };
    }
    else {
    throw new ClassCastException("" + obj + " is not a Session");
    }
}


/**
 * Compares this object to the specified object.
 * The result is <code>true</code> if and only if the argument is
 * not <code>null</code> and is a <code>Session</code> object that
 * contains the same values as this object.
 *
 * @param  obj  the object to compare with.
 * @return <code>true</code> if the objects are the same;
 * <code>false</code> otherwise.
 */
public boolean equals(Object obj) {
  if ((obj != null) && (obj instanceof Session)) {
        Session s = (Session)obj;
        Date d = getStartDate();
        Date d2 = s.getStartDate();
        return d.equals(d2)
              && getName().equals(s.getName());
  }
  return false;
}


/** Test data for the class <code>Session</code>.
 * Creates a new instance of a <code>Session</code>.
 *
 */
public static void main(String args[]) {
Session s = new Session();
System.out.println(s);

s = new Session();
System.out.println(s);

DateFormat df = DateFormat.getDateInstance();
Date d = new Date();
s = new Session(d);
System.out.println(s);

try {
   d = df.parse("19-Oct-98");
}
catch (java.text.ParseException e) {};
s = new Session(d);
```

```
System.out.println(s);
}
} ///:~

default sessionSun Dec 13 16:37:52 GMT 1998
default sessionSun Dec 13 16:37:55 GMT 1998
default sessionSun Dec 13 16:37:55 GMT 1998
default sessionMon Oct 19 00:00:00 GMT 1998
```

Implementing the Sale class

A Sale (Figure 10.13) is a collection of SaleLineItems (Figure 10.14).

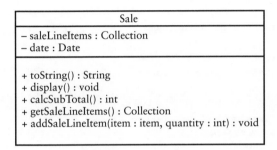

Figure 10.13   Sale UML.

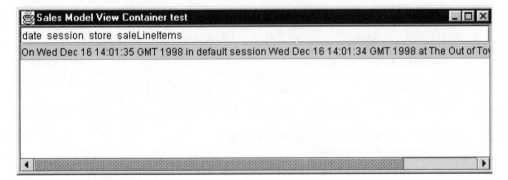

Figure 10.14   Sale Model View Container.

```
//: Sale.java
package chap10;
import java.util.*;
import java.io.*;
import javax.swing.*;

/** The class <code>Sale</code> represents a particular
 * Sale.
 * <pre>Which may have :
 *    Several different SaleLineItems
 *    A Session and Store
 * </pre>Observable to inform any interested observers of
```

```
 * any change of state.
 * @see java.util.Observable
 * @see chap10.PLU
 * @author Stuart F Lewis
 * @version 1.00, 23/10/98
 */
public class Sale extends Observable implements Serializable {

private static Session unknownSession = new Session();

private static Store unknownStore = new Store();

private Session session;
private Store store;
private Date date;

/** The saleLineItems.
 */
private Collection saleLineItems;

//constructor
public Sale() {
this(unknownSession,unknownStore);
}//constructor

//constructor
public Sale(Session session, Store store) {
this.session = session;
this.store = store;
date = new Date();
saleLineItems = new ArrayList();
}//constructor

public void addSaleLineItem(Item item, int quantity) {
SaleLineItem lineItem = new SaleLineItem(item,quantity);
saleLineItems.add(lineItem);
}//method addSaleLineItem

/**
 * Gets the items in the Collection saleLineItems.
 * @return a Collection containing saleLineItems.
 */
public Collection getSaleLineItems() {
  return saleLineItems;
}

public int calcSubTotal() {
SaleLineItem saleItem;
int subTotal = 0;
 for (Iterator i = saleLineItems.iterator(); i.hasNext();) {
   saleItem = (SaleLineItem)i.next();
   subTotal += saleItem.calcSubTotal();
 }//for
return subTotal;
}

public void display() {
}//method display

public String toString() {
return "On " + date + " in " + session + " at " + store;
}//method toString
```

```
/** Test data for the class <code>Sale</code>.
 * Creates a new instance of an <code>Sale</code>.
 *
 */
public static void main(String args[]) {

Collection sales = new ArrayList();

//set up some sales and add them to the collection
Sale s = new Sale();
sales.add(s);

Price p = new Price();

Item i = new Item("first one",p);
s.addSaleLineItem(i,5);

p = new Price(200);
i = new Item("another",p);
s.addSaleLineItem(i,2);

System.out.println(s);
System.out.println(s.calcSubTotal());
System.out.println(sales);

JScrollPane scrollPane = new CollectionViewContainer(sales);
scrollPane.setColumnHeaderView(
   new JTextField("date session store saleLineItems"));
JFrame frame = new
   ClosableFrame("Sales Model View Container test");
frame.getContentPane().add(scrollPane);
frame.pack();
frame.setVisible(true);
}

} ///:~
```

```
On Sun Dec 13 16:36:13 GMT 1998 in default session Sun Dec 13
16:36:10 GMT 1998 at The Out of Town Department Store
   13-Dec-98             500 Sun Dec 13 16:36:13 GMT 1998
   13-Dec-98             200 Sun Dec 13 16:36:13 GMT 1998
2900
[On Sun Dec 13 16:36:13 GMT 1998 in default session Sun Dec 13
16:36:10 GMT 1998 at The Out of Town Department Store]
```

10.13 Why has the value 2900 been displayed?

Implementing the Store class

A Store holds all the sales, items and cashiers as three collections (Figure 10.15).

```
//: Store.java
package chap10;
import java.util.*;
import java.io.*;
import java.text.DateFormat;
```

```
/** The class <code>Store</code> represents a particular
* Store which is a large container of registers (left as an exercise)
* items, sales and cashiers.
* Observable to inform any interested observers of
* any change of state.
* @see java.util.Observable
* @see chap10.PLU
* @author Stuart F Lewis
* @version 1.00, 23/05/98
*/

public class Store extends Observable implements Serializable {

private Collection cashiers;
private Collection items;
private Collection sales;
private String nameOfStore;

private static Cashier unknownCashier = new Cashier("Unknown
Cashier","no password");
private static Item unknownItem = new Item("Unknown Item");

public Store() {
cashiers = new TreeSet();
items = new TreeSet();
sales = new ArrayList();
nameOfStore = "The Out of Town Department Store";
}//constructor

public Collection getCashiers() {
return cashiers;
}

public Collection getItems() {
return items;
}

public Collection getSales() {
return sales;
}
```

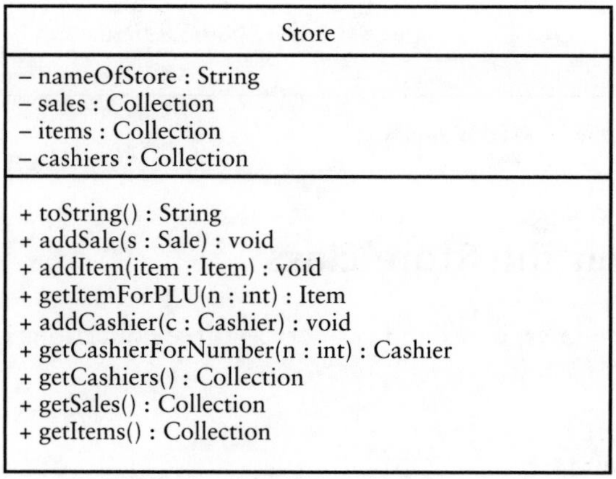

Store
– nameOfStore : String – sales : Collection – items : Collection – cashiers : Collection
+ toString() : String + addSale(s : Sale) : void + addItem(item : Item) : void + getItemForPLU(n : int) : Item + addCashier(c : Cashier) : void + getCashierForNumber(n : int) : Cashier + getCashiers() : Collection + getSales() : Collection + getItems() : Collection

Figure 10.15   Store UML.

```java
public Cashier getCashierForNumber(int n) {
Cashier c;
  for (Iterator i = cashiers.iterator(); i.hasNext();) {
    c = (Cashier)i.next();
    if (c.getNumber() == n) {
          return c;
    }//if
  }//for
return unknownCashier;
}

public void addCashier(Cashier c) {
cashiers.add(c);
}//addCashier

public Item getItemForPLU(int n) {
Item item;
  for (Iterator i = items.iterator(); i.hasNext();) {
    item = (Item)i.next();
    if (item.hasPLU(n)) {
          return item;
    }//if
  }//for
return unknownItem;
}

public void addItem(Item item) {
items.add(item);
}//addItem

public void addSale(Sale s) {
sales.add(s);
}//addSale

public String toString() {
return nameOfStore;
}
/** Test data for the class <code>Store</code>.
 * Creates a new instance of a <code>Store</code>.
 *
 */
public static void main(String args[]) {
Store s = new Store();

//set up some cashiers
Cashier cashier = new Cashier("Stuart","s");
s.addCashier(cashier);
cashier = new Cashier("David","stuart");
s.addCashier(cashier);
cashier = new Cashier("Tess","stuart");
s.addCashier(cashier);
cashier = new Cashier("Nell","stuart");
s.addCashier(cashier);
cashier = new Cashier("Meg","stuart");
s.addCashier(cashier);

//set up some items
Item item = new Item("Kitchen brush");
s.addItem(item);
item = new Item("Garden brush");
s.addItem(item);
```

```
PLU u = new PLU(1234);
Price p = new Price(123);
item = new Item("Wheel barrow",u,p);
s.addItem(item);
u = new PLU(12345);
item = new Item("Garden hose",u,p);
s.addItem(item);

u = new PLU(1111);
p = new Price(10);
item = new Item("Spade",u,p);
u = new PLU(1112);
item.addPLU(u);
u = new PLU(1113);
item.addPLU(u);
s.addItem(item);
u = new PLU(1010);
item = new Item("Patio plant pot 10 inch",u,p);
s.addItem(item);

Sale sale = new Sale();
s.addSale(sale);
sale.addSaleLineItem(item,5);

System.out.println("new store");
System.out.println(s);
//test serialization
  try {
      ObjectOutputStream out =
        new ObjectOutputStream(
          new FileOutputStream("Store.ser"));
      out.writeObject("Store storage");
      out.writeObject(s);
      out.close();
      // All output
  } catch(Exception e) {
      e.printStackTrace();
    }
}//main
} ///:~
```

Generalized ViewContainer for Collections

The task of displaying a Collection of Collections is ideal for a reusable class. The tree-like structure is best captured in a Tree of nodes implementing the TreeModel interface.

```
//: NodeHolder.java

package chap10;
import java.io.*;
import java.util.*;
import java.lang.reflect.*;

/** NodeHolder implementation.
* @author Stuart F Lewis
* @version 1.00, 19/10/98
*/
```

```
class NodeHolder
{
    Object myNode;
    Vector children;
    String description = null;

public NodeHolder(Object f) {
myNode = f;
}

public NodeHolder(Object f, String collectionName) {
myNode = f;
description = collectionName;
}

public Object getNode() {
return myNode;
}

public Vector getChildren() {
System.out.println("get Children for " + myNode);
NodeHolder curHolder;

if ((myNode instanceof Collection) && (children == null)) {
 Object curNode;
 Collection curChildren;
 curChildren = (Collection) myNode;
 children = new Vector();
 for (Iterator i = curChildren.iterator(); i.hasNext();) {
     curNode = i.next();
     curHolder = new NodeHolder(curNode);
     children.addElement(curHolder);
 }
}//if

if (children == null) {
 // Look up methods.
 Method[] methods = myNode.getClass().getDeclaredMethods();
 children = new Vector();
 for(int i = 0; i < methods.length; i++) {    // Display them.
 if (methods[i] instanceof Method) {
    Method m = (Method) methods[i];
    Class returntype = m.getReturnType();
    if (returntype.getName().equals("java.util.Collection")) {
    System.out.println(m.getName() + " returns a Collection");
    java.util.Collection collect;
    try {
     collect = (java.util.Collection)m.invoke(myNode,null);
     System.out.println("Got collection " + collect);
       String collectionName = m.getName().substring(3);
     curHolder = new NodeHolder(collect,collectionName);
     children.addElement(curHolder);
    }
    catch (Exception e) {
     System.out.println("error invoking");
     e.printStackTrace();
    }
   }//if collection
  }//if method
 }//for all methods
}//if no children yet
```

```
      return children;
    }

    public String toString() {
    if (myNode instanceof Collection) {
        return description;
    }
    else if (description != null) {
        return description;
    }
    else {
        return myNode.toString();
    }
    }//toString()

    /** Test data for the file NodeHolder.
     * Creates a new Collection and a NodeHolder to store it
     * and shows it
     */
    public static void main(String args[]) {
    Collection ic = new TreeSet();

    Integer val = new Integer(10);
    for (int i = 0; i < 10; i++) {
            val = new Integer((int)(Math.random()*100));
            System.out.println(val);
            ic.add(val);
    }
    System.out.println();
    System.out.println(ic);

    NodeHolder testNode = new NodeHolder(ic,"Integers");
    System.out.println(testNode);
    System.out.println(testNode.getChildren());
    }//method main
    } ///:~
```

When the program is run, it displays

```
64
50
61
9
50
26
83
64
28
55

[9, 26, 28, 50, 55, 61, 64, 83]
Integers
get Children for [9, 26, 28, 50, 55, 61, 64, 83]
[9, 26, 28, 50, 55, 61, 64, 83]

//: CollectionTreeModel.java
package chap10;
```

```java
import javax.swing.*;
import javax.swing.tree.*;
import javax.swing.event.*;
import java.io.*;
import java.util.*;
import java.lang.reflect.*;

/** CollectionTreeModel implementation.
 * showing how a CollectionTreeModel implements TreeModel.
 * Knows nothing about the state, methods, or interface
 * of the start object
 * @see chap10.CollectionTree
 * @see chap10.NodeHolder
 * @author Stuart F Lewis
 * @version 1.00, 19/10/98
 */
class CollectionTreeModel implements TreeModel {
protected NodeHolder root;
protected Vector listeners;

public CollectionTreeModel(Object r) {
root = new NodeHolder(r,r.getClass().getName());
listeners = new Vector();
}

public Object getRoot() {
return root;
}

public Object getChild(Object parent, int index) {
Object retVal = null;
Vector children;
System.out.println("get Child for " + parent);
if(parent instanceof NodeHolder) {
  children = ((NodeHolder)parent).getChildren();
  if (children != null) {
    if(index < children.size()) {
          retVal = children.elementAt(index);
    }
  }
}
return retVal;
}

public int getChildCount(Object parent) {
int retVal = 0;
Vector children;
if(parent instanceof NodeHolder) {
 children = ((NodeHolder)parent).getChildren();
 if (children != null) {
  retVal = children.size();
 }
}
return retVal;
}

public boolean isLeaf(Object node) {
boolean retVal = true;
Object Node = null;
```

```
System.out.println("is node " + node + "a leaf");
if(node instanceof NodeHolder) {
 Node = ((NodeHolder)node).getNode();
 retVal = !(Node instanceof Collection);
}
// Look up methods.
Method[] methods = Node.getClass().getDeclaredMethods();
// Check them for returning Collection.
for(int i = 0; i < methods.length; i++) {
  if (methods[i] instanceof Method) {
   Method m = (Method) methods[i];
   Class returntype = m.getReturnType();
   if (returntype.getName().equals("java.util.Collection")) {
    retVal = false;
   }
  }
}
return retVal;
}

public void valueForPathChanged(TreePath path,Object newVal)
{
//Do nothing
}

public int getIndexOfChild(Object parent,
 Object child)
{
int retVal = -1;
Vector children;

if(parent instanceof NodeHolder)
{
children = ((NodeHolder)parent).getChildren();

if(children != null)
{
retVal = children.indexOf(child);
}
}

return retVal;
}

public void addTreeModelListener(TreeModelListener l)
{
if((l != null)&&!listeners.contains(l)) listeners.addElement(l);
}

public void removeTreeModelListener(TreeModelListener l)
{
listeners.removeElement(l);
}

/** Test data for the file CollectionTreeModel.
* Creates a new Collection and a CollectionTreeModel
* Adds the CollectionViewContainer to a frame and shows it
*/
public static void main(String args[]) {
Collection ic = new TreeSet();
```

```
Integer val = new Integer(10);
for (int i = 0; i < 10; i++) {
        val = new Integer((int)(Math.random()*100));
        System.out.println(val);
        ic.add(val);
}

CollectionTreeModel testModel = new CollectionTreeModel(ic);
System.out.println(testModel);
Object root = testModel.getRoot();
System.out.println(root);
System.out.println("Child Count is " +
testModel.getChildCount(root));

}//method main
} ///:~
```

When the program is run, it displays

```
chap10.CollectionTreeModel@fc30526d
java.util.TreeSet
get Children for [8, 27, 30, 34, 39, 51, 52, 72, 89]
Child Count is 9
```

After implementing the TreeModel interface in CollectionTreeModel, a GUI interface can be provided by using JTree (Figure 10.16).

```
//:CollectionTree.java
package chap10;

import javax.swing.*;
import java.awt.event.*;
import java.awt.*;
import java.io.*;
import java.util.*;

/** A test class for
 * the CollectionTree implementation.
 * Knows nothing about the state, methods, or interface
 * of the start object.
 * @see chap10.CollectionTreeModel
 * @see chap10.NodeHolder
 * @author Stuart F Lewis
 * @version 1.00, 19/10/98
 */
public class CollectionTree extends JPanel {

public CollectionTree(Object start) {
JTree tree;
CollectionTreeModel model;
setLayout(new BorderLayout());
model = new CollectionTreeModel(start);
tree = new JTree();
tree.setModel(model);
add(new JScrollPane(tree),"Center");
}
```

```
public Dimension getPreferredSize() {
return new Dimension(500, 500);
}

public static void main(String args[]) {
JFrame frame = new JFrame("Collection Tree Example");
CollectionTree panel;
Store s = new Store();
//read from file
    try {
        ObjectInputStream in =
          new ObjectInputStream(
```

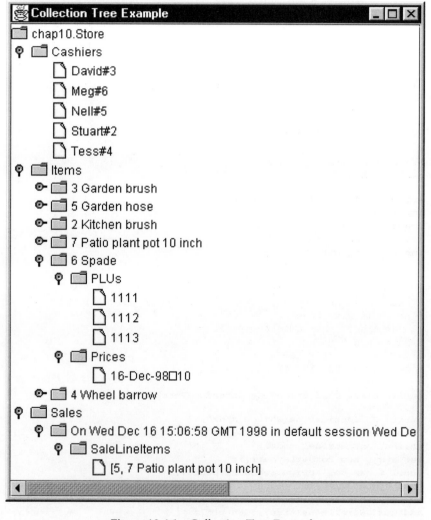

Figure 10.16   Collection Tree Example.

```
                    new FileInputStream("Store.ser"));
                    String info = (String)in.readObject();
                    s = (Store)in.readObject();
                    System.out.println(info);
                System.out.println(s);
            }   catch(Exception e) {
                    e.printStackTrace();
                }
        }

    panel = new CollectionTree(s);

    frame.getContentPane().add(panel,"Center");

    frame.setSize(panel.getPreferredSize());
    frame.setVisible(true);
    frame.addWindowListener(new WindowCloser());
    }//main
    }//Class CollectionTree

    class WindowCloser extends WindowAdapter {
    public void windowClosing(WindowEvent e) {
    Window win = e.getWindow();
    win.setVisible(false);
    System.exit(0);
    }
    } ///:~
```

Summary

The Collection class was described explaining why it is useful and what it can do. A case study for a general point-of-sale system was discussed. Several communicating classes were designed. Objects of these classes are stored using the Collection class from Java 2 (1.2). Full coverage of various options for data management within Java 2 (1.2). The graphical user interface was developed using javax.swing components from Java 2 (1.2).

Answers to in-text questions

1 There are many possible answers from the real world. Any grouping of similar things can be considered as a Collection. A library is a Collection of books. A course is a Collection of modules. A car park is a Collection of cars.

2 The keys and key-value mappings are Sets because they do not contain any duplicates. But the values are a Collection because they may contain duplicates.

3 Left as an exercise for the current API.

4 Additional methods provided by the TreeSet implementation include comparator(), headSet(Object toElement), subSet(Object fromElement, Object toElement), and tailSet(Object fromElement).

5 A ClassCastException is thrown by compareTo if the parameter passed in is not a PLU or one of its subclasses.

6 When the program is run this output will be displayed:

```
1
2
3
4
5
[1, 2, 3, 4, 5]
```

7 There are no duplicates because the PLUs are stored in a Set.

8 The values are sorted according to the natural order of the Integer class (see Comparable).

9 Seven methods windowActivated, windowClosed, windowClosing, windowDeactivated, windowDeiconified, windowIconified, and windowOpened) must be implemented for the WindowListener interface.

10 Using an inner anonymous class rather than adding another class has several advantages. This reduces the number of classes overall annd avoids having to recompile the ClosableFrame class should the superclass change. If the class of the Frame is changed to the standard AWT Frame the inner anonymous class still works.

11 Add the following code to the main method:

```
JScrollPane scrollPane = new ModelViewContainer(thePLUs);
JFrame frame = new ClosableFrame("PLU Model View Container test");
frame.getContentPane().add(scrollPane);
frame.pack();
frame.setVisible(true);
```

12 When the program is run it will display

```
13-Dec-98        500
19-Oct-98        500
29-Oct-98        300
13-Dec-98        200
[13-Dec-98       200, 13-Dec-98 500, 29-Oct-98 300, 19-Oct-98 500]
```

13 The value 2900 is displayed as the subtotal of (5*500) + (2*200).

REVIEW QUESTIONS

Answers in Appendix A.

1 Why are Collections useful?

2 What is the difference between a Set and a List interface to a Collection?

EXERCISES

Answers to exercises flagged with an asterisk appear in Appendix B.

1* What other data structures are used for storing multiple objects?

2 How could the TreeModel API be improved?

11

Building your own reusable class

Overview

One of the major advantages of using an object-oriented approach is the opportunity to develop reusable software components. Already the classes developed for the user interface have been reused with different problem domain classes. The Java language has its own reusable component framework designed to allow developers to build components that can then be reused by other developers in many different applications. This component model is known as JavaBeans. The full specification for the JavaBean component architecture is available on the Sun web site at http://java.sun.com/beans. A JavaBean is an independent reusable software component that can be visually manipulated in builder tools. Before writing a new Bean, be sure to check what is already available. If a new Bean is built, the investment of time and effort in designing for reuse will pay dividends in the long term. Multi-threading and event-driven programming are introduced to build a more sophisticated interface to the Count class before implementing it as a JavaBean. This demonstrates simultaneously active objects within a single system.

Using JavaBeans

Every graphical user interface developed using Java uses JavaBeans because all of the AWT components are also Beans.

11.1 Which AWT components have you used?

One aim in developing your own Bean is to make it as easy to use as the components from the AWT. The essential difference in using JavaBeans as opposed to other reusable software components is that they are portable across many different application designer tools. This is possible because the designer tools can query JavaBean components and ask them what kinds of properties or attributes they have, and what kinds of events they can generate or respond to. This process is known as introspection.

11.2 If you have used an integrated Java development environment, how did it support reusable software components either from the standard API or as imported Beans?

If you have used a visual application builder tool, you will be familiar with the process of selecting a particular Bean from the toolbox, dropping it into a form or design layout, possibly modifying its appearance and behavior by setting some properties or attributes, defining any interaction with other Beans, and combining them into an applet, application, or new Bean. All this can be done without writing a line of code.

JavaBeans are actually classes and can be used without a visual application builder tool in the same way that all components from the AWT are used. There is no requirement for a tool to be able to manipulate the Beans. Most JavaBeans are documented using the javadoc tool.

What JavaBeans can do

There are an increasing number of Beans available ranging from improved versions of the standard AWT components to increasingly sophisticated and complex Beans. At the simpler end of the spectrum are familiar buttons, text fields, list boxes, scrollbars, dialogs, and sliders. These Beans are often sold in component sets, toolkits, or widget libraries for developers to use in their own applications.

More complex Beans may be calendars, spreadsheets, or graphical editors. These are often built from other components and then become components in their own right. Using Beans can speed up the development process, support visual programming tools, reduce the maintenance burden and enable rapid prototyping of new applications.

Writing your own Bean

Rather than starting from scratch, many Beans are the result of converting an existing class into an even more reusable form. For this example, consider how the Count class developed earlier could be provided as a reusable component. Rather than the Choice device for controlling the changing values the button interface will be used as a base for this new Bean (Figure 11.1).

Before converting this CountContainer to a Bean, implement the new view. A more sophisticated layout manager will be required to achieve the desired effect. The

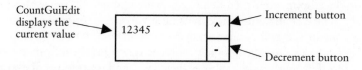

Figure 11.1   Initial design for CountContainer.

GridBagLayout class is a flexible layout manager that aligns components vertically and horizontally, without requiring that the components be of the same size. Each GridBagLayout object maintains a dynamic rectangular grid of cells, with each component occupying one or more cells, called its display area. This is ideal for producing the desired layout.

11.3 What other layout managers are available from the API?

Two API classes combine to specify a GridBagLayout. The gridbag itself and the GridBagConstraints class are used to control how each component is added to the layout. The gridbag is filled from the top left with each component added from left to right and top to bottom. Each component is associated with an object of the GridBagConstraints class that specifies how the component is laid out within its display area. Setting one or more of the instance variables of the GridBagConstraints object changes the way each component is added.

CountContainer is laid out as a gridbag by the private helper method doGridBagLayout(). Setting gridbagconstraint.fill to BOTH makes the component fill its display area entirely by resizing it. The CountGuiEdit text field is added to the GridBagLayout first. Setting gridbagconstraint.gridheight to two means that the CountGuiEdit text field will be twice the height of the two buttons. Before adding the increment button gridbagconstraint.gridwidth is set to REMAINDER completing the first row. Reducing gridbagconstraint.gridheight to one means that the button will be half the height of the textfield. Finally, the decrement button is added after setting the gridbagconstraint.gridheight to REMAINDER completing the second row and last column.

The original CountGuiChoicePanel button interface had four buttons each with an inner class listening for events generated by the button. Reducing the number of buttons to only two will reduce the number of listening classes too. However, the functionality of the exit button will need to be provided at a higher level.

The CountGuiChoicePanel inner classes implemented the ActionListener interface performing the appropriate action when the user generated an ActionEvent by pressing the button.

11.4 How many methods must be implemented to provide the ActionListener interface?

The listener classes for CountContainer MouseAdaptor extend instead of implementing the MouseListener interface which would mean defining all of the methods in it.

11.5 How many methods must be implemented to provide the MouseListener interface?

This will allow the incrementMouseListener, and decrementMouseListener classes to respond at the MouseEvent level rather than the ActionEvent level. The increment and decrement buttons will function in the same way as standard scroll bar buttons do. A single click will change the Count by one, but holding down the mouse button will start the Count changing until the button is released or the cursor is moved out of the button area. If the cursor is moved back into the button area without releasing the mouse button the change will start again. To achieve this effect a separate Thread will be created that keeps changing the count until the mouse button is released. A Thread is a single sequential flow of control within a program.

A number of additional attributes will be added to CountContainer (Figure 11.2). Each has a related set and get method in preparation for converting to a Bean. Specifically a debug switch, delay time, labels for the two buttons, the number of columns for displaying the Count and the Count itself will be attributes of CountContainer.

```
┌─────────────────────────────┐
│       CountContainer        │
├─────────────────────────────┤
│ debug                       │
│ delay                       │
│ incrementButtonLabel        │
│ decrementButtonLabel        │
│ Count                       │
│ CountGuiEdit                │
│ columns                     │
│ increment                   │
│ decrement                   │
├─────────────────────────────┤
│ doBorderLayout()            │
│ doGridBagLayout()           │
└─────────────────────────────┘
```

Figure 11.2   Diagram showing the CountContainer class.

11.6 Why are the get and set accessor methods not shown on the UML class diagram for CountContainer?

11.7 What other aspects of CountContainer could be added as attributes to be modified at design time by a customization tool?

Implementing CountContainer

The CountViewContainer implementation knew nothing about the state, methods, or interface of a Count. CountViewContainer relied on the Choice panel and editable display classes to control the Count. CountContainer combines the Choice, display and editing functions into one class. All attributes are declared as private and can only be changed using synchronised set methods. The full code for CountContainer is

```
//: CountContainer.java
package chap11;

import chap07.*;
import java.io.*;
import java.awt.*;
import java.awt.event.*;

/**
 * CountContainer implementation
 * showing the use of extends to inherit
 * from the Panel superclass, uses two buttons and a CountGuiEdit
 * to control and display a Count
 * @see chap07.Count
 * @see chap07.CountInt
 * @see chap07.CountChar
 * @see chap07.CountDate
 * @see chap07.CountGuiEdit
 * @author Stuart F Lewis
 * @version 1.00, 02/10/98
 */
public class CountContainer extends Panel {

/** debug switch change to false to suppress messages
 */
private boolean debug = false;

/** delay between changes if the increment or decrement button
 * is kept pressed down
 */
private int delay = 300;

/** Label to appear on the increment button
 * @see java.awt.Button
 */
private String incrementButtonLabel = "^";

/** Label to appear on the decrement button
 * @see java.awt.Button
 */
private String decrementButtonLabel = "-";

/** The count to control and display.
 * @see chap07.Count
 */
private Count c;

/** CountGuiEdit to display the Count
 * @see java.awt.TextField
 */
private transient TextField t;

/** Number of columns in CountGuiEdit to display the Count
 * @see java.awt.TextField
 */
private int columns;

/** button for increasing the value of the Count.
 * @see java.awt.Button
 */
private Button increment;
```

```
/** button for decreasing the value of the Count.
* @see java.awt.Button
*/
private Button decrement;

/** Constructs a new <code>CountContainer</code>
* as interface to Count c.
* Creates two new buttons with default labels.
* Create a new CountDate and
* displays the initial value of the count
* using a <code>CountGuiEdit</code> that is editable.
* Adds MouseListeners to the buttons
* lays out the CountContainer using a GridBagLayout
* @see java.awt.Button#addMouseListener
*/
public CountContainer() {
increment = new Button(incrementButtonLabel);
decrement = new Button(decrementButtonLabel);
c = new CountDate();
t = new CountGuiEdit(c);
if (debug) {
   System.out.println("count is" + c + " " + c.hashCode());
}

increment.addMouseListener(new incrementMouseListener());
decrement.addMouseListener(new decrementMouseListener());
if (debug) {
   System.out.println("increment button is" + increment);
   System.out.println(increment.getMinimumSize().toString());
}//if
this.doGridBagLayout();
}

/** Layout a CountContainer using BorderLayout.
* Add buttons above and below the Count.
*/
private void doBorderLayout() {
t.setColumns(columns);
this.setLayout(new BorderLayout());
this.add(increment,BorderLayout.NORTH);
this.add(t,BorderLayout.CENTER);
this.add(decrement,BorderLayout.SOUTH);
}

/** Layout a CountContainer using GridBagLayout.
* Buttons above each other beside the Count
*/
private void doGridBagLayout() {
t.setColumns(columns);
GridBagLayout gridbag = new GridBagLayout();
GridBagConstraints gridbagconstraint = new GridBagConstraints();

this.setFont(new Font("Helvetica", Font.PLAIN, 14));
this.setLayout(gridbag);

gridbagconstraint.fill = GridBagConstraints.BOTH;

//CountGuiEdit is twice the height of the buttons
gridbagconstraint.gridheight = 2;
gridbagconstraint.weighty = 1.0;
this.add(t,gridbagconstraint);
```

```
gridbagconstraint.gridwidth
        = GridBagConstraints.REMAINDER; //end row
gridbagconstraint.gridheight = 1;                      //reset to the default
this.add(increment,gridbagconstraint);

gridbagconstraint.gridheight
        = GridBagConstraints.REMAINDER; //end column
gridbagconstraint.gridwidth = GridBagConstraints.REMAINDER;
this.add(decrement,gridbagconstraint);
}

/**
 * IncrementMouseListener inner class
 * uses extends to inherit
 * from the MouseAdapter superclass as a convenience
 * for creating listener objects. Instead of implementing
 * the MouseListener interface which would mean defining all
 * of the methods in it.
 * @see java.awt.event.MouseAdapter
 * @author Stuart F Lewis
 * @version 1.00, 02/10/98
 */
private class incrementMouseListener extends MouseAdapter
                             implements Serializable {

/**
 * A Thread used to keep the count increasing when the mouse has
 * been pressed on the increment button.
 */
private transient Thread inc = null;

/**
 * A flag used to know if the count is increasing.
 * Set to true when the mouse is pressed on the increment button.
 * Set to false when the mouse is released
 */
private boolean incrementing = true;

/**
 * A flag used to know if the increment button is pressed.
 * Set to false when the mouse is released
 */
private boolean pressed = false;

/** Invoked when a mouse button has been pressed on
 * the increment button. Creates a new Thread and
 * starts it incrementing the Count
 */
public void mousePressed(MouseEvent e) {
if (debug) {
    System.out.println("About to start incrementing count" +
    c + " " + c.hashCode() + " Event" + e);
}
inc = new ThreadInc(c,this);
if (debug) {
    System.out.println("Start thread " + inc);
}
incrementing = true ;
inc.start();
pressed = true;
}
```

```java
/** Invoked when the mouse enters the increment button.
* if the button is pressed a new Thread is started.
*/
public void mouseEntered(MouseEvent e) {
 if (pressed) {
    inc = new ThreadInc(c,this);
    incrementing = true ;
    inc.start();
 }
}

/** Invoked when the mouse exits the increment button.
* The Thread is stopped. But the button may be left pressed.
*/
public void mouseExited(MouseEvent e) {
if (debug) {
    System.out.println("mouseExited " + inc);
}
incrementing = false;
}

/** Invoked when a mouse button has been released.
* The Thread is stopped and the button is unpressed.
*/
public void mouseReleased(MouseEvent e) {
if (debug) {
    System.out.println("mouseReleased " + inc);
}
incrementing = false;
pressed = false;
}

/**
* Returns true if the count is increasing.
* @return boolean true if the count is being incremented.
*/
public boolean isIncrementing() {
return incrementing;
}
}//class incrementMouseListener

/**
* ThreadInc keeps incrementing a Count as long as the increment
* button is pressed.
*/
private class ThreadInc extends Thread {

/** The count to increment.
* @see chap07.Count
*/
private Count countToInc;

/** The incrementMouseListener that created and started
* this thread. This thread will stop and die when the
* mouse button is released
* @see chap11.incrementMouseListener
*/
private incrementMouseListener l;
```

```
/** Constructs a new <code>ThreadInc</code>
 * to increment the Count countToInc.
 * @see java.lang.Thread
 */
public ThreadInc(Count c, incrementMouseListener l) {
if (debug) {
 System.out.println("constructing new thread to increment count " +
                     c + " " + c.hashCode());
}
this.countToInc = c;
this.l = l;
}


/** Keeps incrementing the Count countToInc. This thread
 * will stop and die when the
 * mouse button is released
 * @see java.lang.Thread
 * @see chap11.incrementMouseListener
 */
public void run() {
if (debug) {
    System.out.println("isIncrementing " + l.isIncrementing());
}
while(l.isIncrementing()) {
 /* The code here will increment the Count by one
 * then sleep for delay/3 ms.
 */
 try {
  if (debug) {
    System.out.println("going up ");
    System.out.println(countToInc + " " + countToInc.hashCode());
  }
  countToInc.increment();
  sleep(delay);
 }//try
 catch(Exception e) {
  System.out.println("ThreadInc interrupted " + e);
 }//catch
}//while
}//method run

}//class ThreadInc


/**
 * DecrementMouseListener inner class
 * uses extends to inherit
 * from the MouseAdapter superclass as a convenience
 * for creating listener objects. Instead of implementing
 * the MouseListener interface which would mean defining all
 * of the methods in it.
 * @see java.awt.event.MouseAdapter
 * @author Stuart F Lewis
 * @version 1.00, 02/10/98
 */
private class decrementMouseListener extends MouseAdapter
                        implements Serializable {
```

```
/**
 * A Thread used to keep the count decreasing when the mouse has
 * been pressed on the decrement button.
 */
private transient Thread dec = null;
/**
 * A flag used to know if the count is decreasing.
 * Set to true when the mouse is pressed on the decrement button.
 * Set to false when the mouse is released
 */
private boolean decrementing = true;
/**
 * A flag used to know if the decrement button is pressed.
 * Set to false when the mouse is released
 */
private boolean pressed = false;

/** Invoked when a mouse button has been pressed on
 * the decrement button. Creates a new Thread and
 * starts it decrementing the Count
 */
public void mousePressed(MouseEvent e) {
dec = new ThreadDec(c,this);
decrementing = true;
pressed = true;
dec.start();
}

/** Invoked when the mouse enters the decrement button.
 * if the button is pressed a new Thread is started.
 */
public void mouseEntered(MouseEvent e) {
if (pressed) {
 dec = new ThreadDec(c,this);
 decrementing = true;
 dec.start();
}
}

/** Invoked when the mouse exits the decrement button.
 * The Thread is stopped. But the button may be left pressed.
 */
public void mouseExited(MouseEvent e) {
if (debug) {
    System.out.println("mouseExited " + dec);
}
decrementing = false;
}

/** Invoked when a mouse button has been released.
 * The Thread is stopped and the button is unpressed.
 */
public void mouseReleased(MouseEvent e) {
if (debug) {
  System.out.println("mouseReleased " + dec);
}
decrementing = false;
pressed = false;
}
```

```
/**
 * Returns true if the count is decreasing.
 * @return boolean true if the count is being decremented.
 */
public boolean isDecrementing() {
return decrementing;
}
}//class decrementMouseListener

/**
 * ThreadDec keeps decrementing a Count as long as the decrement
 * button is pressed.
 */
private class ThreadDec extends Thread {
/** The count to decrement.
 * @see chap07.Count
 */
private Count countToDec;

/** The decrementMouseListener that created and started
 * this thread. This thread will stop and die when the
 * mouse button is released
 * @see chap11.decrementMouseListener
 */
private decrementMouseListener l;

/** Constructs a new <code>ThreadDec</code>
 * to decrement the Count countToDec.
 * @see java.lang.Thread
 */
public ThreadDec(Count c, decrementMouseListener l) {
this.countToDec = c;
this.l = l;
}

/** Keeps decrementing the Count countToDec. This thread
 * will stop and die when the
 * mouse button is released
 * @see java.lang.Thread
 * @see chap11.decrementMouseListener
 */
public void run() {
if (debug) {
    System.out.println("isDecrementing " + l.isDecrementing());
}
while(l.isDecrementing()) {
 /* The code here will decrement the Count by one
 * then sleep for delay/3 ms.
 */
 try {
  if (debug) {
   System.out.println("Count is " + countToDec + " and going
   down");
  }
  countToDec.decrement();
  sleep(delay);
 }//try
```

```
   catch(Exception e) {
    System.out.println("ThreadDec interrupted "+e);
   }//catch
 }//while
 }//method run

}//class ThreadDec

/**
 * Set method for the debug switch
 */
public synchronized void setDebug(boolean b) {
debug = b;
}

/**
 * Access method for the debug switch
 * @return boolean the current state of the debug switch
 */
public boolean getDebug() {
    return debug;
}

/**
 * Set method for the delay time
 */
public synchronized void setDelay(int d) {
delay = d;
}

/**
 * Access method for the delay time
 * @return int delay time between changes to Count value
 */
public int getDelay() {
    return delay;
}

/**
 * Set method for the incrementButtonLabel
 * @param l the new label, or <code>null</code>
 *                  if the button has no label.
 * @see java.awt.Button#setLabel
 */
public synchronized void setIncrementButtonLabel(String l) {
if (!incrementButtonLabel.equals(l)) {
    incrementButtonLabel = l;
    increment.setLabel(incrementButtonLabel);
}
}

/**
 * Access method for the incrementButtonLabel
 * @return increment button label
 */
public String getIncrementButtonLabel() {
    return incrementButtonLabel;
}
```

```
/**
 * Set method for the decrementButtonLabel
 * @param l the new label, or <code>null</code>
 *                if the button has no label.
 * @see java.awt.Button#setLabel
 */
public synchronized void setDecrementButtonLabel(String l) {
if (!decrementButtonLabel.equals(l)) {
    decrementButtonLabel = l;
    decrement.setLabel(decrementButtonLabel);
}//if
}


/**
 * Access method for the decrementButtonLabel
 * @return decrement button label
 */
public String getDecrementButtonLabel() {
    return decrementButtonLabel;
}


/**
 * Set method for the Count
 * @param c the new Count.
 * @see java.awt.Button#setLabel
 */
public synchronized void setCount(Count c) {
if (!this.c.equals(c)) {
    this.c = c;
    this.t = new CountGuiEdit(c);
    this.removeAll();
    this.doGridBagLayout();
}
}


/**
 * Access method for the Count
 * @return Count
 */
public Count getCount() {
    return c;
}


/**
 * Set method for the columns in CountGuiEdit
 * @param c the new columns.
 * @see   chap07.CountGuiEdit
 */
public synchronized void setColumns(int c) {
 if (this.columns != c) {
    this.columns = c;
    this.t.setColumns(columns);
    this.removeAll();
    this.doGridBagLayout();
 }
}
```

```
/**
 * Access method for the columns in CountGuiEdit
 * @return columns in CountGuiEdit
 * @see   chap07.CountGuiEdit
 */
public int getColumns() {
    return columns;
}

/** Test code for CountContainer.
 *
 */
public static void main(String args[]) throws IOException {
System.out.println("Create new CountContainer");

CountContainer s = new CountContainer();
Count c = new CountInt();
s.setCount(c);
s.setColumns(8);
s.setDebug(true);

CountContainer s2 = new CountContainer();
c = new CountDate();
s2.setCount(c);
s2.setColumns(30);
s2.setDebug(true);

Frame f = new ClosableFrame ("Test CountContainer ");
f.setLayout(new FlowLayout());
f.add(s);
f.add(s2);
f.pack();
f.setVisible(true);
}//main
} ///:~
```

Note that the testing method uses a class ClosableFrame that was developed in a previous chapter. This ClosableFrame inherits from the standard AWT Frame.

The initial window shows the CountContainer as created. The debugging messages show the effect of pressing and releasing the increment and decrement buttons. The second window shows the CountContainer after the debugging activites (Figure 11.3).

Converting to a JavaBean

The process of converting to a JavaBean involves checking that whenever possible attributes, methods, and inner classes are encapsulated using private, and ensuring that all classes used for instance variables implement Serializable. Any instance variables that are not Serializable must be marked as transient. All methods that set attributes should be synchronised and all attribute accessor methods should be named in get/set pairs following the convention getAttribute and setAttribute. This will enable any tools to recognise the attributes and provide default editors for changing them.

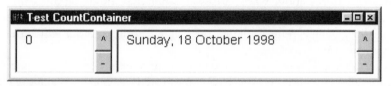

```
Create new CountContainer
mouseExited null
mouseExited null
About to start incrementing count 0 1889355
Eventjava.awt.event.MouseEvent[MOUSE_PRESSED,(12,12),mods=16,clickCount=1] on button0
constructing new thread to increment count 0 1889355
Start thread Thread[Thread-1, 5, main]
isIncrementing true
going up
0 1889355
going up
1 1889355
going up
2 1889355
going up
3 1889355
going up
4 1889355
going up
5 1889355
mouseReleased Thread[Thread-1, 5, main]
mouseExited Thread[Thread-1, 5, ]
mouseExited null
isDecrementing true
Count is Sunday, 18 October 1998 and going down
mouseReleased Thread{Thread-2, 5, main]
isDecrementing true
Count is Saturday, 17 October 1998 and going down
mouseReleased Thread{Thread-3, 5, main]
isDecrementing true
Count is Friday, 16 October 1998 and going down
Count is Thursday, 15 October 1998 and going down
Count is Wednesday, 14 October 1998 and going down
Count is Tuesday, 13 October 1998 and going down
Count is Monday, 12 October 1998 and going down
Count is Sunday, 11 October 1998 and going down
Count is Saturday, 10 October 1998 and going down
Count is Friday, 9 October 1998 and going down
mouseReleased Thread{Thread-4, 5, main]
mouseExited Thread[Thread-4, 5, ]
No process, input ignored\r
```

Figure 11.3   Diagram showing output for CountContainer.

The majority of the above were addressed when the CountContainer interface was improved and the Thread classes added. A Thread is not Serializable because at the time a Serialized bean is reinstantiated, the original context under which the program was running no longer exists.

As a CountBean, CountContainer will need to generate an event when the value of the Count changes and send this to any interested Listeners. To achieve this a new event class is created by extending EventObject from the API package java.util.

```
//: CountBeanEvent.java
package CountB;

import java.util.EventObject;

public class CountBeanEvent extends EventObject {
private Object value;

public CountBeanEvent(Object source, Object v) {
super(source);
value = v;
}

public Object getValue(){
return value;
}

} ///:~
```

To listen for events generated by the CountBean an Event Listener class is required. This CountBeanListener class is created by extending EventListener also from the API package java.util.

```
//: CountBeanListener.java
package CountB;
import java.util.EventListener;

public interface CountBeanListener extends EventListener {

public void countBeanChange(CountBeanEvent e);

} ///:~
```

To complete the conversion to a Bean several additional attributes and methods must be added. Some require extra classes from the API to be imported.

```
//extra imports for Bean support - Observable, Vector
import java.io.*;
import java.util.*;
```

The additional attributes are to store some Bean specific information and a Vector of registered CountBean listeners that will be notified of any CountBeanEvent.

```
//main removed and to convert CountContainer into CountBean
//extra fields added

/*
 * Used for versioning in explicit serialization of the bean.
 * Get the serialVersionUID by executing the JDK tool serialver on
 * the bean class file giving the full package/pathname
```

```
* F:\sflewis\myjava\sflewis\CountB>serialver CountB.CountBean
* gives
* CountB.CountBean:   static final long serialVersionUID = 0L;
*/
private final static long serialVersionUID = 0L;

/** Version number 1 - designed to use only Java 1.1 components
*/
private final static int versionNum = 1;

protected Vector countBeanListeners = new Vector();
```

The additional methods are to implement the Observer interface and fire any CountBeanEvent to all the Vector of registered CountBean listeners. These listeners can be added or removed using the other additional methods. Finally the default readObject() method used for serialization is overridden to ensure that the Count being observed is linked to the controller view provided by CountGuiEdit.

```
//Extra methods added
/**
* Called when the Count c being observed notifies
* observers of a state change.
* @param Observable o the observable object ie. the Count.
* @param Object arg an optional argument passed to the ;
*           notifyObservers method, always null in this case.
*/
public void update(Observable o,Object arg) {
if (debug) {
    System.out.println("update called by Count ");
}
 if (countBeanListeners != null) {
   fireEvent(new CountBeanEvent(CountBean.this,getValue()));
 }
}

/*
* CountBean listeners are notified when a value change occurs
* on the count.
*/
public void addCountBeanListener(CountBeanListener l) {
   countBeanListeners.addElement(l);
if (debug) {
    System.out.println("Listener " + l + " added");
}
}

/*
* CountBean listeners are notified when a value change occurs
* on the count.
*/
public void removeCountBeanListener(CountBeanListener l) {
   countBeanListeners.removeElement(l);
}

/** Send an event to all registered countBeanListeners */
public void fireEvent(CountBeanEvent e) {
// Make a copy of the list and fire the events using that copy.
```

```
// This means that listeners can be added or removed from the
// original list in response to this event.
    Vector list = (Vector) countBeanListeners.clone();
    for(int i = 0; i < list.size(); i++) {
      CountBeanListener listener =
        (CountBeanListener)list.elementAt(i);
      listener.countBeanChange(e);
    } //for
}

/** Overide default readObject to make sure Count is
* linked to the display view */
private void readObject (ObjectInputStream stream)
throws IOException, ClassNotFoundException {
stream.defaultReadObject();
/* link the restored Count to a new TextField on the display
*/
t = new CountGuiEdit(c);
}
/:~
```

To test the CountBean is generating Events successfully a TestCountBean class is used.

```
//: TestCountBean.java
package chap11;

import java.awt.*;

import CountB.CountBean;
import CountB.CountBeanListener;
import CountB.CountBeanEvent;

public class TestCountBean extends ClosableFrame
            implements CountBeanListener {

CountBean s;

/**
* Constructor.
*/

public TestCountBean () {
s = new CountBean();
s.addCountBeanListener(this);
add(s);
}

public void countBeanChange(CountBeanEvent e) {
System.out.println("countBeanChangeBegin " + e);
System.out.println("event value " + e.getValue());
System.out.println("box value " + s.getValue());
}

public static void main(String args[]) {
System.out.println("start main");
Frame f = new TestCountBean();;;
f.pack();
f.show();
}//main

} ///:~
```

In this test (Figure 11.4) the CountBean seems little more than just another imported class. To fully appreciate how a Bean differs from other classes it must be compiled and packaged in a Java Archive (JAR) file. After the JAR file is created, the bean can be imported into a GUI builder tool.

Figure 11.4   TestCountBean.

The command to package CountBean into a JAR file is similar to

> jar cvf CountBean.jar CountB/*.class chap07/*.class

The contents of a JAR file can be listed using a command similar to

> jar tvf CountBean.jar

Which will produce output similar to

```
   0 Fri Dec 11 22:02:28 META-INF/
  25 Fri Dec 11 22:02:28 META-INF/MANIFEST.MF
2039 Fri Dec 11 16:26:24 CountB/CountBean$decrementMouseListener.class
2386 Fri Dec 11 16:26:24 CountB/CountBean$incrementMouseListener.class
1783 Fri Dec 11 16:26:24 CountB/CountBean$ThreadDec.class
2068 Fri Dec 11 16:26:24 CountB/CountBean$ThreadInc.class
6284 Fri Dec 11 16:26:24 CountB/CountBean.class
 581 Fri Dec 11 16:26:24 CountB/CountBeanEvent.class
 366 Fri Dec 11 16:26:24 CountB/CountBeanListener.class
1391 Fri Dec 11 16:26:24 chap07/Count.class
2932 Fri Dec 11 16:26:24 chap07/CountDate.class
1701 Fri Dec 11 16:26:24 chap07/CountGuiDisplay.class
2450 Fri Dec 11 16:26:24 chap07/CountGuiEdit.class
2991 Fri Dec 11 16:26:24 chap07/CountInt.class
```

Now the CountBean can be imported into a Bean tool and customized. The Bean Development Kit (BDK) and BeanBox is the standard reference base for both bean developers and tool vendors. The BDK is not intended for use by application developers, nor is it intended to be a full-fledged application development environment. The BeanBox is used to test out new beans. When BDK is started, three frames are displayed (Figure 11.5). The ToolBox contains a list of imported Beans. The BeanBox is a container for adding beans to. The properties editor frame allows the Bean attributes to be customized using some default property editors.

When CountBean is first instantiated in the BeanBox the properties are the default set defined when CountBean was compiled. These can now be changed without altering any code (Figure 11.6).

The same process can be achieved by using any Bean tool, for example Java Workshop (Figure 11.7).

Other application development environments also support Beans. The details vary from tool to tool but are normally well documented.

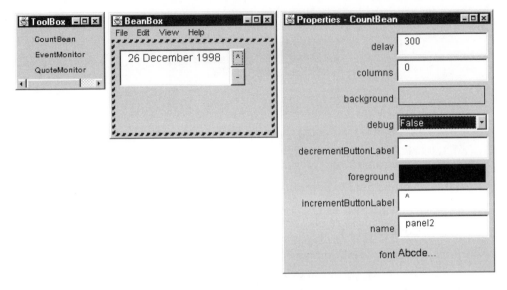

Figure 11.5   CountBean in the BDK before customizing.

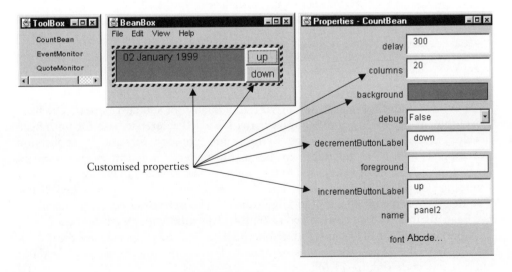

Figure 11.6   CountBean after customizing in the BDK.

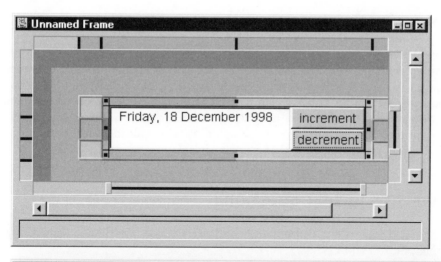

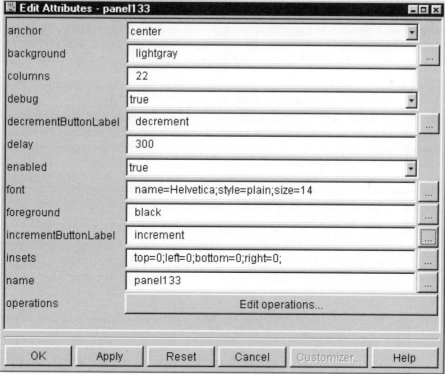

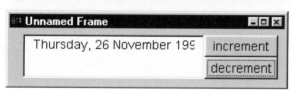

Figure 11.7   CountBean being customized using Java Workshop.

Summary

One of the major advantages of using an object-oriented approach is the opportunity to develop reusable software components. The Java language reusable component framework is known as JavaBeans. A JavaBean is an independent reusable software component that can be visually manipulated in builder tools. Multi-threading and event-driven programming were introduced to build a more sophisticated interface to the Count class before implementing it as a JavaBean. This demonstrated simultaneously active objects within a single system.

Answers to in-text questions

1 In this text, the AWT components used are Choice, TextField, Panel, Frame, Applet, Button and List.

2 Depending on the builder tool used various answers may be given. Either importing a JAR file for one or more beans or by manually writing a shadow class for a component, wrapping it around the component class, and importing the shadow class or by a tool specific variation of either of these approaches.

3 GridLayout, ScrollPaneLayout, ViewportLayout, and FlowLayout all implement the interface java.awt.LayoutManager. BoxLayout, CardLayout, JRootPane.RootLayout, OverlayLayout, GridBagLayout, and BorderLayout all implement the interface java.awt.LayoutManager2 which extends the LayoutManager interface to deal with layouts explicitly in terms of constraint objects that specify how and where components should be added to the layout.

4 Only one method actionPerformed must be implemented for the ActionListener interface. Its signature is public void actionPerformed(ActionEvent e). It is invoked when an action occurs.

5 Five methods, mouseClicked(MouseEvent e), mouseEntered(MouseEvent e), mouseExited(MouseEvent e), mousePressed(MouseEvent e), and mouseReleased(MouseEvent e) must be implemented for the MouseListener interface.

6 The get and set accessor methods are often not shown on UML class diagrams because all accessible attributes need to have these methods.

7 Other aspects of CountContainer that could be added as attributes to be modified at design time include the format of output, title of the frame, colours used and even the layout manager.

8 The full source for a 1.2. ClosableFrame is

```
//: ClosableFrame.java
package chap11;
import javax.swing.*;
import java.awt.*;
import java.awt.event.*;
```

```
/**
 * the public class closeableFrame
 */
public class ClosableFrame extends JFrame {

/**
 * private variable frame to store the frame
 * so it can be disposed of later
 */
private ClosableFrame frame;

/**
 * Constructor for a new ClosableFrame.
 * creates a new FrameListener for this frame
 */
public ClosableFrame () {
this("");
}

/**
 * Constructor for a new ClosableFrame with a title.
 * creates a new FrameListener for this frame
 */
public ClosableFrame (String title) {
super(title);
WindowListener l = new FrameListener(this);
this.addWindowListener(l);
}// Constructor ClosableFrame

/**
 * inner class FrameListener extends WindowAdapter rather
 * than implementing
 * all the methods required by the public interface WindowListener
 */
private class FrameListener extends WindowAdapter {

/**
 * Constructor for a new FrameListener,
 * creates a new FrameListener for the frame
 * to be listened to, and stores the frame so
 * it can be disposed of later
 */
public FrameListener (ClosableFrame listenedToFrame) {
    frame = listenedToFrame;
}

public void windowClosing(WindowEvent e) {
frame.dispose();
System.exit(0);
}
}//inner class FrameListener

/**
 * main application test
 * creates a new frame
 * displays the frame
 */
public static void main(String args[]) {
ClosableFrame f = new ClosableFrame();
```

```
f.setSize(200,200);
f.setLocation(200,200);
f.show();
}// method main
} ///:~
```

9 The full source for a CountBean is:

```
//: CountBean.java
package CountB;

import chap07.*;
import java.io.*;
import java.awt.*;
import java.awt.event.*;

//extra imports for Bean support - Observable, Vector
import java.io.*;
import java.util.* ;

/**
 * CountBean implementation
 * showing the use of extends to inherit
 * from the Panel superclass, uses two buttons and a CountGuiEdit
 * to control and display a Count
 * @see chap07.Count
 * @see chap07.CountInt
 * @see chap07.CountChar
 * @see chap07.CountDate
 * @see chap07.CountGuiEdit
 * @author Stuart F Lewis
 * @version 1.00, 02/10/98
 */
public class CountBean extends Panel implements Observer {

/** debug switch change to false to supress messages
 */
boolean debug = false;

/** delay between changes if the increment or decrement button
 * is kept pressed down
 */
int delay = 300;

/** Label to appear on the increment button
 * @see java.awt.Button
 */
private String incrementButtonLabel = "^";

/** Label to appear on the decrement button
 * @see java.awt.Button
 */
private String decrementButtonLabel = "-";

/** The count to control and display.
 * @see chap07.Count
 */
Count c;

/** CountGuiEdit to display the Count
 * @see java.awt.TextField
 */
private transient TextField t;
```

```
/** Number of columns in CountGuiEdit to display the Count
 * @see java.awt.TextField
 */
private int columns;

/** button for increasing the value of the Count.
 * @see java.awt.Button
 */
private Button increment;

/** button for decreasing the value of the Count.
 * @see java.awt.Button
 */
private Button decrement;

/** Constructs a new <code>CountBean</code>
 * as interface to Count c.
 * Creates two new button with default labels.
 * Create a new CountDate and
 * displays the initial value of the count
 * using a <code>CountGuiEdit</code> that is editable.
 * Adds MouseListeners to the buttons
 * lays out the CountBean using a GridBagLayout
 * @see java.awt.Button#addMouseListener
 */
public CountBean() {
increment = new Button(incrementButtonLabel);
decrement = new Button(decrementButtonLabel);
c = new CountDate();
t = new CountGuiEdit(c);
if (debug) {
   System.out.println("count is" + c + " " + c.hashCode());
}
increment.addMouseListener(new incrementMouseListener());
decrement.addMouseListener(new decrementMouseListener());

if (debug) {
   System.out.println("increment button is" + increment);
   System.out.println(increment.getMinimumSize().toString());
}//if
this.doGridBagLayout();
}

/** Layout a CountBean using BorderLayout.
 * Add buttons above and below the Count.
 */
private void doBorderLayout() {
t.setColumns(columns);
this.setLayout(new BorderLayout());
this.add(increment,BorderLayout.NORTH);
this.add(t,BorderLayout.CENTER);
this.add(decrement,BorderLayout.SOUTH);
}

/** Layout a CountBean using GridBagLayout.
 * Buttons above each other beside the Count
 */
private void doGridBagLayout() {
t.setColumns(columns);
GridBagLayout gridbag = new GridBagLayout();
GridBagConstraints gridbagconstraint = new GridBagConstraints();
```

```
    this.setFont(new Font("Helvetica", Font.PLAIN, 14));
    this.setLayout(gridbag);

    gridbagconstraint.fill = GridBagConstraints.BOTH;

    //CountGuiEdit is twice the height of the buttons
    gridbagconstraint.gridheight = 2;
    gridbagconstraint.weighty = 1.0;
    this.add(t,gridbagconstraint);

    gridbagconstraint.gridwidth
        = GridBagConstraints.REMAINDER;                        //end row
    gridbagconstraint.gridheight = 1;              //reset to the default
    this.add(increment,gridbagconstraint);

    gridbagconstraint.gridheight
        = GridBagConstraints.REMAINDER; //end column
    gridbagconstraint.gridwidth
        = GridBagConstraints.REMAINDER; //end row
    this.add(decrement,gridbagconstraint);
    }

/**
 * incrementMouseListener inner class
 * uses extends to inherit
 * from the MouseAdapter superclass as a convenience
 * for creating listener objects. Instead of implementing
 * the MouseListener interface which would mean defining all
 * of the methods in it.
 * @see java.awt.event.MouseAdapter
 * @author Stuart F Lewis
 * @version 1.00, 02/10/98
 */
private class incrementMouseListener extends MouseAdapter
                                  implements Serializable {

/**
 * A Thread used to keep the count increasing when the mouse has
 * been pressed on the increment button.
 */
private transient Thread inc = null;

/**
 * A flag used to know if the count is increasing.
 * Set to true when the mouse is pressed on the increment button.
 * Set to false when the mouse is released
 */
private boolean incrementing = true;

/**
 * A flag used to know if the increment button is pressed.
 * Set to false when the mouse is released
 */
private boolean pressed = false;

/** Invoked when a mouse button has been pressed on
 * the increment button. Creates a new Thread and
 * starts it incrementing the Count
 */
public void mousePressed(MouseEvent e) {
if (debug) {
    System.out.println("About to start incrementing count" +
    c + " " + c.hashCode() + " Event" + e);
}
```

```
inc = new ThreadInc(c,this);
if (debug) {
   System.out.println("Start thread " + inc);
}
incrementing = true ;
inc.start();
pressed = true;
}

/** Invoked when the mouse enters the increment button.
 * if the button is pressed a new Thread is started.
 */
public void mouseEntered(MouseEvent e) {
 if (pressed) {
    inc = new ThreadInc(c,this);
    incrementing = true;
    inc.start();
 }
}

/** Invoked when the mouse exits the increment button.
 * The Thread is stopped. But the button may be left pressed.
 */
public void mouseExited(MouseEvent e) {
if (debug) {
   System.out.println("mouseExited " + inc);
}
incrementing = false;
}

/** Invoked when a mouse button has been released.
 * The Thread is stopped and the button is unpressed.
 */
public void mouseReleased(MouseEvent e) {
if (debug) {
   System.out.println("mouseReleased " + inc);
}
incrementing = false;
pressed = false;
}

/**
 * Returns true if the count is increasing.
 * @return boolean true if the count is being incremented.
 */
public boolean isIncrementing() {
return incrementing;
}
}//class incrementMouseListener

/**
 * ThreadInc keeps incrementing a Count as long as the increment
 * button is pressed.
 */
private class ThreadInc extends Thread {

/** The count to increment.
 * @see chap07.Count
 */
private Count countToInc;
```

```
/** The incrementMouseListener that created and started
 * this thread. This thread will stop and die when the
 * mouse button is released
 * @see chap11.incrementMouseListener
 */
private incrementMouseListener l;

/** Constructs a new <code>ThreadInc</code>
 * to increment the Count countToInc.
 * @see java.lang.Thread
 */
public ThreadInc(Count c, incrementMouseListener l) {
if (debug) {
 System.out.println("constructing new thread to increment count " +
                    c + " " + c.hashCode());
}
this.countToInc = c;
this.l = l;
}

/** Keeps incrementing the Count countToInc. This thread
 * will stop and die when the
 * mouse button is released
 * @see java.lang.Thread
 * @see chap11.incrementMouseListener
 */
public void run() {
if (debug) {
    System.out.println("isIncrementing " + l.isIncrementing());
}
while(l.isIncrementing()) {
 /* The code here will increment the Count by one
 * then sleep for delay/3 ms.
 */
 try {
  if (debug) {
   System.out.println("going up ");
   System.out.println(countToInc + " " + countToInc.hashCode());
  }
  countToInc.increment();
  sleep(delay);
 }//try
 catch(Exception e) {
  System.out.println("ThreadInc interrupted " + e);
 }//catch
}//while
}//method run

}//class ThreadInc
/**
 * decrementMouseListener inner class
 * uses extends to inherit
 * from the MouseAdapter superclass as a convenience
 * for creating listener objects. Instead of implementing
 * the MouseListener interface which would mean defining all
 * of the methods in it.
 * @see java.awt.event.MouseAdapter
 * @author Stuart F Lewis
 * @version 1.00, 02/10/98
 */
```

```
private class decrementMouseListener extends MouseAdapter
                                  implements Serializable {
/**
* A Thread used to keep the count decreasing when the mouse has
* been pressed on the decrement button.
*/
private transient Thread dec = null;

/**
* A flag used to know if the count is decreasing.
* Set to true when the mouse is pressed on the decrement button.
* Set to false when the mouse is released
*/
private boolean decrementing = true;

/**
* A flag used to know if the decrement button is pressed.
* Set to false when the mouse is released
*/
private boolean pressed = false;

/** Invoked when a mouse button has been pressed on
* the decrement button. Creates a new Thread and
* starts it decrementing the Count
*/
public void mousePressed(MouseEvent e) {
dec = new ThreadDec(c,this);
decrementing = true ;
pressed = true;
dec.start();
}

/** Invoked when the mouse enters the decrement button.
* if the button is pressed a new Thread is started.
*/
public void mouseEntered(MouseEvent e) {
if (pressed) {
 dec = new ThreadDec(c,this);
 decrementing = true;
 dec.start();
}
}

/** Invoked when the mouse exits the decrement button.
* The Thread is stopped. But the button may be left pressed.
*/
public void mouseExited(MouseEvent e) {
if (debug) {
   System.out.println("mouseExited " + dec);
}
decrementing = false;
}

/** Invoked when a mouse button has been released.
* The Thread is stopped and the button is unpressed.
*/
public void mouseReleased(MouseEvent e) {
if (debug) {
   System.out.println("mouseReleased " + dec);
}
```

```
decrementing = false;
pressed = false;
}

/**
* Returns true if the count is decreasing.
* @return boolean true if the count is being decremented.
*/
public boolean isDecrementing() {
return decrementing;
}
}//class decrementMouseListener

/**
* ThreadDec keeps decrementing a Count as long as the decrement
* button is pressed.
*/
private class ThreadDec extends Thread {
/** The count to decrement.
* @see chap07.Count
*/
private Count countToDec;

/** The decrementMouseListener that created and started
* this thread. This thread will stop and die when the
* mouse button is released
* @see chap11.decrementMouseListener
*/
private decrementMouseListener l;

/** Constructs a new <code>ThreadDec</code>
* to decrement the Count countToDec.
* @see java.lang.Thread
*/
public ThreadDec(Count c, decrementMouseListener l) {
this.countToDec = c;
this.l = l;
}

/** Keeps decrementing the Count countToDec. This thread
* will stop and die when the
* mouse button is released
* @see java.lang.Thread
* @see chap11.decrementMouseListener
*/
public void run() {
if (debug) {
    System.out.println("isDecrementing " + l.isDecrementing());
}
while(l.isDecrementing()) {
 /* The code here will decrement the Count by one
* then sleep for delay/3 ms.
 */
 try {
  if (debug) {
   System.out.println("Count is " + countToDec + " and going
   down");
  }
  countToDec.decrement();
```

```
   sleep(delay);
 }//try
 catch(Exception e) {
  System.out.println("ThreadDec interrupted "+e);
 }//catch
}//while
}//method run

}//class ThreadDec

/**
* Set method for the debug switch
*/
public synchronized void setDebug(boolean b) {
debug = b;
}

/**
* Access method for the debug switch
* @return boolean the current state of the debug switch
*/
public boolean getDebug() {
   return debug;
}

/**
* Set method for the delay time
*/
public synchronized void setDelay(int d) {
delay = d;
}

/**
* Access method for the delay time
* @return int delay time between changes to Count value
*/
public int getDelay() {
   return delay;
}

/**
* Set method for the incrementButtonLabel
* @param l the new label, or <code>null</code>
*        if the button has no label.
* @see java.awt.Button#setLabel
*/
public synchronized void setIncrementButtonLabel(String l) {
if (!incrementButtonLabel.equals(l)) {
   incrementButtonLabel = l;
   increment.setLabel(incrementButtonLabel);
}
}

/**
* Access method for the incrementButtonLabel
* @return increment button label
*/
public String getIncrementButtonLabel() {
   return incrementButtonLabel;
}

/**
* Set method for the decrementButtonLabel
```

```
 * @param l the new label, or <code>null</code>
 *                  if the button has no label.
 * @see java.awt.Button#setLabel
 */
public synchronized void setDecrementButtonLabel(String l) {
if (!decrementButtonLabel.equals(l)) {
    decrementButtonLabel = l;
    decrement.setLabel(decrementButtonLabel);
}//if
}

/**
 * Access method for the decrementButtonLabel
 * @return decrement button label
 */
public String getDecrementButtonLabel() {
    return decrementButtonLabel;
}

/**
 * Set method for the Count
 * @param c the new Count.
 * @see java.awt.Button#setLabel
 */
public synchronized void setCount(Count c) {
if (!this.c.equals(c)) {
    this.c = c;
    this.t = new CountGuiEdit(c);
    this.removeAll();
    this.doGridBagLayout();
}
}

/**
 * Access method for the Count
 * @return Count
 */
public Count getCount() {
    return c;
}

/**
 * Set method for the columns in CountGuiEdit
 * @param c the new columns.
 * @see  chap07.CountGuiEdit
 */
public synchronized void setColumns(int c) {
  if (this.columns != c) {
    this.columns = c;
    this.t.setColumns(columns);
    this.removeAll();
    this.doGridBagLayout();
  }
}

/**
 * Access method for the columns in CountGuiEdit
 * @return columns in CountGuiEdit
 * @see  chap07.CountGuiEdit
 */
```

```java
public int getColumns() {
   return columns;
}

//main removed and to convert CountContainer into CountBean
//extra fields added

/*
* Used for versioning in explicit serialization of the bean.
* Get the serialVersionUID by executing the JDK tool serialver on
* the bean class file giving the full package/pathname
* serialver sflewis.CountBean.CountBean
* gives
* sflewis.CountBean.CountBean:static final long serialVersionUID =
0L;
*/
private final static long serialVersionUID = 0L;

/** Version number 1 - designed to use only Java 1.1 components
*/
private final static int versionNum = 1;

protected Vector countBeanListeners = new Vector();

//Extra methods added

/**
* Called when the Count c being observed notifies
* observers of a state change.
* @param Observable o the observable object ie. the Count.
* @param Object arg an optional argument passed to the ;
*               notifyObservers method, always null in this case.
*/
public void update(Observable o,Object arg) {
if (debug) {
    System.out.println("update called by Count ");
}
 if (countBeanListeners != null) {
   fireEvent(new CountBeanEvent(CountBean.this,getValue()));
 }
}

/*
* CountBean listeners are notified when a value change occurs
* on the count.
*/
public void addCountBeanListener(CountBeanListener 1) {
   countBeanListeners.addElement(1);
if (debug) {
   System.out.println("Listener " + 1 + " added");
}
}

/*
* CountBean listeners are notified when a value change occurs
* on the count.
*/
public void removeCountBeanListener(CountBeanListener 1) {
   countBeanListeners.removeElement(1);
}
```

```
/** Send an event to all registered countBeanListeners */
public void fireEvent(CountBeanEvent e) {
// Make a copy of the list and fire the events using that copy.
// This means that listeners can be added or removed from the
// original list in response to this event.
    Vector list = (Vector) countBeanListeners.clone();
    for(int i = 0; i < list.size(); i++) {
      CountBeanListener listener =
        (CountBeanListener)list.elementAt(i);
      listener.countBeanChange(e);
    } //for
}

/** Overide default readObject to make sure Count is
* linked to the display view */
private void readObject (ObjectInputStream stream)
throws IOException, ClassNotFoundException {
stream.defaultReadObject();
/* link the restored Count to a new TextField on the display
*/
t = new CountGuiEdit(c);
}
} ///:~
```

REVIEW QUESTIONS

Answers in Appendix A.

1 How does a builder tool know what methods and attributes a JavaBean has?

2 What is the simplest JavaBean in the API?

3 What are the advantages of using layout managers?

4 What other event could CountBean generate?

EXERCISES

Answers to exercises flagged with an asterisk appear in Appendix B.

1* Why does the object-oriented approach fit so well with the concept of reusable software components?

2 What are the advantages and disadvantages of storing Beans in JAR files?

3* How are commercially produced Beans distributed?

4 What other reusable software component frameworks are available?

5 Why would a software development organisation prefer to develop their own in-house Bean rather than purchase one?

6* What is the major advantage of the Bean framework over other reusable component frameworks?

Appendix A: Answers to review questions

Chapter 1

1 Mouse, keyboard, digitising pad, scanner, bar code reader, etc.

2 Different events are generated by each input device.

3 Operating system.

4 Each is suited to a different task or type of problem.

5 Syntax error.

6 Comments add some meaningful explanations in natural language.

7 An interpreter translates one line of source code at a time. A compiler translates the entire source code file into machine code that can be executed independently.

8 Sequence, selection and iteration.

9 The arrival of the web made the Internet much easier to use with the graphical user interface and embedded hypertext links.

10 http://java.sun.com/.

Chapter 2

1 A CD player, a bottle of wine, a one penny piece, could all clearly be considered as objects.

2 We can request a CD player to play, stop playing, change CD, change track, open, close and much more. We can open a bottle of wine, pour from it. We can toss a one penny piece.

3 The CD player has many possible states: on, off, empty, playing etc. A bottle of wine may be open, closed, full, partially full or empty. A coin can be showing either a head or a tail or it may even be in the air.

4 A plumber may be interested in the water supply, hot and cold storage tanks, locations of stop taps, pipes, drains, water-heating system, and outlet points.

5 The interface presented by the mains electrical system includes the sockets, light switches, thermostats and other control devices.

6 CD players, homes, money and friends could be considered as classes.

Chapter 3

1 The amount of storage used for all primitive data types is the same for all Java platforms because Java runs on a virtual machine.

2 Byte is the class that is used to instantiate objects that are wrappers for variables of primitive data type byte.

3 The primitive integral data types are the four integer types byte, short, int, long plus the char type.

4 The primitive floating-point data types are float and double.

5 For all integral data types the predecessor and successor values are known for every value and the values have the same ordinal sequence on all platforms. The primitive floating-point data types are only a very close approximation to their true values.

Chapter 4

1 Round brackets.

2 Either using a switch statement or multiple if statements.

3 An array of String objects.

4 switch.

Chapter 5

1 (a) Object – class, hashcode and String representation.
       String – value and length (plus what Object knows).
       StringBuffer – value, length and capacity (plus what Object knows).
       System.out – Slightly tricky; System.out is a reference to an object of the class java.io.PrintStream. A PrintStream knows the OutputStream that it is connected to.
   (b) stack – size (if fixed), number of items, status.
       list – maximum length (if fixed), current length, status.
       queue – maximum length (if fixed), current length, status, first item, last item.
       array – size, elements.

(c) invoice – date, reference, customer, lines, value.
     bank account – customer, balance, overdraft limit, transactions.
     address book – names, phone numbers, addresses.

2 (a) We can request an object of each class to
     Object – display its hashcode and string representation.
     String – display its length, convert to an array of char (plus do what Object
     does).
     StringBuffer – display its length, convert to an array of char, append or insert
     another item to the buffer (plus do what Object does).
     System.out – print out a value.
     stack – push, pop, report status using isFull.
     list – add, remove, find items, report status using isEmpty.
     queue – remove first item, add last item, report status using isEmpty.
     array – get or set elements, report status using length or capacity.
     invoice – send, pay, make overdue, change value.
     bank account – deposit, withdraw, change overdraft limit, list transactions.
     address book – find name, find phone number, print addresses.

3 Some of these requests would alter the object state by updating the instance
variables. Other requests may not change the state.

Chapter 6

1 Considered more intuitive to use than text-based interfaces. The rapid fall in the
cost of hardware and move away from vector graphics devices to the ubiquitous
high-resolution raster display of the modern personal computer has made the GUI
the *de facto* standard interface.

2 (a) Choice – list of possible choices, number of choices, current choice.
     Panel – list of components, current location.
     Applet – name, list of components.
     TextField – name, current contents, if editable.
   (b) locator – current x,y position, cursor shape.
     pick – selected object.
     menu – as Choice above.
     point – x and y co-ordinate, units.
   (c) student – name, enrolment number, course, address, tutor, timetable.
     savings account – balance, interest rate, maximum investment allowed,
     transactions.
     address – number, street, area, city, county, post code, country.

3 Choice – add, remove, get or select choice item. Get count of items.
   Panel – add component, get list of current components, get current location.
   Applet – name, list of components.
   TextField – name, current contents, if editable.
   locator – current x,y position, cursor shape.

pick – selected object.
menu – as Choice above.
point – x and y co-ordinate, units.
student – name, enrolment number, course, address, tutor, timetable.
savings account – balance, interest rate, maximum investment allowed, transactions.
address – number, street, area, city, county, post code, country.

4 Choice – change choice items.
   Panel – change current components.
   Applet – change components.
   TextField – change current contents, if editable.
   locator – change cursor shape.
   pick – as locator above.
   menu – as Choice above.
   point – change x and y co-ordinate.
   student – change name, enrolment number, course, address, tutor, timetable.
   savings account – change balance, interest rate, maximum investment allowed, transactions.
   address – change number, street, area, city, county, post code, country.

Chapter 7

1 (a) Date – year, month, day, hour, minute, second.
        Calendar – current date, start date, end date, all the dates between the start and end.
        DateFormat – widths of various fields to be displayed.
   (b) file – name, access date, create date, size, access permissions.
        directory – files, subdirectories, access permissions.
        text – see String.
   (c) date – as above.
        calendar – as above.
        appointment book –appointments (date, who, where, what).

2 The services these objects could provide may include:
   Date – day of the week, set new date.
   Calendar – add time, next day.
   DateFormat – formatting (date to text) and parsing (text to date) to and from different style formats SHORT, LONG etc.
   file – open, close, read, write.
   directory – create, copy, rename, delete files, sort, list.
   text – see String.
   Real-world classes.
   date – day of the week.
   calendar – first day of the week, next day.
   appointment book – book new meeting, cancel appointment, check if free.

3 Those requests may alter the object state in these ways:
Date – value may change
Calendar – current date may change
DateFormat – current format may change
file – from open to closed, file status may change
directory – add or remove files from the directory
text – see String
Real-world classes
date – no state, today is today!
calendar – current date may change
appointment book – add or remove appointments in the future

Chapter 8

1 When serializing the state of an object there may be some attributes that should not be stored.

2 A skeleton problem domain class can be used to provide a rapid prototype interface or to separate the interface development from the problem domain development.

3 The stages in developing a GUI interface are: define the components, add them to a container, handle the events generated by the components.

4 Simple structure charts and pseudo code can help in developing the detail flow of control within methods for more complex classes.

5 The Random class provides services to initialize the random sequence with a different seed and return the next value as any one of the primitive data types.

Chapter 9

1 Truth tables or a summary of all possible combinations of input are useful for ensuring that all cases are covered when testing a class.

2 The JDK API provides a number of classes that perform locale-sensitive operations. For example, the NumberFormat class formats numbers, currency, or percentages in a locale-sensitive manner. DateFormat helps to format and parse dates for any locale. The code can be completely independent of the locale conventions for months or days of the week.

3 The locale-sensitive classes are useful in reducing the problems of localisation (modifying software for different international markets).

4 The advantages of subdividing the GUI into separate panels are that the same panels can be reused in several different applications.

5 GridLayout, ScrollPaneLayout, ViewportLayout, and FlowLayout all implement the interface java.awt.LayoutManager. BoxLayout, CardLayout, JRootPane.RootLayout,

OverlayLayout, GridBagLayout, and BorderLayout all implement the interface java.awt.LayoutManager2 which extends the LayoutManager interface to deal with layouts explicitly in terms of constraint objects that specify how and where components should be added to the layout.

Chapter 10

1 The Collection classes provide a generalized storage mechanism for objects with a common interface that can be specialized to implement a particular interface or use a particular underlying data structure.

2 The Set interface ensures that no duplicates appear in the Collection.

Chapter 11

1 A builder tool knows what methods and attributes a JavaBean has by a process of introspection. This is possible because the designer tools can query JavaBean components and ask them what kinds of properties or attributes they have, and what kinds of events they can generate or respond to.

2 The simplest JavaBean in the API is probably the Button.

3 The advantages of using layout managers are that applications are portable across many platforms.

4 CountBean could generate an ActionEvent.

Appendix B: Answers to exercises

Chapter 1

1 Programs stored in memory are no longer available when the machine has been turned off, rebooted or the memory has been reused by another application. Programs stored on disk can be reloaded from disk many times.

4 Other diagrammatic notations that can be used for expressing the low level design constructs sequence, selection and iteration include flow charts, Nassi-Schneiderman charts and Structured Systems Design Method Entity Life History.

Chapter 2

1 Here are two – coin and die.

2 Coin – flip, die – roll.

3 Coin may change from showing heads to showing tails. Die may change value in the range one to six.

4 Coin – as a boolean, e.g. headIsShowing. Die – as an integer (byte).

5 Both are server objects, providing the service of a random value in a narrow range.

Chapter 3

1 java.lang

2 indexOf in the String class has the signature public int indexOf(int ch). Returns the index within this string of the first occurrence of the specified character. If a character with value ch occurs in the character sequence represented by this String object, then the index of the first such occurrence is returned – that is, the smallest value k such that:

$$this.charAt(k) == ch$$

is true. If no such character occurs in this string, then -1 is returned.

3 trim in the String class has the signature public String trim() and removes white space from both ends of a string.

6 Integer inherits from the abstract class Number.

8 Yes, the class Integer has a constructor that has a String argument.

Chapter 4

1 true or false.

4 The scope of i is only the body of the for loop.

5 Switch is a class but switch is a Java reserved word used for forming multi-way selection statements.

Chapter 5

1 Simple command-line arguments, a standard console interface and graphical user interfaces (GUI) for both applets and applications.

2 The three methods usually overridden by classes extending Object are toString, equals, and hashCode().

3 The three styles of commenting available in Java are // to the end of a single line, /** starts a javadoc comment, and /* starts a C like multi-line comment. Both multi-line comments are terminated by a */.

6 The tagged paragraph @see is used when referring to another class which javadoc will convert to a hypertext link.

7 The two questions that can help when designing or extending classes are what does an object of that class know and what services can it provide to potential clients.

Chapter 6

1 Valuator, stroke, pick, locator and text are logical input devices.

2 They provide a number, a sequence of points, a graphics object, a single point and a string of characters.

Chapter 7

1 At least one abstract method.

3 In instance variables that may be supplemented by concrete subclasses.

Chapter 8

3 The method random() has the signature public static double random(). Returns a random number greater than or equal to 0.0 and less than 1.0. Returned values are chosen pseudo randomly with (approximately) uniform distribution from that range. When this method is first called, it creates a single new pseudo random number generator, exactly as if by the expression

    new java.util.Random

This new pseudo random number generator is used thereafter for all calls to this method and is used nowhere else.

4 The Random class differs from the method in the Math class in that it can supply a stream of pseudo random numbers from one of the primitive data types boolean, byte, integer, long, float, or double. Many applications will find the random method in class Math simpler to use.

Chapter 9

3 The methods that are most straightforward to generate are the get and set accessor methods for class attributes.

4 The main advantage of using a layout manager is that the programmer does not need to be concerned with the absolute positions of components within containers. Each time a container is displayed the components are laid out according to the size, space, and location available.

Chapter 10

1 Other data structures that are used for storing multiple objects include Vector, Stack, List and serialized files.

Chapter 11

1 Both the object-oriented approach and reusable software components require methods and data to be stored together.

3 Many commercially produced Beans are distributed using the Internet.

6 The major advantage of the Bean framework over other reusable component frameworks is the power of introspection and serialization that allow Beans to be customized at design time without altering the original Bean code.

Glossary

Abstract base class Common superclass that has been specialized to provide several subclasses but cannot be used to instantiate objects.

Abstract class Superclass that can be specialized to provide subclasses but cannot be used to instantiate objects.

Abstract method Method with a signature defined by an abstract class, which is then implemented by all concrete subclasses.

Abstraction Ignoring the inessential details of something and concentrating only on those that are relevant to the current problem.

Access time The time taken to retrieve an element from a collection.

Accessor Method that allows access to an attribute, informal standard for naming is get or set followed by the attribute name.

Argument Information supplied by the client object to the server object to customize the way in which the server carries out some request (*see* **Parameter**).

Assignment Setting or defining the value of an identifier.

Attribute Part of an object state.

Behavior (1) List of the requests that an object can respond to.

Behavior (2) The methods that an object provides.

Binary (1) A value stored using only zero and one.

Binary (2) An operator requiring two operands.

Binary (3) The number base 2.

boolean Something having one of exactly two values, true or false.

Browser Software package used to view .html format documents.

Casting Converting a value of a variable of one type to another type.

char Integral type whose values are 16-bit unsigned integers (0 to 65535) representing Unicode characters.

Class (1) Grouping of similar objects.

class (2) Java reserved word indicating the start of a new class definition.

Class hierarchy A tree structure similar to a family tree with the root at the top known as the superclass.

Client (1) An object that sends requests to a server object.

Client (2) An object that uses the resources of another object.

Collection A group of objects, known as its elements.

Comment Text added to source code to aid readability

Component (1) GUI building block provided by the Abstract Windowing Toolkit (AWT) used to compose complex GUIs.

Component (2) UML uses the term to refer to a representation of a source file, a library or an executable.

Composition Assembling simple components from more complex ones.

Concatenation Adding one string of text to another to produce a longer string.

Constant A variable which cannot be changed. Defined in Java using static final.

Constructor Method used to instantiate an object.

Container GUI component provided by the Abstract Windowing Toolkit (AWT) that can contain other GUI components.

Data structure Attribute of a class that contains zero or more elements.

Declaration Program statement(s) that give the compiler information about a class or variable.

Definition Program statement(s) that causes the compiler to allocate some storage by assignment of a value to an identifier.

Delegate Class that combines the view and controller classes from the MVC pattern (*see* **Model-View-Controller**).

Dependency (1) A client server relationship between two classes.

Dependency (2) Link between two objects.

Design pattern Reusable piece of object-oriented design.

Editable view Delegate class that provides access to change the attributes of another class

Embedded Class that runs inside another virtual machine, often refers to applets.

Encapsulation Hiding detailed information about something (information hiding).

Enumeration An interface that specifies methods to generate a series of elements from a collection one at a time (*see* **Iterator**).

equals() For all objects the equals() method returns true if both objects are equal.

Event driven System controlled by the user generating events by interacting with a GUI; the user dictates the flow of control.

extends Java reserved word used to inherit from a generalized class to provide a more specialized class.

final Java reserved word preventing the modification of a value. Makes a variable constant. Makes it impossible to override a method.

Floating-point Float or double data type, representing the single-precision 32-bit and double-precision 64-bit format IEEE 754 values and operations as specified in IEEE Standard for Binary Floating-Point Arithmetic, ANSI/IEEE Standard 754-1985 (IEEE, New York)

Generalized Superclass that can be specialized to provide subclasses.

Handle Identifier that provides access to an object, sometimes referred to as pointer or reference type.

Hash table The original mapping class from JDK 1.0 containing a pair of key and value for every object in the Hash table.

Hashcode A unique value generated for every object.

Hierarchy Tree structured organisation.

Host Program or machine that runs an embedded applet or application.

Identifier Name of variable, class, object or method.

if Java reserved word used in conditional statements.

Implement Write appropriate methods defined by an interface or an abstract class.

Indexed storage A data structure with elements that can be accessed directly by their position.

Inheritance To specialize a generalized superclass and provide subclasses.

Initialize Assigns a first value to an identifier defining the initial value.

Instance An object of a particular class.

Instance variables Variables used to store the attributes that make up the state of an object.

Instantiate To create an actual instance of an object.

Instantiation Process of creating a new object from the class definition.

Integer Variable of type byte, short, int, or long.

Integral Having discrete values so the predecessor and successor are always know.

Interact To allow the user to use an interface.

Interface (1) A Java class that can be implemented by other classes.

Interface (2) The boundary between two things.

Introspection The process of querying a JavaBean to discover its properties.

Intuitive Simple to understand without reasoning or analysis.

Iterator An interface to deliver each element from the Collection to a client (*see* **Enumeration**).

javadoc Tool for generating documentation from source code.

Key A unique value that provides access to an object.

Lightweight persistence When objects can be written to and read from long term storage, but the programmer must manage the process.

List An unordered Collection that may contain duplicates and multiple null elements and the elements can be accessed directly by their position.

Locale-sensitive Class that is aware of national conventions for handling data.

Map A Set of key-value mapping pairs.

Method Operations or requests that the object can accept.

Model A problem domain object, often Observable.

Model-View-Controller A common design pattern used for implementing GUIs by separating the problem domain object from its user interface.

Multiline Spanning several lines.

Not-a-Number The result of arithmetic operations whose result is not a number.

Notify To inform an interested observer that a state change has occurred.

null Java reserved word that refers to an object that has not been initialized or defined as referring to any particular instance of a class.

Object An instance of a particular class.

Observer An object (often a view) that watches for changes in another object (often a model from the problem domain).

Operand A value or variable involved in an expression.

Operator A special symbol used to perform an operation on one or more operands involved in an expression.

Overloaded A symbol that has different meanings in different contexts.

Overriding Providing a method with exactly the same signature as an inherited method.

package Group of Java classes.

Parameter Variable listed in the round brackets of a method declaration which has local scope to the method (*see* **Argument**).

Persistence Enabling objects to be written to and read from long-term storage.

Pointer Identifier that provides access to an object; sometimes referred to as reference type or handle.

Polymorphic Method that provides different functionality according to context.

Portable A system, component or language that can run on many different platforms with little or no modification.

Postfix Operator appearing after the operand.

Predecessor Previous value in the sequence of values for an integral primitive data type.

Prefix Operator appearing before the operand.

Primitive data type One of the eight types provided by the Java language that are not references to objects.

private Java reserved word limiting access to the defining class only.

Problem domain Area of a system concerned with meeting the core requirements and providing a solution independent of the interface.

properties Another term for attributes, often used when referring to JavaBeans.

protected Java reserved word limiting access to the defining class and subclasses only.

Public Java reserved word giving access to this method or variable from any other class.

Query To request information from a class about itself.

Queue A data structure where elements are added to the back and taken from the front.

Reference type Identifier that provides access to an object; sometimes referred to as pointer or handle.

Resources Memory, disk space or methods of another object.

return Java reserved word used to return some value from a method to the client that called it.

Reusable software component A piece of software that can be used in several different applications.

Sequential stream A flow of input or output bytes ordered by time; may come from or go to a file, memory, a network, or another object.

Serializable An interface defined by the Java API; objects of all classes that implement Serializable can be written to and read from long-term storage.

Server (1) An object that provides resources.

Server (2) An object that responds to requests from a client object.

Set An unordered Collection that contains no duplicate elements.

Signature A method signature is made up of the visibility modifier, return type, method name and parameter list.

Skeleton Partly completed class that provides only enough functionality to develop other dependent classes.

Specialize To extend a generalized class giving a more powerful subclass.

Stack A data structure that can only be accessed at the top.

State Summary of the attributes of an object.

static Java reserved word indicating that this is a class variable or method as opposed to an instance variable or method.

Store To keep the value of an identifier for future use.

String Java library class providing immutable character strings.

Successor Next value in the sequence of values for a integral primitive data type.

switch Java reserved word for a multiway selection.

Template Describes the attributes that make up the state of an instantiated object and the methods which that object performs.

this Java reserved word used in a class definition to refer to an instance of the class.

Type A range of values and set of operations defined by the Java for eight primitive data types.

Unary An operator requiring only one operand.

Variable Name of a location in the computer memory used to store a data value.

Vector The Vector class implements a growable array of objects.

View A text or graphical representation of the state of a model object.

Visibility Scope or availability of an identifier, either public, protected or private.

void Java reserved word indicating that a method does not return any information.

Wrapper Class to enable a primitive value to be stored as an object.

Bibliography

Anuff, Ed, 1996, *The Java Sourcebook: a complete guide to creating Java applets for the Web*, New York and Chichester: Wiley Computer Publishing.
After comparing Java to other languages, O-O basics are followed by Java basics. The appendices reproduce the API documentation for the applet, awt and awt.image packages.

Arnold, Ken (with James Gosling), 1996, *The Java Programming Language*, Reading, MA: JavaSoft Addison-Wesley.
Part of the Java series from JavaSoft in association with Addison-Wesley (Sun Microsystems). Very limited coverage of O-O design. Assumes familiarity with O-O concepts. Concentrates on examples to demonstrate the language features. Very few diagrams.

Bell, Douglas (with Mike Parr), 1999, *Java for Students*, 2nd edition, Hemel Hempstead: Prentice Hall.
Aims to start from scratch but quickly introduces graphical applets using the paint() method. Uses scrollbars to enter numbers and flow charts to illustrate control structures. Uses a Balloon class to introduce objects and the MVC design pattern before an extensive disscussion of arrays. Uses the 1.1 ActionListener interfaces but handles events in a single actionPerformed(ActionEvent e) similar to the 1.0 approach. After exploring console applications and the AWT, returns to applets to cover more graphics and sound before addressing basic O-O design methods, program style, testing, debugging, threads and packages. Concludes with some advanced O-O concepts, 1.1 and 1.2 enhancements, and several appendices covering C++, some API libraries, HTML, GUIs, keywords and scope rules. Extensive bibliography and glossary.

Ben-Natan, Ron, 1997, *Objects on the Web: designing, building and deploying object-oriented applications for the Web*, New York and London: McGraw-Hill.
Places Java in context among the other developing technologies for Web applications.

Booch, Grady, 1994, *Object-oriented analysis and design: with applications*, Redwood City, CA and Wokingham: Benjamin Cummings.
Classic OOA and OOD text. Includes five applications each partially implemented in a different O-O language: Smalltalk, Object Pascal, C++, Common Lisp Object System (CLOS), and Ada.

Campione, Mary and Walrath, Kathy, 1996, *The Java tutorial: object-oriented programming for the Internet*, Reading, MA: JavaSoft Addison-Wesley.
Well organised tutorial linked to CD-ROM and regularly updated web site at http://java.sun.com/docs/books/tutorial/index.html.

Coad, Peter (with Jill Nicola), 1993, *Object-oriented programming*, Englewood Cliffs, NJ and London: Yourdon Press/ Prentice-Hall.
Excellent introduction to OOP with examples in both Smalltalk and C++.

Coad, Peter, 1997, *Java design: building better apps and applets*, Upper Saddle River, NJ: Yourdon Press.
Plenty of class diagrams in both UML and Coad's own notation. Includes CD with source code, Playground (a OOD tool), and patterns handbook. Two case studies run through the text: a charter airline and a zone/sensor monitoring system. Derides the Java Observer/Observable API implementation preferring to develop his own (amazingly similar version but using an ObservableComponent as one of the attributes of the Observed Class). The source code appears to contain some minor errors and is not easily imported into separate Java files (lots of cut and paste, all the filenames need to be entered). Has a significant design content stressing composition via interfaces rather than inheritance that leads to more flexible implementations.

Cohen, Shy (*et al.*), 1996, *Professional Java Fundamentals*, Olton: Wrox Press.
A book for programmers by programmers. Full of example code.

December, John, 1995, *Presenting Java*, Indianapolis: Sams.net.
An introduction to Java and HotJava for animation and interactivity on the World Wide Web. Lots of screen shots of early Java applets. Some simple Java code for essential control flow and operations. Example classes include: Safe – a lockable storage device to illustrate scoping, modifiers and access to instance variables; Drama – a short play involving some Person, Dialog and Action to show object interaction; Scene – a multi-threaded Applet based on a similar theme. Simple diagrams show classes as ellipses sometimes inside one another with public and private methods or attributes floating. Minimal attention to design.

Eckel, Bruce, 1998, *Thinking in Java*, Upper Saddle River, NJ: Prentice Hall.
Comprehensive coverage of Java also available online at http://www.BruceEckel.com.

Flanagan, David, 1997, *Java Examples in a Nutshell*, O'Reilly & Associates.
An excellent tutorial companion to *Java in a Nutshell*. Packed full of useful, well written code demonstrating many elements of the Java API.

Flanagan, David, 1997, *Java in a Nutshell: a desktop quick reference*, 2nd edition, O'Reilly & Associates.
A compact summary of the online documentation of Java 1.1.

Gamma, Erich (*et al.*), 1995, *Design Patterns: elements of reusable object-oriented software*, Reading, MA and Wokingham: Addison-Wesley.
The original design patterns handbook.

Garside, Roger (with John Mariani), 1998, *Java: first contact*, Cambridge, MA: Course Technology.
A student teaching text. Uses a rather dated flow-chart notation for selection and iteration within object methods.

Geary, David M. (with Alan L. McClellan), 1997, *Graphic Java: mastering the AWT*, Reading, MA: SunSoft Press.
Concentrates on the Abstract Window Toolkit (AWT) and extending its functionality. Includes excellent colour images and demonstrations but assumes considerable Java knowledge.

Gosling, James (with Bill Joy and Guy Steele), 1996, *The Java Language Specification*, Reading, MA: JavaSoft Addison-Wesley.
The original authors attempt a complete specification of the syntax and semantics of the Java language. Also available online at http://java.sun.com/docs/books/jls/html/index.html

Gosling, James (with Frank Yellin), 1996, *The Java Application Programming Interface, Volume 1: Core packages*, Reading, MA: JavaSoft Addison-Wesley.
Excellent class hierarchy diagrams. Covers each of the core packages in the application programming interface in detail giving classes, interfaces, exceptions and errors. A useful reference, but not suitable for learning the language.

Gosling, James (with Frank Yellin), 1996, *The Java Application Programming Interface, Volume 2: Window toolkit and applets*, Reading, MA: JavaSoft Addison-Wesley.
Concentrates on the Abstract Window Toolkit (AWT) and applets.

Hopson, K.C. (with Stephen E. Ingram), 1996, *Developing Professional Java Applets*, Indianapolis, IN: Sams.net.
Shows how to build reasonable applications including a spreadsheet, catalogue and http server but with limited design.

Ince, Darrel (with Adam Freeman), 1997, *Programming the Internet with Java*, Harlow: Addison-Wesley.
Teaching textbook concentrating on Internet technologies. Previous knowledge of programming in C or Pascal is assumed.

Jackson, Jerry R., 1996, *Java by Example*, Upper Saddle River, NJ: Prentice Hall.
A programmer's book with plenty of example code on CD including: CountLines – showing the close relationship with C and C++ in the text processing of a file; Card – standard playing cards with a static initializer that creates a deck as a class variable to illustrate the difference between instance and class methods; a simple BankAccount as an abstract class; BigNum and LongMult used to illustrate constructors; TreeSort – a binary tree sort from first principles using enumeration and interfaces; Arrays – exceptions and io are explained in depth before multiple threads are introduced. A simple Person class demonstrates overriding toString. A stack based Calculator with console interface concludes the first part.
The Puzzle and Memory Applet games help explain event handling and thread for applets. Both feature a grid of colours and mouse interaction. OccupationalOracle, a form-based Applet. TikerTape, the classic animated Applet configurable using HTML. Extensive examples of cell automaton, from the game Life, evolving. Short appendix of O-O features and a quick reference to the language including a list of reserved words. Good overall, minimal design included.

Jardin, Cary A., 1997, *Java Electronic Commerce Sourcebook: all the software and expert advice you need to open your virtual store*, New York and Chichester: Wiley Computer Publishing.
Includes a fully developed shopping cart Applet.

Jaworski, Jamie, 1997, *Java 1.1: developer's guide*, 2nd edition, Indianapolis, IN: H.W.Sams.
Plenty of examples on accompanying CD-ROM.

Jaworski, Jamie, 1998, *Java 1.2 Unleashed*, Indianapolis, IN: Sams.net.
An updated, revised and expanded edition that includes coverage of new Java add-ons and third-party development tools; this volume is aimed at the experienced programmer.

Jepson, Brian, 1997, *Java Database Programming*, Chichester: John Wiley & Sons.
A specialized database textbook written in a quirky style. Starts with a Vector of Hashtables before introducing database design, SQL and JDBC. Combines these to develop the tinySQL database management system.

King, Peter (with Patrick Naughton, Mike DeMoney, Jonni Kanerva), 1996, *JavaSoft Code Convention*.
JavaSoft internal programming standard available on the World Wide Web.

Lewis, John (with William Loftus), 1997, *Java Software Solutions: foundations of program design*, Reading, MA and Harlow: Addison-Wesley.
Comprehensive programming text with plenty of examples, self-review questions and exercises.

Marketos, Joshua, 1997, *The Java Developer's toolkit: techniques and technologies for Web programmers*, Chichester: John Wiley & Sons.

A brief review of O-O concepts and rapid coverage of Java basics is followed by simple applications using the java.lang package. Applets, graphics, the AWT, threads, io and networking are all covered by examining the classes in each API package including reproducing the API documentation. Despite advising against using native code over 40 pages are devoted to interfacing native methods to Java. A minimal shopping cart and JDBC example precede a brief look into the future.

McGraw, Gary, 1997, *Java Security*, New York and Chichester: John Wiley & Sons.
A specialized security textbook concentrating on web based Java users rather than programmers.

McGregor, John D, 1992, *Object-oriented Software Development: engineering software for reuse*, New York and London: Van Nostrand Reinhold.
An early O-O book emphasising reuse.

Morrison, Michael (*et al.*), 1996, *Java Unleashed*, Indianapolis, IN: Sams.net.
Opening section by John December (*Presenting Java*) sets the scene followed by a slightly dated review of various Java development tools. Numerous simple examples introduce the basics with flow charts used to illustrate control structures. A general OOP primer includes the Alien class and Enemy interface. Threads and exception handling are briefly disccusses before the API libraries lang, util, and io are covered in detail. Applets are developed for a simple calculator, phone book, and ColorPicker. Subsequent parts cover network programming, games and VRML, debugging, documentation, native methods, the virtual machine and security. Finally JavaScript is described. See similar text by Jaworski for Java 1.2.

Niemeyer, Patrick (with Joshua Peck), 1996, *Exploring Java*, O'Reilly & Associates.
Starts with applets and concentrates on networked applications. Very readable.

Parsons, David, 1998, *Introductory Java*, London: Letts Educational.
An excellent introduction to OOP with Java. Starts with some history but quickly introduces classes based on everyday items such as a Clock, Lift (elevator) and Coin. Combines a Dice, Board, Square, Snake and Ladder to develop a basic game. Other good examples feature logic gates, a distance table, courses and modules, the Rock, Paper Scissors game and a multithread race between the Tortoise and the Hare.

Pew, John A., 1996, *Instant Java*, Upper Saddle River, NJ: Prentice-Hall.
Concentrates on providing general purpose applets for web pages on accompanying CD-ROM. Includes a few useful tips for programmers and selected source code listings but does not attempt to teach Java.

Quatrani, Terry, 1998, *Visual modeling with Rational Rose and UML*, Reading, MA and Harlow: Addison Wesley.
Very practical introduction to the UML supported by the Rational Rose object modelling and diagramming tool.

Ritchey, Tim, 1995, *Programming with Java!*, Indianapolis, IN: New Riders Publishing.
Includes Beta 2.0, which is interesting, as Java version 1.2 Beta4 was the latest version as of October 1998. Lots of information about HotJava and Java with plenty of history and background. No design as such. Classes include a Rectangle drawn on the console using # symbols. Some simple applets and a network application.

Tapley, Rebecca (*et al.*), 1996, *The Official Gamelan Java Directory*, Emeryville, CA: Ziff-Davis.
A companion reference to the Gamelan online Java directory describing the best Java applets available there.

Unicode Consortium, The, 1996, *The Unicode Standard: Worldwide Character Encoding*, Version 1.0. Reading, MA: Addison-Wesley.
The international superset of ASCII including many of the world's languages.

Weber, Joseph L., 1998, *Using Java 1.2 Edition*, 4th Special edition, Indianapolis, IN: Que.
Concentrates on Java 1.2 changes that affect graphics and GUI programming to create multimedia applications.

Weiner, Scott (with Stephen Asbury), 1998, *Programming with JFC*, New York and Chichester: John Wiley & Sons.
Excellent coverage of the Java Foundation Classes now integrated into Java 2 (1.2).

Winder, Russel (with Graham Roberts), 1998, *Developing Java Software*, New York and Chichester: John Wiley & Sons.
Detailed treatment of fundamental programming concepts from first principles using Java.

Winston, Patrick Henry, 1996, *On to Java*, Reading, MA and Harlow: Addison-Wesley.
Based mainly on a single applet for viewing a movie rating that is developed from scratch to completion. Clearly explains many basic Java concepts including Observer and Observable used in the MVC design pattern.

Index